PRAISE FOR

SPLIT☉PIA

"The essential and supremely practical guide to the good divorce . . . Filled with history and research on child development and mediation, loneliness, and resilience, *Splitopia* makes a compelling case that it's high time for a new definition of Happily Ever After—for everyone."

—Brigid Schulte, author of *Overwhelmed: Work, Love, and Play When No One Has the Time*

"A good divorce is possible. Through *Splitopia*'s compelling stories and deep research, we gain insight into marriage, separation, and life well-lived."

—Shane J. Lopez, author of *Making Hope Happen*

"A smart, thoughtful, and well-written antidote to the idea that divorce is a toxic event for parents and children. Think of it instead as a family reorganization—a period not just of crisis but also of opportunity for growth and development that can result in a better quality of life for parents and children."

—Andrew Schepard, Max Schmertz Distinguished Professor of Law; Director Emeritus of the Center for Children, Families and the Law; and editor, *Family Court Review*, at the Maurice A. Deane School of Law at Hofstra University

"A smart and interesting guide, extremely helpful for those going through divorce."

—Tal Ben-Shahar, positive psychology lecturer and teacher, and author of *Happier*

"Finally, a book that shows there really can be a good divorce (even after the marriage has turned bad). *Splitopia* is a great resource and an engaging, moving read by a wonderfully subtle, skilled writer. It has useful advice, helpful hints—and much humor."

—Naomi Cahn, Harold H. Greene Chair,
GWU Law School, and coauthor of *Marriage Markets*

"*Splitopia* is an important book. Divorce is hard, but there are approaches that minimize the pain and set people on a path to healing. *Splitopia* suggests how to do this."

—Joan Blades, cofounder of MoveOn.org,
MomsRising.org, and LivingRoomConversations.org

"*Splitopia* is a wonderful blend of storytelling and social science—a book that amuses and captivates while dispensing shrewd advice based on solid psychological research. It's a practical guide that also lifts the spirit."

—John Tierney, coauthor of *Willpower:
Rediscovering the Greatest Human Strength*

"In many ways, this may be the most comprehensive approach to relationships that I've seen."

—Tonio Epstein, host of WGDR's *The Magical Mystery Tour*

"Paris is like an older, wiser friend who cheerfully shares her advice and counsel. Particularly useful as a guide for clients, *Splitopia* also provides valuable insights for lawyers on the types of non-legal advice we might provide to support them outside of our offices."

—Naomi Cahn and Jana Singer,
Family Law Quarterly, Spring 2016

SPLIT◯PIA

DISPATCHES FROM TODAY'S
GOOD DIVORCE
AND
HOW TO PART WELL

Wendy Paris

ATRIA PAPERBACK
New York   London   Toronto   Sydney   New Delhi

ATRIA
PAPERBACK

An Imprint of Simon & Schuster, Inc.
1230 Avenue of the Americas
New York, NY 10020

First Atria Paperback edition May 2017

ATRIA PAPERBACK and colophon are trademarks of Simon & Schuster, Inc.

Certain names have been changed.

The lines from Rainer Maria Rilke's "The Spanish Trilogy" translated
by Michael Hamburger are reprinted by permission from *Turning-Point*
published by Anvil Press Poetry in 2005.

For information about special discounts for bulk purchases,
please contact Simon & Schuster Special Sales at 1-866-506-1949
or business@simonandschuster.com.

The Simon & Schuster Speakers Bureau can bring authors to your
live event. For more information or to book an event, contact the
Simon & Schuster Speakers Bureau at 1-866-248-3049
or visit our website at www.simonspeakers.com.

Designed by Paul Dippolito

Manufactured in the United States of America

10   9   8   7   6   5   4   3   2   1

The Library of Congress has cataloged the hardcover edition as follows:

Names: Paris, Wendy (Journalist) author.
Title: Splitopia : dispatches from today's good divorce and how to part well /
Wendy Paris.
Description: First Edition. | New York : Atria Books, 2016. | Includes index.
Identifiers: LCCN 2015029939
Subjects: LCSH: Divorce. | Marriage. | Families. | BISAC: FAMILY &
    RELATIONSHIPS / Divorce & Separation. | SOCIAL SCIENCE / Sociology /
    Marriage & Family. | FAMILY & RELATIONSHIPS / Marriage.
Classification: LCC HQ814 .P367 2016 | DDC 306.89—dc23
LC record available at http://lccn.loc.gov/2015029939

ISBN 978-1-4767-2551-2
ISBN 978-1-4767-2552-9 (pbk)
ISBN 978-1-4767-2553-6 (ebook)

For my parents, Joy Paris and Sanford Paris,
and my son,
Alexander Paris-Callahan

Contents

PART FOUR: SIGNS OF LIGHT

Contents

Note to Reader

What We Talk about When
We Talk about Divorce

'd been complaining about my marriage for years. When my husband and I announced our decision to separate in November of 2011, I assumed my friends would bring champagne and chocolate truffles, or at least express relief. "Finally," they'd say. "You've been frustrated for ages. Good for you for doing something about it."

Instead, I got pushback. "Are you sure you want to do this? Maybe you're just unhappy in your career," said a single male friend, a fellow freelancer who'd been griping about work along with me for a decade.

"I know a number of attractive women your age who are single and have been unable to meet anyone. This could happen to you, too," offered a happily married female friend.

"This may be the last party you two throw," sniffled another married friend. We were standing around the farm table in my warm, yellow-walled kitchen, picking at the crispy edges of potato pancakes I'd fried for the holidays. Kids were running up and down the stairs. My husband, who hadn't yet moved out, was drinking wine with friends in the front room. "Aren't you so sad?" she asked.

I wasn't so sad. At least, not until she suggested I should be.

No matter how wrong our marriage was, divorce couldn't be better, or so these peers believed. Neither my husband nor I like to fight, but once we entered the twilight zone of divorce, they assumed, we'd lose our personalities and values and transform into raging lunatics of hate.

1

Our son would be irrevocably damaged. I'd be destitute, too miserable to work. My life would unravel, unroll, deliquesce.

Why were my friends so reluctant to let my marriage go? At first, I assumed they were simply concerned for me, and respectful of my husband. Some shared bad divorces they'd seen, including those of their own parents. But as I questioned them further, and began to read more about divorce, I realized that their worries largely dated to an earlier era—back when the only legal way to end a marriage was to prove your spouse a reprobate, when women had few ways to support themselves while property laws conspired against them, and fathers often were excluded from the daily care of their children.

Society and laws have changed dramatically since the 1960s and '70s, back when divorce was less common and judgment widespread. No-fault laws were new and few. Many kids lost frequent contact with their fathers and felt the stigma of having the only divorced family on the block. But today—nearly half a century later—the "average family" has completely changed, as have our roles. The family next door might easily be divorced, or headed by a single father. It might feature an unmarried couple with children, a biracial or same-gender couple, a transgender pair.

My friends' fears also were inflamed by biased reporting about divorce, it turned out, and blatant misrepresentations of the facts. Writers bemoaning today's changing family often conflate stats on social problems, such as the poverty of unwed mothers, with those on divorce. Unwed mothers are among the poorest people in our society, in part because about half of unwed mothers are adolescents. The fate of a tenth grader raising a baby tells us nothing about the economic future of two married professionals divorcing in their forties. But if you read an article claiming that divorce plunges mothers into poverty, you've just been hoodwinked into thinking it does. In their desire to promote good marriages, some writers and pundits seem determined to scare people into staying in bad ones.

Then there's the early study about childhood adjustment—begun in 1971, based on 131 kids from sixty families—by social worker turned psychologist Judith S. Wallerstein. She concluded that ten years after their parents' divorce, "almost half of the children entered adulthood as worried, under-achieving, self-deprecating and sometimes angry young men and women."

Wallerstein, a caring and dedicated advocate for children, continued flagging the risks of divorce until her death in 2012. But family scholars criticize the methods and conclusions of her early work, and an accumulation of evidence shows that her negative claims were overblown. There have since been hundreds of studies on childhood adjustment showing far rosier outcomes. Four decades of research show that 75 to 80 percent of kids whose parents divorce adjust fine and have no ongoing psychological, social, or academic problems. Yet anti-divorce ideologues still haul out Wallerstein's to "prove" the ills of divorce, probably because it's the only one they can find showing such dire results.

Contemporary studies of divorce that show a dip in health or longevity also can be misconstrued to augur fear. As with all types of loss or disruption, not everyone bounces back from divorce—such as some divorcees who had a preexisting condition of clinical depression. This subset of sufferers lowers the numerical average, but it has no actual bearing on the vast majority of us. Most people get through divorce fine; some become far happier.

While divorce has become as common as staying married, it's been re-stigmatized in some circles. Our hyper focus on healthy lifestyle choices has spawned a dark side—an unconscious judgment of any act that seems to deviate from Perfect Living. If using a plastic cup that may leach BPAs can harm your children, the reasoning goes, divorce must be worse. My friends' concerns also derived from this kind of thinking, as if ending a marriage were the relationship equivalent of existing on a diet of fried pork rinds and orange soda, the long-term ramifications sure to be grave.

* * *

I always had an optimistic view of divorce. My parents divorced in 1973, and I remained close to both. My mother spoke about divorce alongside women's liberation. Shortly before my husband and I split, my sister divorced, and became notably happier and more productive than when married. My father was living with his third ex-wife as a roommate in a far more symbiotic, laughter-filled friendship than the power struggle that had characterized their legal union.

My husband, the youngest of six, had almost no experience with divorce. His own parents had been married more than fifty years. He'd gleaned the idea from friends that it would be difficult for about two years. "Better to get those two years out of the way sooner rather than later," he said.

As we dived into those two difficult years, I discovered another reason why divorce has such a bad reputation. It's mind-bogglingly difficult to untangle a shared life. "It's like trying to take apart a rubber-band ball, every band woven in and around the others," one woman said. In some ways, our divorce should have been easier than most. Neither of us had had an affair. We didn't labor under the guilt of violating a cherished religious tradition. My husband has an almost preternatural calm, like Spock from *Star Trek*.

We did not devolve into enmity or despair, as friends forecasted, but I experienced many of the lowlights that divorce can and often does include: feeling socially insecure, needing to move yet being unable to choose a new home, and watching our five-year-old son hurl metal cars off the top of a stepladder and wondering, *Uh, is he upset about something?* I had the nauseating experience of witnessing my almost ex-husband enter an exclusive relationship with another woman quickly after moving out. I also had a minor medical crisis during that first year of separation, which is not atypical. Stress can cause real physical problems, as I would learn.

Divorce remains difficult, far more so than I realized. But the *external* reality has changed in ways that can help us all get through it more smoothly, and better protect those we love. Divorce brings inevitable sadness but also very *avoidable* pain, and we have many choices about how we handle the aspects over which we do have sway. We can support our children through this transition and help them feel stable, secure, and happy—rather than lost and alone. We can use a cooperative, sensitive legal approach, one of the new options that might actually improve our relationship, post-marriage—rather than spend tens of thousands of dollars on a vicious lawsuit spiraling out of control. Even an unwanted divorce can lead to surprising personal growth, new strengths, and closer connections with others—rather than a sense of ever-fraying bonds. Whether we like it or not, some of our greatest gains and most profound insights come through loss.

I began to appreciate my future ex-husband more with some distance. Our incompatibilities as spouses had obscured his good qualities, and effaced mine. I had so much anger and hurt in my marriage. We hold our feelings for others inside ourselves, and my resentment, painful to him, bored tunnels through me. Now, my burgeoning well of goodwill felt like a font of strength.

This book focuses on the early stages of divorce and tracks those difficult first two years in my own life, starting when my husband moved out in March 2012. That year was exactly forty years since my parents had separated. In that time, the world of divorce had completely transformed, as I would see, due to changes in laws and customs, new insights and new resources.

In 1969, California's then governor, Ronald Reagan, signed the nation's first no-fault divorce law, California's Family Law Act, which went into effect in 1970. No-fault is one of the most significant improvements in divorce law and a major reason so many divorces are less contentious today. Before no-fault, divorce basically had to be a domestic battle. The exact definition of "permissible grounds" varied from state to state, but the idea was the same across the states for centuries—divorce was an action taken by a "good" spouse against a bad one. The suing party generally had to prove not only that her spouse was morally bankrupt—had kept a mistress or slugged her numerous times, say—but also that she'd done nothing wrong herself.

People who wanted to divorce merely because they were desperately unhappy had few options. Some chose to lie in court, before witnesses—to fabricate vice. In New York, for example, a couple might collude with a friend to come to the apartment in skimpy lingerie and act like a mistress. The wife could then "discover" her husband frolicking with this other woman, and testify about it.

By the 1960s, these "legal fictions" were making a mockery of the nation's courts. In California, where cruelty could be grounds, Supreme Court of California Associate Justice Stanley Mosk described being lied to regularly before no-fault: "Every day, in every superior court in the state, the same melancholy charade was played: the 'innocent' spouse, generally the wife, would take the stand and, to the accompanying cacophony of sobbing and nose-blowing, testify under the deft guidance of an attorney to the spousal conduct that she deemed 'cruel.'"

Those who could afford it, such as my parents, traveled to places like the Dominican Republic, with short or nonexistent residency requirements and a version of no-fault. But most people had to commit the criminal offense of perjuring themselves in court—or remain stuck in their marriage. No-fault paved the way for an honest, cooperative divorce. Even if you're just making it up, an accusatory volley can easily breed mistrust and escalate into a verbal and financial war. No-fault allowed couples to end their marriages without destroying their relationships.

No-fault also saved lives. If a woman in an abusive marriage worked up the nerve to make a case against an aggressive husband in court, a judge could still deny the divorce. She now had to return home with her violent husband, after shaming him in public. Economists Betsey Stevenson and Justin Wolfers analyzed family violence surveys in the 1970s, before no-fault legislation, and again in the mid-1980s, after no-fault legislation had passed in some states. After no-fault divorce became an option, *the number of women murdered by their partners dropped by 10 percent in states that adopted no-fault divorce*. Domestic violence dropped by one-third. Suicide rates among women dropped by 8 to 16 percent in some states. Suicide rates among women continued to fall for more than a decade in the states the economists tracked.

No-fault led to the development of other ways to un-marry, legal approaches that *can actually improve the relationship on the other side of marriage*. But legal improvements are only part of the good divorce story. In the past four decades, advances in psychology have begun helping adults and children in divorce. We now know more about resilience, the power of gratitude, and how our thoughts affect our feelings. We have more tools for coping, ways to not just spring back but also spring forward. The field of positive psychology has blossomed, offering insights into happiness and methods for creating meaning and crafting lives in line with our strengths and values.

The active inclusion of fathers also has improved divorce. We now have decades of research confirming the notion that fathers *do* play a role in the social and emotional development of kids. This awareness has spurred new practices and policies that support co-parenting.

Meanwhile, new technology gives divorcing couples unprecedented access to information and support. You can look up the child- and spousal-support guidelines in your state, saving time and money by educating yourself. Online co-parenting programs offer new ways to track expenses and overnights, and to share photos, notes, and doctors' numbers. A distant or traveling parent can connect with her children on Skype. Social networking sites make it easier than ever for a newly single person to replace her former jogging partner (aka her husband), as well as to reconnect with old friends, meet other new singles, and even find dates.

Nearly every state now has staffed self-help centers at courthouses to answer questions, as well as parenting programs for those facing divorce. Many offer peer sessions for children. The options continue to expand for fee-based help such as divorce therapists, coaches, workshops, and for-profit programs such as one called "Divorce Detox."

• • •

In my career as a journalist, I'd written about love and marriage, dating and family, but never divorce, a topic that had been with me my whole life. Now that I was entering it from the adult's side, I realized I wanted to know more. How had my parents' divorce affected me, *really*? What actions lead to a decent, reasonably calm divorce, rather than a firestorm of anger? I wanted to learn about divorce in general, and about good ones, specifically.

I began by reaching out to family and friends, asking about their divorces, and those of people they knew. Then I visited online divorce support groups and chat rooms, and contacted lawyers, researchers, clergy, and family-focused nonprofits. I also read books about marriage and divorce in the Western world, and tracked down relevant studies in psychology, law, demographics, evolutionary biology, and neuroscience.

The most exciting part of the research, however, was not this systematic investigation but rather the chance encounters, often with strangers, who shared intimate details about their divorces—and lessons they'd learned. I love those seemingly random interactions that spark the surprising insight, the tossed-off phrase that sticks with you for years. I'm the kind of person who enjoys talking, to pretty much anyone, preferably about fundamental life concerns. I'll often find myself in an intense dialogue with someone I've just met. I'll talk to a garden hedge if no one else is around. One of the joys of ending a bad marriage is the chance to reconnect deeply not only with others but also with yourself, with your own strengths and tendencies.

I talked about divorce on airplanes over the Midwest, commuter trains on the East Coast, ferries chugging to and from Manhattan. I spoke to divorced people in coffee shops and hair salons, at a tango in South Florida, a cohousing community in rural New Hampshire, a think tank in Washington, DC. I discussed divorce—and listened to others' tales—while picking up my son from school, Hula-Hooping in the park, corresponding on OkCupid, going on dates.

I spoke to a couple hundred people in the midst of divorce or long past it. My approach was immersive. I was going through a divorce; it was constantly on my mind. I wanted to hear what other people had to say, to *feel* this experience fully.

Divorce, of course, is all around us—and there are plenty of good ones in the mix. My friends hadn't heard about them because the horror stories suck up the airtime.

Ending a bad marriage can be a better choice than staying in it—better for the adults, better for the kids. Probably better for the pets and the houseplants, too. But researchers and therapists I spoke to complained about a shroud of ignorance cloaking divorce, and the persistence of false beliefs.

"The negative impact of living in a bad marriage is incredible, on your health, on your career, on your social life," said Lawrence Birnbach, a psychoanalyst in private practice in New York and Connecticut, and the author of *How to Know If It's Time to Go.* "The conclusions of researchers fly in the face of so much of the negativity around divorce. This information is sorely, sorely needed."

• • •

We need to change how we talk about divorce. It's time to shuck off shame and accept divorce as a reality, using the vast knowledge available today to do it better. Why? Because the mismatch between perception and reality continues to make us angrier than we might be. Saddled with misplaced guilt or blame, we turn on each other and on ourselves at a time we need compassion, self-compassion, and cooperation.

One of the great advances in psychology since the 1960s has been the realization that our *thoughts* about events affect us, perhaps even more than the facts. If you *believe* you're going to be working two jobs while your ex-husband strides across the rolling courses of Bermuda, swinging a golf club and hoisting another beer, that perception can increase feelings of injustice, make you more combative and suspicious, and push a decent parting into a damaging, expensive fight. To put it another way, if fear makes you lash out at your ex in front of your kids, drink too much alcohol, and gorge on brownie-batter-filled Dunkin' Donuts while hiding under the covers, you're creating a reality that may be a little too lonely for a little too long. Assuming divorce must be dreadful often ensures that outcome.

It's easy to blame divorce for the friction generated during a marriage. A marriage may end because one spouse had affairs for a decade, using cash from the children's college fund. Friends lament the "bad divorce," but the affairs and the lying happened *during the marriage*. The divorce is the final snapped link in a weak relationship chain, the public unveiling of a long-stewing private conflict.

Sometimes "bad behavior" continues during the divorce. About 20 percent of American adults suffer a diagnosable mental illness over the course of a year, according to the National Institutes of Health. This likely explains some of the "crazy" divorce behavior we see. But people who are otherwise sane and logical can behave like Mr. Hyde during divorce. Fear and anxiety exacerbate anger, especially when combined with guilt or embarrassment—and a battery of lifestyle changes taking place all at once. It takes real work to hold the nuances in your head, to remain kind and considerate, to remember why you married in the first place and yet push forward to separate.

There are policy changes that still need to happen to protect divorcing families, and unmarried separating ones. Being dragged through court wreaks its own havoc; moving more divorces and related services out of the courts would help many. For the poor in particular, unrealistic child support obligations and aggressive enforcement can create a form of debtors' prison, sending indigent parents to jail, and right out of their children's lives. But a cultural shift, a deploring of anger-fueled escalation, a conviction that this behavior *is not okay* would help.

There are books to help you decide if you should stay married or get divorced. This is not one of them. It doesn't attempt to figure out the *if* but rather the *how*. Nor does it cover remarriage and stepfamilies, important realities for many. But my focus here is on transitioning *out* of the existing marriage rather than into a new one.

Some marriages end due to addiction, abuse, or mental illness. These problems erode intimacy and destroy trust on their own, and are also beyond the scope of this book. I believe you can have a decent divorce even when serious issues exist. You probably won't be eager to spend time with your ex. Your good divorce may look more like establishing your own life, minimizing conflict, and extricating yourself gracefully and kindly from the chaos of the other.

Throughout the book, I use the terms "divorce" and "separation" interchangeably. I'm focusing on the emotional and practical issues at a marriage's end, rather than the signing of the papers. I refer to my partner in divorce variously, too, as my husband or ex-husband, my future ex-husband or almost-ex, my husband emeritus, my *wusband*. Many people I spoke to wished for a term without the negative overlay of "ex," one that honors the union as a time-limited bond, something equivalent to "my high school girlfriend," or "my first love." I tried "my first husband," but without a second, it sounded overly aspirational. "Even the word 'divorce' sounds too negative," my father insisted. "There should be another word."

About two million people divorce in the United States each year, and the numbers are growing around the world. Everyone likes to say that marriage takes work. Why not work equally hard to have a good divorce?

Divorce is a journey, as nearly all the difficult phases of life seem to be termed these days. If your marriage is strong and adheres through the years, that's a journey, too. But if it ends, your life cracks open, maybe just a sliver, or maybe in a great, gaping maw. New light comes in. As scary as that is, it's also a chance for evolution. How often do you get to start over, hit the "reset" button, examine your beliefs and habits and how you live? It's perhaps more scary than anything else to date, and it goes on and on, until the new life you're creating feels like your "real life," solid and set. But don't let anyone tell you that nothing good can come from this, or that there won't be moments of wisdom and insight and even exhilaration.

• • •

We've grown up with stories of love and marriage. *Romeo and Juliet. Father Knows Best. Cinderella.* The coach and his wife on *Friday Night Lights.* Our marriages exist under the long shadow of the more perfect unions in our minds. They can feel thin and dry when compared to the greatest love songs, inspiring novels, passionate poetry, *When Harry Met Sally.*

There is, however, no Canon of Divorce. There's the occasional story, but the good divorce is largely an unwritten tale. There's no grand, misty vision that our own falls short of meeting. Which is great, because it means we can write the narrative of the new divorce now. We can toss aside the tragic tales, remain open to the myriad possibilities for relationships, and assert the good divorce as the new norm.

LOVE, NEW AMERICAN STYLE

PART ONE

LOVE NEW AMERICAN STYLE

CHAPTER ONE

The Joy of Ex

My Quest for a More Perfect Disunion

❂

Many people assume divorce destroys relationships, but some former spouses get along better after they part. Fears about being single, miserable, and broke tend to be overblown. My husband and I set off on a quest to separate, together.

We are stardust, we are golden . . .
And we got to get ourselves back to the garden.
— Joni Mitchell, Canadian folk singer, "Woodstock"

THE ENLIGHTENED DIVORCÉE

I met Chloe in the spring of 2011. We were sitting on the floor in a parent-toddler class at a Waldorf-inspired school in Manhattan's East Village, knitting narrow scarves from dye-free wool for our children to roll together in creative play. The Waldorf movement, begun by the Austrian philosopher Rudolf Steiner in 1919, propagates a nature-based, earth mother approach to child-rearing. Waldorf parents aspire to a simple, old-fashioned way of life. Or so I thought.

I was new to the group, having recently moved back to the New York City area after three years in the countryside, relocation being among the many attempts my husband and I had made to get along better. Now we were living in Hoboken, a charming town of nineteenth-century town houses across the Hudson River from Manhattan. Hoboken is kayaking distance from Midtown. But in the way that no place ever quite fit in that marriage, I felt somehow "less than" the hip Manhattan moms due to my New Jersey address.

After class, the other mothers headed to a small-batch pretzel bakery on a gentrifying stretch of Avenue B. I went along, pushing my son in his stroller, listening to them discuss summer plans. Chloe, tall and thin, sat at a metal table wearing large sunglasses, her caramel-colored curls tossed over one shoulder. She was going to France for a month with her tall, curly-haired daughter and her daughter's father, whom she was in the process of divorcing.

"Wait. You're divorcing and going to France together?" I asked.

"Yes," she said, seemingly exasperated by my slow grasp of European travel with one's ex. "His family is from France, and we want our daughter to see them," as if spending a month abroad with the man she was divorcing was totally normal.

I was dumbfounded, and something within me stirred. I'd begun fantasizing about being free of my marriage, but I didn't want to cut my husband out of my life entirely, and certainly not out of our son's. He was a good father. He mattered to our son, and to me. Also, I wanted to maintain some of the activities we enjoyed together as a family. Chloe's situation was a revelation: You could divorce and still vacation with your ex? Where do you sign up?

"We had a really good therapist," Chloe said. "She also told us not to get apartments in the same building, as we'd planned, but nearby instead. She thought we needed more privacy."

Chloe was my introduction to today's new, good divorce. Certainly I'd seen decent partings. When my parents divorced, they remained polite to each other. They didn't fight. My father supported all of us while my mom went back to school to get her bachelor's degree in engineering. But they weren't *pals*. We didn't have dinner together as a family, or travel to visit relatives in Cleveland, let alone Europe. I rarely said "my mother and father" in the same sentence, a linguistic omission that now sounded tragic when considering how my own child might fare if we divorced.

Yet here was Chloe, maintaining an active family with her ex. Was there some new kind of divorce styling happening?

I started asking around, casually at first. I began hearing more stories of former spouses remaining actively connected. A friend-of-a-Facebook-friend in Colorado, Anne, said that after four years of a friction-filled marriage, she and her husband divorced, and finally formed a great relationship. Anne said she felt gratitude for her once-husband, whereas when they were married, his inconsiderateness and erratic emotional life constantly frustrated her. "The thing is, we weren't great married. But he's the best ex-husband you could ever ask for. I'm the happiest divorced person on the planet," she said.

"Everyone's jealous on the playground. Everyone says, 'Anne has the best life. She gets to live across the street from her husband, and have a boyfriend.'

"I think maybe we shouldn't try to fit ourselves into being one way. We should just find situations that work."

Up late one night trolling the Internet, I stumbled upon the blog of Susan Orlins, a sixty-something writer in Washington, DC, who writes about divorce and other topics in her blog and book *Confessions of a Worrywart: Husbands, Lovers, Mothers, and Others*. Susan had divorced in 1998 and eventually begun taking annual summer vacations with her former husband and their three daughters. "The only thing that feels odd," Susan wrote about their 2011 trip, "is that it feels so normal to be all together."

Later, I reached out to Susan, and she became something of a Good Divorce Mentor. When we finally met, she said that when a hurricane had sent a tree flying into her house, she and her daughters moved in with her ex-husband for three weeks during repairs. This was six years after they'd separated. She could turn to him in crisis because they'd maintained a good relationship. She felt confident she'd be there for him, too, if he needed aid.

• • •

My husband and I started talking about divorce seriously at my friend Sara's wedding. It was the last weekend of May, too cold to be sitting on folding chairs on the beach in cocktail dresses, yet visually perfect, like one of those magazine ads for a destination wedding so evocative, you tear up with emotion just reading the room rates. Standing before the Atlantic in her strapless gown, her thin shoulders hunched against the cold, my friend looked vulnerable yet secure, as if she knew this man would always hold back the tide.

Sara's groom read his vows, shivering a little as he promised to try to listen to everything she had to say, to support her dreams and ambitions, to continue improving his mind to remain interesting to her. Sara also made promises, but her husband's moved me more. His vision of marriage as a super-connected joint project sounded like what I'd long wanted.

I sat on my chair, huddled under my husband's borrowed suit jacket, and looked from the marrying couple to the man I'd married. We hadn't written our own vows, but if we had, we would not have made those promises. Their expectations of marriage were compatible, whereas ours were not. Yes, people change, but if two people in the same union can't agree on a vision of marriage, they aren't likely to change in ways that will make them happier together.

After the ceremony, the guests picked their way through the powdery white sand toward the hotel. I slumped against the sand dunes rising up along the shore. My husband sat down next to me. "You know," I said, "what are we doing? Why are we still doing this?"

He wasn't expecting me to suggest divorce on this rare romantic weekend, our son back home with my mother. But it wasn't totally unexpected, either. We gazed out at the chilly ocean for a while. Then we pulled ourselves up and joined the reception, a little glassy-eyed. But that seemed normal at a wedding; as usual, we *looked* fine.

The next afternoon, we drove around, car touring. "I met a guy last night with a great custody arrangement," my husband said. "He takes his daughter to school every morning and plays with her afterward until the mom gets home. It made me feel hopeful." I looked at him, driving responsibly, hands at ten and two. I felt hopeful, too.

But then it was summer. Who wants to divorce in the summer when there are so many fun things to do that seem to require a partner? Divorce rates actually drop in the summer, as do online searches for information about it. They rise in the fall, taper off over the holidays, then begin climbing toward Valentine's Day and peak in March.

We focused on our marriage again. Our repeated efforts to salvage our union are typical. Others may proclaim that divorce is the "easy way out" or that new laws make it as simple to divorce as it is to get a driver's license, but once I began investigating in earnest, I didn't find one divorcing couple that hadn't put in the hard work first, prioritized their children's needs over their own, decided to live with less than they wanted for years or even decades, insisting to themselves and everyone else that it was fine, they could do it, they didn't need more. It's incredibly hard to accept that you can't love each other well, bound in this way, and it often takes years to admit.

We decided to see a New York City therapist who'd been counseling couples for nearly fifty years and specialized in the effects of marriage and divorce on children. My husband and I took our bikes on the ferry from Hoboken, then rode up the path along the Hudson River to her office in a tall apartment building on the Upper West Side.

"You really need to be more flexible about how you think about relationships," the therapist said. "I've seen couples who live in separate apartments but remain married, couples who divorce but share all major holidays, couples who have open marriages. Marriage and divorce aren't any one thing."

I liked this notion of a more flexible view of how we wed and how we part, an idea that relationships exist on a spectrum between the two poles of soul mates and enemies for life, and that there are viable and worthy arrangements in between.

I also liked her assurance that if we did split, we'd likely remarry, given our ages and the age of our child. She gave us a statistic that sounded hopeful—in a study looking at U.S. census data from the mid-1990s, 69 percent of women and 78 percent of men remarried after divorce. The official remarriage rate dropped in the short time between this conversation and our own divorce, as more people began opting out of marriage at all stages, but the number of *unmarried* couples living together doubled. Whatever the legal structure, we'd likely both fall in love again.

I was flat-out scared about supporting myself alone. This is a realistic concern for many of us, even those who don't live in the most expensive city in the country, as I did. Cohabiting creates economies of scale: one cable bill, one comfy couch, one order of Thai food that clearly feeds two people. But my fears of poverty, and the worries of some friends, also were informed by another widely cited, flawed study—this one so faulty its own author eventually retracted it.

In 1985, Harvard sociologist Lenore Weitzman published a book based on a study of parents who divorced in Los Angeles in 1977. It claimed that the mothers' standard of living plummeted after divorce *by nearly three-quarters*. Their once-husbands, meanwhile, were living twice as well. These numbers were so provocative, so scary, and frankly so in line with the growing concerns about gender inequality, that journalists and others cited them, unquestioned, for years. They appeared in newspapers and magazines, social science and law review articles, and at least two dozen state appellate and Supreme Court cases. As Arizona State University professor emeritus Sanford Braver noted, they were "the most widely known and influential social science results" of the '80s and '90s.

There was just one problem with these figures. They were wrong.

As Braver describes in his page-turning whodunit, *Divorced Dads: Shattering the Myths*, his own calculations showed that divorced women *retained* about three-quarters of their prior standard of living, rather than lost it. Other researchers at the time were reaching the same conclusion. Weitzman's study, meanwhile, continued to gain attention.

Finally, in 1996, Weitzman allowed sociologist Richard R. Peterson to view her records. Peterson recalculated, based on Weitzman's own data, and found what Braver and others had suspected: Weitzman had flipped her numbers, showing what she *believed* to be true.

Weitzman published an acknowledgment of her mistake in the *American Sociological Review*. But who reads sociology reviews? The idea had become part of the common store of knowledge, and many people continue to believe it.

Even the amended results paint an inaccurately bleak picture, when factoring in details such as tax breaks for the custodial mother, and expenses the father might pay. There is no one indisputable figure about the economics of divorce, as Braver notes, because there are a variety of ways to calculate both expenses and advantages. But divorce isn't the de facto plunge into poverty many people assume.

The outlook is also better for women today because along with no-fault divorce came "equitable distribution" property laws, a fairer way of dividing property. In the past, in many states, a couple's property belonged to the titleholder, which basically meant the man. Today, every state views marital assets as subject to either equitable distribution or community property laws, both of which split property accumulated in marriage equally or fairly, as opposed to going to the man, who will then dole out what he sees fit.

Some people earn more money after divorce because they can concentrate on their careers once their negative, critical spouse leaves the building. For others, the pressure of having to fend for themselves snaps them into action. Maybe not right away; stress can scatter focus, compromise performance, and cause illness resulting in missed days. But person after person I spoke to told me about "kicking it" at work, finally being motivated to take charge of their finances, or even watching their former spouse succeed.

I gained two hours a day after my husband moved out—time I'd formerly spent ruminating about our problems. I landed a fellowship to do communications work in the South Bronx, then quickly discovered I wanted to write again, after years of a marriage-induced creative lull. My career, and my enthusiasm for it, felt re-railed.

That summer after my friend Sara's wedding, before we split, my husband and I took our bikes on the ferry from Hoboken to Manhattan every other week, riding up along the river together to the therapist's office. In a tiny foreshadowing of how separation would feel, counseling became something we did together, the breezy riverfront ride, the weird hyperreality of walking out of her office and up the wide, bustling sidewalk an hour later, holding our innermost concerns in our hands. The intensity helped me see my partner more clearly, and with more compassion. In an odd way, it made me feel closer. Years later, I would look back at this strange time and say, "He was there with me. He went through it, too."

HOW WE GOT HERE, PERSONALLY

We married in July 2005 on Manhattan's Lower East Side. Friends and family gathered on the red concrete steps outside the romantically dilapidated historic temple, drinking coffee from to-go cups. My slender mom and beautiful aunt Judie looked glitzy, even at 9 a.m., in their fitted suits, leaning against the chipped metal balustrade, smoking cigarettes.

We'd chosen a popular venue, a Gothic-style synagogue built in 1847. The unrenovated space evoked a palpable sense of history. The violet light filtering through the stained-glass windows, the filigree decay of the sanctuary—always cool, smelling of clay—radiated a feeling of capaciousness, of hope, the way that ruins, wreckage, even the abandoned dreams of a marriage can conjure up not only sadness for the past but also excitement for the future. It assures you that this synagogue, this city, this life, is not set in stone, not fixed and established and spoken for. Anything can happen, and still may. I felt a thrilling sense of possibility in that space.

So did others. People started requesting the synagogue for weddings and large events. We got a good deal on the room because we accepted an early-morning slot.

I'm telling you about the place I wed because while the synagogue held personal significance for me, I also liked how stylish it was. Sarah Jessica Parker had married there! I cared even then, in those halcyon wedding-planning days, how my marriage looked to others. Of course, most brides care about their weddings. We've been sold for so long on the notion that the cut of the dress and the frosting on the cake affect, in some alchemical way, the quality of the marriage. I contributed to this fantastical formula, having spent years of my journalism career writing for bridal magazines.

For me, though, the typical wedding-day concern about appearances lasted into my marriage, reflecting a lack of solidity at the core. I felt, at times, that we were building our marriage from the outside in, erecting the scaffolding of a life and hoping the foundation would pour itself in. Other times, our marriage seemed like one of those molten chocolate lava cakes. So delicious in a dessert, that wobbly center can give you an ulcer in a marriage. Intimacy, it turns out, doesn't accrete from the outside—at least, it didn't for us.

Worrying about what others think also derives, I now believe, from discomfort with how we appear to ourselves. Living with an action that counters our sense of integrity, such as sustaining an undermining or loveless marriage, can make us search for reassurance from without.

My ex and I were so attracted to each other. We enjoyed the same people and parties. We cared about writing and ethics. We wanted a homey home life. We wanted it to work. We worked at our marriage with an almost Calvinist zeal, believing more effort could yield a better match. Or he did; I was probably channeling the sculptor Rodin, as if by constantly chipping away at each other, we'd reveal an edifice of perfect love.

I was alone, without family, in a large and competitive city, working as a freelance writer, an insecure profession. All these factors, perhaps, made me need so much from my husband, so much intimacy and connection, so much participation and involvement and enthusiastic love. He, in contrast, had spent his life in and around New York City and was deeply embedded in his super-stable life. He lived forty minutes away from his still-married parents, who still spent afternoons reading in their peaceful living room overlooking the Hudson River. Perhaps it was this solidity that felt like a persistent coldness to me, a repeated brushing-off. Or maybe, as he thought, we simply had different notions of emotional intimacy.

I complained that he ignored my preferences, strong-armed his will in wide, searing swaths across my interests and desires. And I failed him, too, because while I meant to protest the independent way in which he made decisions that affected us both, I wound up criticizing his decisions instead. In my complaining about this house or that town, I was telling him, day in and day out, that he'd failed to make me happy. And as modern as we thought ourselves to be, and indeed are, he, the Husband, wanted to take care of his wife. And I, the Wife, wanted to be cared for by my husband.

I was thirty-eight and he was thirty-nine when we wed. We'd left marriage until the last minute, prioritizing work, socializing, and freedom above starting a family. It's easy to look at our lifestyle as causing our divorce, creating in us an insufficient reverence for marriage. Every time a marriage breaks up, it's tempting to launch a wholesale condemnation of your choices or values. But you have to fight against this self-critique, because people leave marriages from all lifestyles, from all religions and no religion at all. This fact can be discouraging to those of us who love matrimony; if there were one cause for divorce, there might be one way to protect marriage. But no matter what you think you should have done differently or how you suspect your partner failed, there's a couple breaking up who spent their time and tended to their marriage in exactly the opposite way.

People divorce across the States, in every age group, and increasingly in countries around the world. In the U.S., divorce rates are highest in the Bible Belt and the West, where so-called traditional family values reign. In the 2004, 2008, and 2012 elections, the highest divorce rates were in the Republican-voting "red" states. Researchers cite the early age of marriage in these communities that emphasize abstinence. Youthful marriages, between spouses who perhaps haven't completed college and lack the income and self-knowledge that come with age, are more vulnerable to divorce. As of 2010, the states with the highest divorce rates were Nevada, Arkansas, Wyoming, Idaho, and Kentucky.

And yet, sixty-year-olds living on hippie communes in California divorce, too.

As our union continued to fail, my work suffered. I acquired aches and pains and a sinus infection that lasted two years. I grew sluggish and enervated. My husband grew defensive and then quite critical. I felt he'd adopted a pessimistic, coldhearted, narrow-eyed view of me, and a suspicion about my capabilities. This attitude probably violated his values as much as my own sluggish negativity affronted mine.

We also had a baby, and as anyone with children will tell you, parents catch the cold-of-the-week fifty-two weeks a year, with those toddlers crawling about the floor, teething on strangers' tennis shoes. But we had almost no disagreements about parenting. We never believed that the presence of our small child contributed to our unhappiness together.

When we wed, on that sunny, Sunday morning in July, my rabbi read marriage vows with this vision: "When you come to the end of your life, may you look at each other and say, 'Because of you, I lived the life I wanted to live. Because of you, I became the person I wanted to be.'" Six years into our marriage, eleven years into our relationship, we looked at each other and felt the opposite to be true. Our marriage had made each of us more adrift in a life we didn't want to lead.

We were locked in that kind of marriage, one in which I felt shamed in my own eyes, and this with a man I respect and admire, who I truly believe is a valuable person with significant work to do in the world. When you're in that kind of marriage, one that's driving the helium out of your spirit, divorce beckons like a hot-air balloon ride over a wild-flower valley. Even when you know about the crazy headlong crash that can happen when you finally have to bring that balloon down, divorce looks like all the best parts of freedom.

HOW WE GOT HERE, HISTORICALLY

Divorce is the flip side of marriage, and as a culture, we keep changing what we want and need from the marital state. While we experience our marriages as private affairs, they exist within the framework of society. We marry in a time and place; broad cultural movements affect our most intimate relationship.

We've been arguing about divorce probably as long as we've been marrying. "What a violent and cruel thing it is to force the continuing of those together, whom God and nature in the gentlest end of marriage never joined," wrote the seventeenth-century British poet John Milton in *The Doctrine and Discipline of Divorce*, a pamphlet railing against England's virtually nonexistent divorce laws in 1644. England's King Henry VIII had helped usher in the English Reformation more than a hundred years earlier in his own attempt to end his first marriage. Yet, a century later, in this same country, British subjects still had no real way to divorce.

It wasn't much different on this side of the Atlantic. In colonial America, divorce was extremely rare. You could divorce in certain cases, such as if your husband had deserted you, remarried, and started a new family, as happened to Anne Clarke, a mother of two in the Massachusetts Bay Colony. In 1643, a judge granted her the very first divorce in the colonies, based on these grounds.

If you were *merely* mismatched, desperately unhappy, consumed by hate? Well, that was marriage.

Divorce laws in the U.S. remained largely the same for the next three hundred years. Divorce was a punishment for egregious moral failing in the courts. It was a sacrilege in the church. It wasn't done in polite society. Of course people did it, but not without shame and serious social and economic repercussions.

This hostility toward divorce makes sense if you consider the vulnerability of families, and of women in particular, for most of human history. For thousands of years before the birth of Christ, and afterward, well into the Middle Ages, life was about survival more than satisfaction. Marriage was part of the extended family effort to stay alive.

A spouse was meant to be a helpmate, not a soul mate, and men and women fulfilled vital, gender-defined roles. Someone else, such as your parents, probably chose your partner. They could be forgiven for not weighing in factors such as whether or not he shared your love of French poetry or boasted the muscle-rippled torso you admired. In our hardscrabble agrarian past, a spouse needed to contribute—and to stick around for the long haul.

With the rise of industrialization in the West, opportunities arose in burgeoning cities, good jobs that required men to relocate to get them. Parents began to lose their authority over their grown children's decisions, including the choice of spouse. Marriage became a more intimate arrangement, between the two involved. But even within this smaller, fleeter unit, men and women had well-defined, truly critical roles to play.

Flash-forward to the twentieth century. In the West, rapid advances in wealth and public health brought new comfort and safety. If you were to visit a typical middle-class family in the United States after World War II, you would see a home life that was growing ever safer and easier. Babies were making it through childhood. Adults were living longer. New luxuries proliferated—dishwashers, toasters, percolators, Hamburger Helper. The age-old struggle for basic survival had largely been met, and then some. Food? *Check.* Clothing? *Check.* Wall-to-wall carpeting? *Take off your shoes and get comfortable.* Marriage's urgent role waned—though the fear and loathing of divorce clung on with sticky fingers for much of the century.

As an adult, I often wondered, *What happened in the 1970s, anyway?* After the storied nuclear-family life of the 1950s and early 1960s, why did so many couples, such as my parents, suddenly want out of marriage?

Johns Hopkins University sociologist Andrew Cherlin offers one way to think about how material and cultural developments in the middle of the twentieth century and onward changed marriage and contributed to divorce. As our external reality improved, what young people needed from a partner changed. There began to be an "emphasis on emotional satisfaction and romantic love," as Cherlin put it.

While most of us dream of a romantic, passionate marriage, love-based matches are vulnerable in a way that those early, survival-based unions were not. The glue is emotional connection, friendship, *depth of feeling.* Unlike the daily struggle for existence, these needs can change.

• • •

As home life grew easier, homemaking became more mundane, largely "administrative," to use the term of William Goode, an influential mid-century sociologist. Many women began to chafe at their traditional roles. Talcott Parsons, another leading sociologist of the day, wrote about his concern that being shut out of the world of work created "role strain" for women.

In 1963, journalist Betty Friedan published *The Feminine Mystique,* a huge bestseller that is often credited with galvanizing the modern women's rights movement. *The Feminine Mystique* said what both men and women were beginning to notice—the role of wife and mother was no longer working for all women.

My mother talked about reading about *The Feminine Mystique* with her sister, my aunt Judie, and dismissing it as hogwash. Then, slowly, living it. She'd married in one era, and matured during another. As my mother said, "I never heard my own name. I was always introduced as my husband's wife or my children's mother." For my mother and women like her, the late 1960s and early 1970s marked the beginning of a long quest for a new kind of autonomy. For some, this meant leaving marriages begun on obsolescent terms.

Lawmakers began passing reforms to meet women's growing desire for expanded options, and to grant more rights to minorities of all types. The 1960s and '70s were a dynamic time socially and legally. In 1963, Congress passed the Equal Pay Act requiring employers to pay women as much as men. Most didn't jump to comply, but the idea had been introduced that women's efforts *should* be equally compensated. The following year, Congress passed the Civil Rights Act, outlawing major forms of discrimination based on sex as well as on race, ethnicity, religion, and nationality. A decade later, the Equal Credit Opportunity Act made it illegal to refuse credit to women simply because they weren't men—something banks could previously do.

No-fault laws began to emerge at this time. No-fault does not *cause* divorce, as some like to claim. There is no legal process so enticing that people leave perfectly good marriages merely to experience it. There was a spike in divorce rates after the passage of no-fault here and in other countries as they followed suit. But the numbers leveled off and have begun dropping in recent years.

The United Nations declared 1975 International Women's Year, with its own theme song: Helen Reddy's "I Am Woman." I'd choreographed dance steps to this lilting, upbeat tune as a child, stomping and swaying in the parking lot of the apartment complex we lived in after my parents divorced.

But women weren't the only ones who began wanting more from life. Men did, too. As we moved into the 1970s and onward, our collective vision of marriage continued evolving beyond romantic love, into something even more challenging—a passionate team committed not only to the union, but also to each individual's *personal growth*. Both men and women began hoping that marriage would support their development and dreams. As Cherlin wrote about this shift, "An even more individualistic perspective on the rewards of marriage took root."

One way to think about the continual ratcheting up of expectations for ourselves and our marriages is through psychologist Abraham Maslow's hierarchy of needs. Maslow argued that after we meet our basic needs, we don't spend our days snoozing and playing with chew toys; we turn toward *higher-order* needs, such as self-actualization. In marriage, this meant women and men seeking to leave those who prevented them from becoming all that they could be.

Today, as much as we revere the *idea* of marriage, we don't need it as we once did. We make our commitments in a swirl of conflicting ideals. We value individuality and partnership, responsibility and passion, family and freedom. We live in a postmodern assemblage, like a James Rosenquist painting, slices of various visions slammed together in a composition that feels energizing and exciting, but also discordant and hard to grasp.

We still want to wed; in polls, most people say they want to marry. But as our expectations for love, intimacy, and happiness have increased, so has our willingness to leave a mediocre marriage in pursuit of a better match.

I believe most people are happier and more productive with a solid partner. But marriage isn't a *prerequisite* for a full adult life. We don't need marriage to have sex; since the FDA's approval of the birth control pill in 1960, and its eventual widespread availability, we've been free to be intimate without fear of unwanted pregnancy. Women don't need husbands to leave their parents' house, and men can create perfectly comfortable homes without wives. We don't need marriage to have children; with the development of new reproductive technology such as in vitro fertilization, even parenting is a partner-optional affair for those who can afford it. While gay couples finally won the long battle for the right to marry in 2015, many others fail to see the point.

As the number of gay marriages increases, we'll likely see a rise in gay divorces. It's not hard to imagine the articles and blog posts to follow, decrying the "breakdown of the homosexual family!" But this will be a ludicrous claim. When marriage is a *choice*, we are also free to choose out of it.

· · ·

Two years before meeting Chloe, my husband and I were still married, living in the country north of Manhattan in a big cedar house in the little woods. My mother called one afternoon to tell me that she and my stepfather were divorcing. After thirty-four years of marriage, he was leaving.

Though divorce rates have declined in recent years, some groups are seeing a spike. During the past twenty years, the divorce rate has doubled among baby boomers, and tripled for those over the age of sixty-five, due in part to another public health gain—increased longevity.

My mother did not want to be part of this particular trend. She was reeling, in shock. She had no interest in being single at sixty-nine, sought no liberating life makeover this time around. She told me that she'd spent the past year trying to convince my stepfather to stay.

My mom and stepfather had been married since the time I was eight. He'd taught me to throw a softball, use a power drill, drive a car. I'd grown up with him, and his two boys. Now he wanted out of the marriage. I wasn't as surprised as I might have been, or as upset. My mother and stepfather hadn't been getting along for years, maybe since all of us kids finished high school and left home, leaving behind an empty *Brady Bunch*–style nest, no studio audience, and a laugh track that grew fainter each year. My first thought was that she was now free to meet someone she got along with better—an unempathetic reaction, I later realized. We all can have these empathy glitches, these moments of being unable to feel another's pain, or grasp their joy. With time, watching my mother try to cope with this unwanted split gave me an intimate look at just how wrenching divorce can be.

That night, my husband and toddler asleep, I logged onto JDate to look for single men her age. The house was silent except for the cicadas outside and the clacking of my keyboard. I decided to create an online dating profile for my mom. I began working on the "activities" section. My mother dislikes all sports, but she'd recently bought jogging pants for walking her dog. I looked for "walking the poodle" under "athletic activities you enjoy." Not an option. Nor was redoing the kitchen cabinets. Or shopping for the grandkids. Where was the box for "shopping for grandkids" on this stupid site?! I resented the implication that my mother was a loafer because she didn't throw a football. Football? This was JDate, for heaven's sake. We throw around ideas, witticisms, references to the Holocaust at times when others can't fathom the connection. We're the people of the book, not the pigskin. My mom smokes a couple of packs of cigarettes a day; that's a thrill sport. Where was "smoking cigarettes" on the list of activities? I was offended for my mother, angered by the implication that she wasn't a "catch" because she didn't throw balls.

I recognized this sense of defending my mother against some broader societal disapprobation. It reminded me of how I felt after she and my dad separated. Divorce was on its way to becoming as common as staying married, but as a kid, I'd felt an unspoken censure I needed to dispute.

I scrolled through the photos of single septuagenarians in South Florida, silently fuming. Why didn't I *know* any attractive, smart, older men?

Wait a minute! I did know an attractive older man, I suddenly realized. *My father.*

My father was single. He was still pretty tall, which my mother would appreciate. My dad didn't look a day over . . . sixty-seven. He was funny. Smart. Fun-loving.

Maybe this would be their chance to reunite, perhaps move back to that great house we once owned in Ohio with the swimming pool!

When I called my dad to tell him, I discovered he already knew. "If there's anything I can do to help, of course I'm happy to," he said, with a lack of self-interest I found chilling.

Of course you can help! I thought. *Fly down to Florida and woo my mother with the boyish humor you're known and sometimes loved for!* It obviously hadn't occurred to my dad that this was his big reunification opportunity.

I know this might sound like I never recovered from my parents' divorce. It was nearly forty years later, and I was still fantasizing that they'd reunite. But I wanted my parents to be happy. If I thought about who was worthy of my excellent mother and funny father, the people I came up with were my parents. Clearly their divorce didn't poison me against marriage, or against either of them.

TOWARD A MORE PERFECT DISUNION

The fall after my friend Sara's wedding, my husband again raised the idea of splitting up. Whereas I'd been the one to bring up the topic of divorce during conflicts in the past, he now led the charge.

In November, we announced our plans for a trial separation. In January, my husband and I sat on our big, squashy couch under the window in our front room, our legs tucked under a soft orange blanket we'd bought when we had a country house, and reaffirmed our commitment to split, at least on a trial basis. We sat on the couch every evening for a week, refining the details—who'd watch our son when, how we'd talk about it at parties. We agreed that we could share friends, attend the same parties, drive out to the beach with our son as a family. We vowed not to discuss dating. While we never agreed on marriage, we had a nearly identical view of separation.

Still, I was scared. What if my naysaying friends were right? Would I end up spending nights alone with my parti poodle, Paco, who liked to roll in goose poop in the park and then nibble on my hair? My husband said we should focus on the good parts of our marriage and consider it a success that had run its term.

"No one else seems to see it that way," I said.

"This is really between you and me," my future ex insisted. "It's not really their business."

In our separation, he finally voiced that us-against-the-world unity I'd long desired. He argued for getting out while we were still relatively young, while we could still find other partners. We had one child, and owed him happier parents. "Better to get the two awful years out of the way sooner rather than later," he said, repeating his notion that the tough part would last a couple of years.

This coolheaded stoicism, often squelching in marriage, felt reassuring and uplifting now that we were contemplating divorce. When he'd been my husband, I'd found him too spottily present in the face of my shifting moods. But I needed a lot less from him in his role as a future ex, and he seemed far more able to give it. I gazed across the couch at this man I'd known for years and thought, *I'm going to wind up loving him more during our divorce than when we were married.*

I began looking around in earnest for stories of good divorces, seeking wisdom I could glean. Many people told me they'd learned from their parents' errors. A forty-something single father of four from California said his parents had stopped speaking after they divorced. This allowed him, as a rowdy teen, to stay out all night by lying to both. Years later, when he and his wife separated, he was determined to keep a tighter rein on his boys. He rented a place down the street from the family home, and transitioned into a close friendship with his ex.

A mother of two in Oregon named Vicki said her mother's criticism of her father had always seemed self-serving. "It just made me feel more negative toward her than toward him." She made a personal commitment to not bad-mouth her children's father, or even use the term "ex" when speaking of him. Today, happily remarried, she has a good relationship with her children and with her first husband.

I talked to grown children of divorce who said they appreciated these kinds of efforts from their parents. "I always feel like they really love me, but they were just two different people," said Elizabeth, a twenty-something fashion buyer from a small Southern Baptist town outside

Dallas. Her parents had met shortly after high school, married, then divorced when she was two. Elizabeth grew up in town with her mother and grandfather; her dad moved to a ranch house twenty minutes away. Both parents made an effort to remain friendly, her father dropping by for a southern meal swimming in butter when he was in town. "My mom, even to this day, will say, 'I love your daddy, but I can't be married to him.' My dad says the same thing. That is comforting to know."

I also began paying attention to the good marriages around me, to what made them work. In some ways, seeing great marriages made me more aware of how hard my husband and I had been working, and how fruitlessly.

"I hate this idea that marriage takes 'work,'" said my friend Andrew, married for nearly two decades in a relationship I see as a solid example of the Good Marriage. "I consider myself the steward of my wife's happiness, as she is of mine. Sometimes I have to do things that I wouldn't have chosen otherwise, but it's to help her be happy and that just isn't a sacrifice. It's what I want to do."

I agree with Andrew. I think active consideration matters in marriage—responsibility for another, care and concern and compromise. But I also think we get carried away with this idea of work, overly confident in its power, believing any two people can be happily married if they just keep at it with hammers and claws.

If we divorced, I'd return to being alone. But at that time, with twelve years of "working on it" having yielded more resentment and less love, being alone sounded less lonely than staying wed.

• • •

My ex and I believed we could do it, alter the terms of our relationship, change it into something less enmeshed. After years of disconnection in marriage, together we crafted a vision of our new, unmarried lives. We wanted to scale back our interactions and expectations, and thus become happier adults and better parents. We set off to see whether this dream could be made true.

PART TWO

DOING IT WELL

CHAPTER TWO

Principles of Parting

Laying the Groundwork for a Good Divorce

Many of us feel overwhelmed or helpless in the midst of divorce, in part because we face this major life transition totally unprepared. Adopting principles of parting can help us regain a sense of control and purpose.

Change your opinions, keep to your principles; change your leaves, keep intact your roots.

—Victor Hugo, nineteenth-century French novelist

A month after my husband moved out, I went to a networking event in Manhattan with a vague notion of getting out, meeting new people. I was speaking to the group's cofounder, a woman named Cole, a late-forty-something professional in an impeccable black suit, waves of brown hair tumbling down her back. Cole was draped like a kudzu vine over a handsome, fit man I'd spotted earlier and hoped was single. He was dating Cole, it turned out. They'd met years ago but gotten together only recently, after they'd both divorced.

"Divorce is awful!" Cole said, beaming like she'd been named homecoming queen, won the lottery, and inherited a classic-six apartment on Manhattan's Upper West Side.

"What are you talking about?" I said. "You're glowing."

"Awful," she repeated.

Maybe her divorce was dreadful, but the aftermath certainly looked appealing. I was reminded of one reason my future ex and I had started out on this scary, sometimes tear-inducing path; we each wanted to be in a loving, comforting, exhilarating relationship—with someone else.

When people talk about the horror of divorce, they're generally referring to the transition itself. No one breaks up a marriage for the divorce. No one says, "My marriage is miserable. I'm going to move out of the house I love and live on half my income for a while. That will make me happy!" The divorce is the part to get through so you can build a better life on the other side. It's a *transition*, not a permanent state.

My husband had the idea that it would be difficult for two years. I've since heard other estimates about how long it takes to move through divorce. One year. Five years. If you have children, challenges may arise throughout their lives, as well as opportunities for reconnection and relationship improvement. But the immediate high-wire anxiety of the early months will pass.

All transitions are difficult, but divorce brings unique challenges. Many people arrive at this difficult transition with a preexisting condition of Irritable Spousal Syndrome—that state of pessimism, fatigue, and flu-like symptoms that accompanies the waning days of marriage or wallops you at the end. This spiritual exhaustion drains even the peppiest among us, and can make small speed bumps feel like high hurdles.

Some of us are seized by loss aversion. Despite the notion that we covet the greener grass on the other side of our fence, most of us fear losing what we have twice as strongly as we relish gaining something new. As now-classic studies in behavioral economics show, we don't jump at the better lawn; we cling to our own parched plot, perforated with mole holes though it may be.

I was holding on to my house, unable to part with the one stable factor in my life. We had no valuable antiques, no couches covered in Thai silk. But everything in it represented the hope for a dreamy home life we'd cherished—the veneer-on-particle-board bench in the kitchen, the little end table that had arrived flat in a box with its own Allen wrench for erecting it. One night, before my husband moved out, I sat in bed looking at a large, leafy plant sitting in a shiny white pot from IKEA. "I love you, plant!" I said, tears in my eyes. "I'll never leave you!"

The rent on the house plus that on my husband's new studio apartment quickly exceeded our joint earnings. I took in a roommate to defray the cost. I already had one college student/part-time au pair living in the guest room. I rented the office to another student. So now I was basically living in a dorm. I was the forty-five-year-old resident advisor. My son was delighted to have college girls around who liked to color; I'd be awakened weekend nights by my young roommates tromptoeing to their bedrooms overhead.

This is just a transition, I'd remind myself. *I will not be an adult RA for the rest of my life.*

We plan ahead for most major life passages, but divorce can erupt like a volcano. Some people describe it as being "shot out of a cannon," or "swept up in a tsunami." Even those of us who have been discussing it for months don't spend the waning years of marriage flipping through glossy divorce magazines or choosing items for our divorce registry and stacking the gifts in the corner as they arrive. We don't zip down to the bank to open a Divorce Savings Account. We continue to invest in our marriage, as we should. It can feel disrespectful to a marriage or even morally suspect to actively plan for the next stage. The lurking history of divorce as a sin can contribute to this willful lack of preparation. *Who are we to strategize for a happy ending?* we may think. This not-planning is understandable, but it contributes to the chaos.

Some people get a surge of energy and excitement at the end of marriage, what courage researcher Shane Lopez calls a "hope bump." "When you partner with someone and it's not working out, your future starts to get smaller and smaller. You have to give up hopes and goals to stay together," he said. "Now that you're parting, those old dreams can reawaken." But it can take time for the animosity and disappointment to lift, for people to shift from survival mode to a more optimistic "promotion approach."

• • •

On a flight to Detroit, I struck up a conversation with a professor from the Midwest who'd experienced an extreme example of transition resistance—and the power of preparation. "Mandrake," as the professor asked to be called, had married in his late twenties. Two kids and two decades later, the long-standing problems between him and his wife had grown intolerable. They tried therapy for three years. Then Mandrake began sleeping in the den. Then he tried "a niceness campaign" to see if they could live as friends.

By 2012, he wanted to separate. His wife's response was, "If you move out and destroy the family, I will never speak to you again." He was afraid of what she might do. "She was so vehemently against it that no cooperation was possible. I worried she'd try to close our credit cards or freeze our assets."

He told me this story as we sat strapped in our seats on the airplane, grounded on the tarmac. I'd just begun conducting my own unscientific survey of the State of Family Today, based on people sitting next to me on airplanes in coach. At the time, my family lived in seven states and one European country, and I flew around a lot to see my relations. Based on my Airplane Poll, three out of four people traveling between midsize cities in the U.S. are touched by divorce—theirs or that of their parents, children, or spouse—pretty much as the Census Bureau reports.

Mandrake said that with the help of a therapist, he decided to buy a home for himself, six blocks away, without telling his wife, then push forward with the legal separation. "It was the hardest decision I'd ever made. I had to, in a small city, buy a house and announce separation nearly simultaneously. The whole thing was incredibly stressful."

He closed on the house on a Friday and told his wife about it that evening. Sunday morning, she handed him a separation agreement, neatly typed. No violent outburst, no financial retaliation. After years of threatening the worst, she accepted his decision within two days, once he made it. She drafted a reasonable agreement that wound up forming the basis of their final settlement.

I can't imagine doing something so secretive, but his decisive action pushed his wife into acknowledging that she could, in fact, live without this man she'd grown to loathe. As Mandrake discovered, even the angriest spouse may surprise you with her ability to adapt. Your own decisive action may help others realize their own strength.

Marshaling your focus toward a much-desired goal can yield magical-seeming results, and provide a shocking sense of personal efficacy after years of treading in the mire of a bad marriage. Later that same summer, I made a small but bold decision myself—to spend a month on the West Coast, where I'd long wanted to live. This move initiated a similar shift in my own future ex's vision of what might be possible in divorce.

Even if you don't buy your own house, Mandrake's story points to the need to plan ahead for divorce. "A lot of times I ask people, 'How long did you prepare for your wedding?' Most people spent seven or eight months, to a year and a half," said MJ Murray Vachon, a licensed clinical social worker in South Bend, Indiana, who has been seeing couples and teenagers for thirty years. "I say, 'It's a similar process, except you're preparing to undo it.'"

I loved this wedding-planning analogy. If there's one thing I learned in my years of writing about marriage, it's this: if you're throwing a party for two hundred followed by a honeymoon to Tahiti, you need an overarching vision to help you through it. Divorce needs a vision, too. Not a seating plan or schedule for passed hors d'oeuvres, but practical strategies and overriding *principles* to help manage the logistical and emotional changes. Principles are guideposts that help keep us on course in trying times.

I began formulating my principles of parting, refining them over the following two years. I finally settled on seven. While your principles might be different, establishing them can protect you and smooth the way toward a positive parting.

SEVEN PRINCIPLES OF PARTING

1. Commit to self-compassion.
2. Take ownership of the future (and the past).
3. Don't confuse filing with closure.
4. Build a tool kit for the transition.
5. Combat anger with empathy.
6. Resist the urge to compare.
7. Create positive moments.

Principle One: Commit to Self-Compassion

When something goes awry, we often conclude that we must have done something wrong to cause it. Self-blame may come naturally, but self-compassion, it turns out, is the key to moving forward after divorce.

During the past fifteen years, there's been a great deal of research from the growing field of positive psychology about happiness, strengths, and virtues—how basically well-adjusted people thrive. This work has generated insights that improve people's daily lives. We've all heard how cultivating gratitude, for example, can counteract a tendency toward negative self-comparison and increase your appreciation of your assets. You might have read about the benefit of savoring—stopping to fully relish a positive moment or sensation. David Sbarra at the University of Arizona wanted to know if these practices or others like them helped during divorce, and what role self-compassion played, in particular.

To find out, Sbarra and his team ran an ad in *Tucson Weekly* and on Craigslist.com, and distributed flyers to family lawyers and divorce recovery groups. They were seeking separated or divorced people willing to share their feelings with strangers in a laboratory setting at a university dotted with palm trees. They found 105 willing divorcées who'd been married an average of thirteen and a half years, and separated about four months.

Sixty-seven women and thirty-eight men came to the psychology department lab, cradled under the Santa Catalina Mountains. Participants were asked to recall an image of their ex and then speak freely for four minutes about their divorce. They also answered questionnaires about how they were recovering.

Four judges listened to the tapes, coding the degree to which the participants expressed self-compassion when speaking. They cross-referenced this attitude with the participants' other positive practices and self-reported well-being, and with logistical realities such as length of the marriage and time since separation.

At the initial interview, and three, six, and nine months later, those with high self-compassion reported fewer intrusive negative thoughts, fewer bad dreams about the divorce, and less negative rumination. Self-compassion had a greater impact than other traits, habits, or even practical details. "If you pick all of the variables that predict how people will do after their marriage ends, self-compassion really carries the day," said Sbarra.

Self-compassion is a composite idea borrowed from Buddhism that includes three parts: seeing your problems as part of the universal human struggle, remaining calm and mindful in the face of a negative experience rather than letting it overwhelm or define you, and viewing yourself with understanding and forgiveness. Self-compassion is not a fixed quality like eye color. You can develop it.

Why is it so helpful in divorce? "The research shows that self-compassionate people are more likely to take responsibility for their misdeeds, apologize for what they did wrong, and repair whatever harm they've caused," said Kristin Neff, a professor of psychology at the University of Texas, Austin, who is largely credited with codifying the concept in Western psychological terms. Neff writes about her own divorce in her book *Self-Compassion: The Proven Power of Being Kind to Yourself.* Self-compassion protects us from identifying completely with our divorce; we see it as one piece of our present, and can still enjoy other positive aspects and build on them.

Self-compassionate people also have better romances, according to at least one study, which is another reason many of us might want to build it. Here's how:

See the universality of your experience: Suspecting that our suffering, failure, or loss is abnormal alienates us from others. In fact, suffering is part of the human experience, as is committing acts we later regret. Even your most successful, chipper friends have lost a loved one, made mistakes, or failed at a lifelong dream. You probably did behave less than perfectly in your marriage; it's the rare person getting divorced—or staying married—who didn't. But you also likely did many loving, lovely things over the years.

The easiest way to feel the normality of divorce is to talk to any of the other two million people in the U.S. who divorced this year. While divorce rates in the U.S. are slowly dropping, it's still a part of life for the vast majority of Americans, and growing numbers of people worldwide. "As the time went by, I'd see friends and family members going through the same thing. I figured, it happens to a lot of people," said Carmen, a twenty-something hairdresser and mother of two from a close-knit Puerto Rican community in New Jersey.

After her husband cheated for the second time, Carmen decided she wanted out of the marriage. She said seeing others do well after divorce gave her courage. "I always said, 'I could never make it without a guy.' But seeing them made me think, 'If they did it, why can't I?' I'm very proud of myself now. Sometimes you don't think you can do it until you actually go through it." Success after divorce also is universal, it turns out.

Another way to put your own struggles in perspective? Volunteer. Serving dinner at a homeless shelter or spending time in a childhood cancer ward is an instant reminder that we live in a world with many troubles, and that we can manage our own. Volunteering also reminds us that we have much to contribute.

Practice mindfulness: Mindfulness is that deep state of "being in the moment," as opposed to, say, having waffles with your child while mentally rehearsing a fight you plan to pick later. Mindfulness in divorce can be as simple as truly noting how you feel. "A lot of people aren't aware that they're suffering. The suffering comes from harsh self-criticism, a harsh voice in their head they don't even notice," said Neff. "Or they go right to fix-it mode, and don't feel it. Mindfulness means seeing things as they really are, turning toward it rather than running from it."

Research links mindfulness with a slew of benefits we could all use at the start of divorce. Mindfulness reduces stress, boosts health, increases self-knowledge, promotes emotional regulation, assuages loneliness, and even improves sleep.

Meditation is one popular method of achieving mindfulness. Meditation can deactivate the brain's "default mode," the energetic state the brain is in when it's not focusing on a specific task. In default mode, your brain might dwell on past regrets or future worries. "One of the most important things meditation does is reduce that activity, both when you're mediating and not meditating. It reduces that constant focusing on ourselves and ruminating. A little bit of self-focus and worry is useful, but not to the degree that we do it," said Neff.

If, like me, you plan to get to meditation sometime in the future that is *not now*, there are other ways to achieve mindfulness. Ellen Langer, a psychologist at Harvard University, often considered the "mother of mindfulness," stresses the calming effect of genuine observation of your physical surroundings, the "stop and smell the flowers" approach to being mindful. Her research shows that *mindlessness* creates stress, in part because it allows for unquestioned negative assumptions and prior convictions to reign unchecked. If you engage with your physical surroundings, you can detach from that ruminative cycle to fully absorb the scent of the roses, or the splash of the fountain, or the taste of the chocolate cake, then revisit troubling events with a fresh, more creative perspective.

View yourself with understanding and forgiveness: Self-forgiveness is a fundamental aspect of nearly all religious traditions, and for good reason. While we're generally skilled at showing kindness to a friend in crisis, we often speak to ourselves as we would to an enemy. Our harsh words can act like internal fangs, causing our body to respond as if to a physical threat, letting loose cortisol and adrenaline. When sustained, this can lead to stress, anxiety, and even illness—not the best state for making amends or moving forward.

One way to bolster self-forgiveness is to write yourself a supportive letter, the type you might send a friend. A recent study showed that people who wrote a short, compassionate letter to themselves about a distressing situation every day for a week felt better, and had lower symptoms of depression and higher happiness rates even six months later.

You also can hug yourself, as sappy as it may sound. Touch is rooted in the mammalian caregiving system, said Neff, which evolved to keep infants close to their mothers. We're wired to respond positively to being held or rocked, even if we're the ones doing the cuddling ourselves.

If you're seeking divine forgiveness, self-forgiveness is a necessary first step, said Mordecai Finley, a rabbi and spiritual counselor in Los Angeles who teaches courses on comparative religious ethics. When you desire absolution from above, yet still blame yourself, that forgiveness will feel false, a coat of paint over a crumbling wall. "It's really understanding that you could not have done otherwise. We are frail, not evil. Reconciling is accepting that. You might say to yourself, 'I had not yet ripened as a human being,'" suggested Finley.

Some religious people I spoke to said that knowing they did everything possible to save their marriage allowed them to finally accept the divorce. Vince, a successful restaurateur from a Catholic family in a working-class section of New Jersey, went to couples counseling for years with his wife. "My aha moment was when we were with our counselor and he said, 'I'm done taking your money. If you did not have kids, right now, would you still be sitting here?' She and I, in less than thirty seconds, both said, 'No.' That was the switch for me. I knew I was done. I think my kids deserve more than two people who are miserable all the time. If I live by what I believe, that's what I'm concerned about. At the end of the day, if I'm judged for that, that's what it is. I have a personal connection to God, and He knows what I've done and how I've done it."

Morgan, a twenty-seven-year-old Evangelical Christian from Georgia, married four days after turning twenty. She said that in her community "divorce is never okay." Things had been hard the whole time, but for years, divorce didn't cross her mind as an option. Then, seven years into her marriage, "something clicked"; she realized she had to get out. She found solace in the Bible. "There are so many other things the Bible wants us to do—to love, be patient, kind, self-controlled, forgiving, hopeful, joyful, serving others. All of those other positive things I couldn't find in that relationship. The way I had to live in it, I couldn't honor those other things. I don't have the strength. I know that God loves me just the same. When I realized that, it just blew me away."

Principle Two: Take Ownership of the Future (and the Past)

"What?!" you may be asking. "Didn't you just say not to blame myself?" Yes, but taking ownership of what happens next—and claiming your role in your marriage's demise—is not the same as wallowing in self-recrimination.

"It is a way of seeing yourself, of creating a context for your life based on choice instead of on the flow of occurrences and events you can't control," notes relationship author Nita Tucker in *How Not to Screw It Up*. Yes, Tucker's book is about how to have a great marriage, not a great divorce, but many of the factors are the same. It's still a unique relationship that arouses deep emotions, and one in which the main thing you can control is yourself.

By seeing your contributions to the downfall of your marriage, you cast yourself as someone with *agency*. A feeling of agency directly correlates with resilience after loss. While a bad marriage can sap your personal power, divorce is a chance to take it back. You want to notice your role in your circumstances, see how you exert influence over your own life. Even if your previous efforts mainly involved sticking with your marriage long past its expiration date, focus on that. Reframe it as a positive example of the dedication you bring to your relationships and commitments. It's easy to see ourselves in the worst possible light in divorce. But we all had good, noble reasons for decisions that may later look deeply flawed.

Ownership of the past helps guide future choices, as I discovered when I tried it myself. As we were nearing the end of our marriage, still living up in the countryside, my career beached itself upon the shore, barely breathing, the end near. I'd occasionally haul myself up to dribble water over its rubbery skin—sending out a résumé to an online job listing, having lunch with a former colleague down in the city—but I could not find a job.

My husband, perhaps worried about his own earning power in our increasingly shaky economy, began finding fault with my work ethic, my focus, my time management skills. I rushed to my defense: I'd been through fertility treatments and was still recovering emotionally; my industry had changed and there were practically no well-paid magazine positions; I wanted to work only part-time to be home with our baby.

That was all true. But with him gone, I decided to consider the other side. My first "maybe it's me" conversation went like this:

Me: "You didn't really hold up your weight financially in your marriage."

Myself: "Really?"

Me: "Your husband earned more than you the entire time. He was writing a book in addition to holding down a full-time job, while you were sitting on the couch, sewing felt balls for the baby. You were supporting yourself when you met him, but you also had that cheap, rent-controlled apartment. One year you racked up so much debt 'supporting yourself' as a freelance writer, you had to spend the next eighteen months paying it off."

Myself: "But I did pay it off! Anyway, I don't care about making a lot of money. I'm driven by creative expression, not wealth. I've never been a big earner, and I don't want to be held to a standard that isn't mine."

I: "Aha!"

My ex-husband was right! I didn't pull my weight, according to *his* values. I was focused on care, not career, when our son was little. Before that, my high-point work experiences involved stimulating interviews and writing projects. My first real job was as a part-time art reporter for the local National Public Radio affiliate, as optional and low-paid a vocation as any. I loved it. Granted, I usually put only a gallon of gas in my car at a time so I could keep my cash longer, but this felt fine to me.

I can certainly see the benefits of fiscal responsibility now that I'm in my forties. But my "maybe it's me" conversation led to an important insight I'd been too defensive to admit: I need a partner who either makes enough money that my income is extra, or who is willing to risk running out of gas on the side of the road with me into our golden years.

A number of people I met talked about the power of taking ownership even after their spouse had an affair. Marcelle, a multilingual, fifty-something jeweler of European descent, said her husband came home one day and handed her a typewritten request for divorce, including detailed plans for dividing up their property. He sat there while she read it. "He gives me the letter. I'm devastated. I don't even know what's happening to me. He'd clearly thought about it a long time."

Later, she learned there was another woman. "Everyone looked at me as the victim. 'Poor you! How could this happen to you?' I was fifty and my husband left me. But I didn't want to be the victim. I felt like I was involved. We worked together and we were going to continue working together."

She found a spiritual guru/therapist, and attended a three-day personal empowerment workshop. The workshop stressed intense forgiveness as a way to release oneself from anger's grip. For Marcelle, taking some responsibility, even for her husband's defection, gave her energy to move on. "I think it was a shared decision, even though it may not look like that at all."

William Glasser, a psychiatrist who pioneered a form of self-reliance therapy in the late 1960s, talked about how working at a veterans' hospital in Los Angeles showed him that being cast as a victim paralyzes people, even if they've been truly wronged. "What they taught, in effect, was that you aren't responsible for your miserable problems because you are the victim of factors and circumstances beyond your control. I objected to that. My question is always, 'What are you going to do about your life, beginning today?'"

Alex, a forty-year-old technology activist in Washington, DC, found that taking ownership of the past was critical to cooperative co-parenting. He'd moved with his wife from Illinois for his work. A few years later, after their daughter was born, his wife fell in love with someone else. She wanted out of the marriage.

Alex said that while he thought cheating was "absolutely a horrendous thing," he also had to admit that he'd contributed to the overall breakdown of the marriage. "The way it came apart was pretty disastrous, but it was definitely a joint fail, of which she did the most spectacular failing," he said. "I think the notion of the designated wrongdoer is too simple. You have to move beyond that, and you can't let that be the defining element of your relationship."

Still, it took him two years before he was willing to face the other man. I met all three of them at their little girl's first ballet recital—Alex, his ex-wife, and her boyfriend-turned-second-husband. They sat together in a back row in the dark auditorium, watching the little girl twirl about in her "autumn leaves" costume. Alex had worked hard to move past the affair for the sake of his daughter. I could see the emotional effort that he was making—that they all were—even two years later. Still, cooperation was ultimately less difficult than dragging all four of them through years of anger and retribution.

Principle Three: Don't Confuse Filing with Closure

While it can be tempting to hurry through the legal process to achieve a sense of completeness, it takes time to get over a divorce, no matter how quickly you dispense with the legal details. "There are five levels of separation: sexual, physical, emotional, financial, legal. You could be legally separated and still totally emotionally enmeshed," said Forrest Mosten, a Los Angeles–based collaborative attorney and mediator who has been practicing since 1972, and has authored four books on law and divorce.

Early separation can be exactly the wrong time to divvy up your assets, let alone make critical decisions about your future. It's hard to think objectively the week after your spouse moves out, particularly if you have no job and no idea where she kept the cable bills. You're in survival mode, scared or angry. *Maybe I can't support myself,* you might think. Or, *She's going to pay for my unhappiness, in cash.* Other people are relieved to the point of imprudence. Rushing to tie up loose ends can create lasting conflicts generated by short-term fears. It can lead to a cash grab based on uncertainty and confusion, or make you give away too much in a fit of freedom-induced euphoria.

The fall that we decided to split up, we sat on our back porch under our blossoming apple tree, discussing our furniture and our finances. My mom was visiting. The three of us sitting together at night reminded me of another family moment, the winter after our son was born. My husband and I had stayed at my mother's house in Florida for two months. Evenings, we'd sip coffee on her patio overlooking the golf course, our infant son sleeping upstairs, and plan his happy future— when we'd start him on solid food, what kind of childcare we might want. It had been so cheerful and anticipatory, our future together unfolding.

Now we were discussing how to shut down that dream. My mom, a two-time divorcée with a law degree, explained the basics: every state requires parents to support their children, and has guidelines for the amount of child support a noncustodial parent should pay; possessions and debts acquired during marriage are basically considered shared, to be divided as such; you can alter the terms later if circumstances change, but your settlement is an attempt to make the best plans, given your situation now.

I got angrier and angrier. Not at my mother, exactly, but at the legal reality she brought with her, at the anticipation of having to fill out forms, at the fact that I was in this spot, that my husband would bounce back in a week while I'd wind up living in a one-room studio over a *panaderia*, with a view of a brick wall.

"You are not taking the bookcases to your apartment!" I snapped at my husband. Then I stormed inside. Then I gave myself a time-out. *I was yelling about bookcases?* I couldn't believe I'd exploded over objects of very little real or sentimental value. But contemplating the *specifics* pierced straight through me.

We decided to postpone discussions about who got what and simply begin living apart—moving toward being unmarried practically and emotionally. We wrote up a basic separation agreement that spelled out how many nights our son would be with each of us, and a child and spousal support arrangement we could both manage. It wasn't a legal contract, but rather a set of personal guidelines we committed to following. I spoke to a couple of lawyers for general knowledge and advice, but didn't hire anyone. Filing and formalizing, we agreed, would be the last stage of our divorce, not the first.

Several lawyers warned me about the possible complications of this approach: debts acquired while we remained legally married would technically be joint, as would earnings. Decisions we made about our son could affect our parenting agreement if we wound up fighting over custody. But we were not going to fight about custody, and I'd seen too many bad divorces caused by rushing to decide and divide.

This interregnum turned out to be one of the most helpful things we did. It let our post-marriage relationship evolve naturally—improve—without divisive input from professionally suspicious third parties. It let me start up a career again, regain confidence, and then consider whether or not I truly needed a microwave we bought in 2005 to match a kitchen in a country house I never wanted in the first place.

"But everyone's telling me to lawyer up!" you might say. We all need information about the laws in our state, but learning the law is not the same as filing for divorce before you're ready emotionally and practically.

Certainly some people need to make it legal quickly. I met a woman who was eight months pregnant with her new boyfriend's child, while her husband tarried over legalities. She felt an urgent need for legal resolution that I understood. I've also spoken to people eager to cut legal ties to spouses who were irrational, addicts, or mentally ill.

But I also met a pharmaceutical executive in Houston who spent $200,000 on his divorce. He'd worked out a settlement plan with his wife, who'd initiated the split. But then she hired a new lawyer, one who encouraged her to mistrust her husband and only communicate with him *through the lawyer herself.* Was a lawyer she'd just met, a legal professional billing for every phone call and e-mail drafted, really more trustworthy than the man she'd been married to for twenty years? In those early months of separation, she couldn't tell.

Many reasonable, sane couples hurl themselves immediately into the legal process, generating a crazed Tilt-A-Whirl of viciousness. I know you may be angry enough to hit something, but you're better off hitting something than trying to exorcise your anger by hiring the first lawyer you meet. Smash tennis balls into a wall. Hit a punching bag.

Stomp through a thousand-calorie-burning aerobic workout, then start the DVD over and do it again. Scream at automated response systems on the telephone.

What's the risk of filing in the fog of resentment? The risk is that your divorce will take on a life of its own, a mean one, a sour green one that looks nothing like your marriage or like the person you've been or hope to become. The risk is that any fears you have will multiply like Hydra heads while your confidence will wither, as will your ability to communicate productively with this person who, by the way, you'll be seeing for the rest of your life if you have children. The risk is that you've laid the groundwork for a future of mistrust and anger.

The other risk is that you'll miss out on the chance to try one of the newer collaborative legal processes that can make your divorce easier, and your life far more manageable.

I'd assumed that lawyers caused most of the awful divorces we see, circling flailing marriages like sharks, salivating, eager to snap up desperate partners' lifelong earnings. We've all heard of greedy-seeming divorce lawyers egging on couples to fight, or inept counselors who somehow passed the bar and then went on to inflict their incompetence on unsuspecting families. But as I began to talk to thoughtful, family-minded lawyers, mediators, legal scholars, and reformers, I discovered that some of the *most helpful innovations in divorce are coming from the legal professionals*. These are people dedicated to helping you get through, and to using the legal process itself to create a blueprint for a solid, stable, happy life unwed.

I know this sounds like a radical notion, particularly when you talk to most people about divorce, including many divorce lawyers, or anyone embroiled in an ugly fight. But as more states began to pass no-fault in the 1970s and 1980s, lawyers and legal scholars around the country realized that the adversarial approach was out of sync with the spirit of the new laws. They began forging more cooperative, more *appropriate* options—different forms of "alternative dispute resolution." Today, legal approaches such as mediation and collaborative divorce allow you to work past anger and fear, learn new communication skills, engage in financial planning—and sometimes even improve your relationship, post marriage.

"The more you can befriend this person, that's your best safeguard against ever having to go back to court," said Regina DeMeo, a family lawyer and commentator in the Washington, DC, area. Like many legal innovators and activists I spoke to, DeMeo once prided herself on being a "pit bull" lawyer. Then she faced her own divorce. She realized that battling with her spouse—as she'd long advised others to do—could seriously scar her son. She signed up for mediation and collaborative law training, and completely changed how she practiced family law. In her new practice, she said, her divorced clients shake hands at the end. They "own" the outcome. "The more I saw the fruits of my labors, the more I saw this as a much better way to divorce."

If we were going to spend the time and money to file for divorce, I decided, the experience should do more than merely render us unwed. The process should be ameliorative, protecting and even improving our future.

Principle Four: Build a Tool Kit for the Transition

The immediate period of separation and early divorce can resemble a hurricane hitting your house—winds are surging, water is leaking under the doors, and you have no idea where you put the extra towels. As with a natural disaster, an emergency-preparedness kit, a "tool kit," can help you weather the storm. I decided mine should contain three things: new routines for daily chores, plans for dousing emotional flare-ups (mine), and an emergency responder.

New routines for daily chores: In marriage, we tend to divvy up the duties. One cooks; the other does the books. The stronger partner lifts the carry-ons into the overhead compartment; the more fastidious one swipes the tray tables with disinfectant wipes. Now you have to figure out how to handle both partners' tasks—or line up others to help.

Two logistical details worried me in the months before my husband moved out: (1) How would I have the energy to make my morning coffee before my first cup of coffee? (2) Who would take out the trash? I worried that I'd forget, week after week. Trash would overflow from under the sink, spill out into the hallway, mount the stairs.

A year later, I couldn't believe I worried about such trivia. But we accept negative caricatures of our quirks and weaknesses in a contentious relationship, and forget our own strengths.

After my husband left, I posted sticky notes about the trash pickup schedule around the kitchen. Some mornings, I left the recycle bin in the hallway, where I'd trip over it unless I dragged it outside that night. These tactics mostly worked. But also, it turns out, if you miss a trash day, nothing bad happens. I didn't need to be Super Responsible Trash Woman, especially now that I had a third less trash to toss.

For the morning coffee, I asked my sister to buy me one of those pod coffeemakers that brews individual cups as a house (re)warming present for my newly single home. I put it in my bedroom, and found that I could push the "start" button while still more or less asleep.

Some people easily turn to a spouse for help but cringe at the thought of asking others. Hollie, a thirty-year-old mother of three in Colorado, said that the media decrying single mothers made her feel like a burden to society. She didn't want to ask anyone for anything. During the divorce, she'd moved from Denver to a smaller, rural town to economize. Her ex, meanwhile, moved to Alaska, where he had work and his new girlfriend—the woman for whom he'd left the marriage. He sent money to Hollie every month.

She was spending days watching their young children, nights pursuing her bachelor's degree online. She also talked to other single moms in chat rooms. Many of the women online admitted that asking for help made them "feel like leeches. It's hard to accept help. You feel like maybe you're not doing it yourself, like you're not doing well enough if you accept help," she said.

I felt awed, and somewhat exhausted, just listening to her eighteen-hour days. *How do people work so hard?* Still, reaching out to other adults for help would have benefited her children, and made her more responsible, not less. By expanding her support system—maybe swapping babysitting hours with another mother, for example, or taking turns cooking meals for the week—she'd have had time to refresh herself and return to the jobs of parenting and studying with more creativity, responsiveness, and joy.

Plans for dousing emotional flare-ups: Connection with others helps us regulate our emotions. This is one reason your former spouse might act "crazy"; he's missing out on the salutary connection he had with you. In divorce, our emotions can ricochet wildly, and we no longer have another adult in the house to catch them—or talk us down.

When we feel bad, the natural reaction can be to lash out. Picking a fight is a common response to an inner whorl of negativity; you want to shove that feeling out of you and onto someone else. But strong, seemingly uncontrollable emotions come in waves; they rise and then recede. Riding out moments of anger rather than acting on them can prevent a decent divorce from devolving into a disaster.

"It's always the emotions that complicate the case," said attorney Regina DeMeo. "It doesn't matter if you have a billion dollars or ten dollars. The complicating factor is never the money. The complicating piece is when people haven't reined in their emotions."

One man told me he'd sent nasty e-mails to his ex in the midst of their divorce. She showed them to their children, something it had never occurred to him she might do. "Those e-mails still affect my relationship with my kids," he said. "I apologized to her, but they still have those e-mails in their minds. They're in college, and it stands between us."

Note to self: Never hit "send" in anger.

For most of us, sharing feelings acts as a pressure-release valve. In divorce, we may need to identify a new verbal support partner or team, perhaps a close friend or family member. Many people turn to a professional counselor, coach, or spiritual guide. Some find help from cognitive-behavioral therapy, a form of talk therapy based on the premise that our worst feelings often arise from twisted thinking and can be argued down by marshaling real evidence against it. Emotions are feelings, not facts. They feel like facts, but they aren't.

We probably also have to expand our repertoire of self-soothing techniques, physical and mental activities that reliably shift our mood. Different things work for each of us—reading, running, listening to music, napping, or seeing art.

To help me control my tendency to share every single negative thought I had with my ex, I started a running list of "issues to discuss" on my computer, then waited until the next time we spoke to mention them. Writing down my complaints often made me feel heard before I voiced them. Sometimes the problem rectified itself, or I'd realize I had a specific, rather minor request he could easily address. In the past, I'd call or text immediately every time I got mad. I still did this on occasion, but less frequently, and I could see now how it had contributed to conflict in our marriage.

As I discovered, divorce can be a great chance to practice all those wonderful communication techniques marriage counselors love to encourage, but that elude even the most verbally adroit when locked in contentious residency with an infuriating spouse. Now we have more space, more distance—and maybe more ability to act on a former marriage counselor's good advice. In separation, I became better able to listen without reacting. I could finally avoid using the "four horsemen of the apocalypse," as well-known marriage researcher John Gottman has famously called common, corrosive communication habits: criticism, contempt, defensiveness, and stonewalling. Destructive in marriage, they're also damaging in divorce

Financial clarity can be another piece of an emotional management plan—a clear-eyed view of your financial situation and a strategy for becoming self-supporting, if you're not. Fear of poverty can be like lighter fluid on smoldering conflict.

Your financial plan may involve relying on your ex while you go to school, start a business, or reenter the workforce. It could mean working longer hours while your ex has your children so you can increase your earnings and savings. It might be investing a large settlement wisely. Many people find that downsizing, even temporarily, brings huge emotional relief. Recognize that money worries can trigger anxiety, see a financial counselor if necessary, and make a plan for gaining solvency.

An emergency responder: Who will take you to the ER at 2 a.m., or stay with one child while you take the other? In marriage, it's usually that live-in emergency responder, your spouse.

For many, myself included, our ex remains our emergency responder, at least in the immediate aftermath of separation. A year later, I could see that it would be empowering to write a name other than my ex-husband's on the "in case of emergency" line on standardized forms. But "being responsible" was one of his top-five signature strengths; should I not utilize this, even theoretically, just because we were divorcing? In general, though, we need to plan ahead who will come to our aid, should we need help.

Principle Five: Combat Anger with Empathy

In June of my second summer alone, I spent two weeks at the Mac-Dowell Colony, an artists' retreat in New Hampshire. I'd never been accepted to such a society, let alone applied. The opportunity felt like one of those new beginnings you hope a scary transition will bring. My ex insisted that he welcomed two weeks of solo parenting, which eased my mind about leaving my son behind while I went.

There I was, in a private cabin in the woods, all meals included, two weeks with no responsibilities beyond writing. Instead of working, I was lying on the bed, looking out at the rain-drenched forest, fuming about the country house my ex had insisted we build in a similarly waterlogged woodsy location seven years earlier.

I was growing angrier by the minute, convinced we needed to see a divorce therapist to discuss how he never apologized for coercing me to live high atop a mountain in the frigid north woods. I was scrambling to find my cell phone so I could call him up and yell, when it buzzed from under a stack of papers. It was a text from my ex with a video of our son's preschool graduation. He was at the school on a Tuesday morning, taking time off work, so I could loll around at an artists' colony, resenting him.

Then I was chagrined. Then I was laughing at our son twirling alongside the "class dance" in some nonconformist pre-K personal choreography. Then my ex sent a photo of the two of them smiling while holding our son's certificate of completion. They were both adorable, and equally proud, and I was glad I hadn't pick a fight about some country house vision quest he'd cherished in 2005, a pursuit that brought him no end of grief and quite possibly hastened the end of our marriage.

Then I remembered that he *had* apologized, actually; had acknowledged making a mistake in insisting we build that house. In my rage in the rain, I'd forgotten.

This is one problem with harboring anger: the more you dwell on the insult, the deeper it burrows. You've dug a massive ditch, like a channel for ships. Some little apology is a tiny piece of flimflam tossed atop all that water. It has no ballast, no weight.

Probably everyone is angry at some point in a divorce. We're angry at our spouse, ourselves, life in general. Anger may be protective in small doses. A burst of intentional, managed anger can shift the power dynamic, put a bullying spouse on notice that the terms *will now change*. Anger can inhibit amnesiac second-guessing. My own mother encouraged me to "be angry!" at one point in my separation, thinking fury would bounce me out of sadness.

Anger can give you a turbo-boost of energy, but a crash usually follows. When prolonged, anger destroys relationships and health. Anger's adrenaline rush served a critical role out on the savannah, if a tiger attacked, or even in the modern world, when a real physical threat looms over your child. "That's the real purpose of anger. We've recycled it to protect fragile egos," said Steven Stosny, an anger expert and family violence consultant in Maryland, and author of *Love Without Hurt: Turn Your Resentful, Angry, or Emotionally Abusive Relationship into a Compassionate, Loving One.*

Stosny has spent years helping maximum-security prisoners learn to manage the anger that landed them behind bars, and his Compassionate Parenting course is mandated in some courts. Anger, he asserts, is basically hurt wearing a mask. Even criminal aggression can stem from feeling wounded, and from a fragile sense of self-worth. Many people mistakenly equate anger with power, which Stosny calls "a tragic substitution of power for value. The urge to devalue other people comes from feeling devalued yourself."

Stosny focuses on compassion as a way to lessen anger. He advises clients to identify the pain under the rage, and to reconnect with their values and compassionate, loving acts, such as their efforts to care for their children. "Compassion and kindness make you feel more humane and valuable. Then you don't feel as vulnerable, and you don't need the resentment. It doesn't justify someone else's bad behavior. You still need to address the behavior. But you can do it in a compassionate and kind way."

Many divorced people I met spoke about the healing power of another surprisingly powerful internal shift—forgiveness. More than one person told me they'd come to forgiveness through Al-Anon, the support group for friends and family of alcoholics. "There I began to understand that not forgiving the other person would make me sick, and that I would be unable to go on with my life unless I came to peace with what happened," said a sixty-something man in Texas. "I would make myself ill if I held on to this much anger. It just really made sense to me."

Stephanie, a twenty-something mother of two from a Mormon community in the Midwest, had met her future husband at church in middle school. They married after they both finished high school and he completed his mission, quickly had two children, and began foster-parenting a third. Then her husband had an affair, which he continued even after she learned of it.

Stephanie decided she wanted a divorce, a rarity in her community. Her religion's focus on forgiveness convinced her that anger or retaliation would hurt the wrong people. "Would I have been justified in acting like a psychotic jerk? Maybe. But how much of that wrath or anger would have affected him? Not much, because he wasn't really around. In terms of who really would have been feeling the outcome of that, it would have been me. And my girls."

Conjuring up kindness, especially for a spouse who has been unfaithful, may feel like "giving in" or giving up well-warranted indignation. "My friends would say, 'He's such an asshole. You should screw him over,'" said Chloe, the Manhattan mom who'd traveled with her ex and their daughter to France, where his parents lived. Chloe's good divorce had inspired me; I was shocked to learn, later, how hard it had been, and that her husband had left her for another woman. "My therapist warned me that there are people who don't get over these things for twenty years. It really comes down to having empathy for the way I was feeling and for the way he was feeling. I don't think the affair ruined our marriage. I think the marriage ruined our marriage."

Letting go of even warranted anger is a potent survival skill. We often assume that "survival of the fittest" means that those who fought hardest lived and passed on their aggressive genes. But social scientists from various disciplines increasingly highlight the evolutionary value and downright *might* of pro-social traits such as empathy, cooperation, forgiveness, and compassion. "We think the origin of empathy is the maternal instinct, which is as old as the mammals, two hundred million years old," said Frans de Waal, Emory University's legendary primatologist and ethologist.

Historically, parents who could forgive had an evolutionary advantage. A brother who wronged you might be a key part of your caregiving team. The mother who could forgive the brother would continue to receive his help. Today, divorced parents often share childcare, basically functioning as a village of two. Encouraging and even contributing to your former spouse's well-being is *in your best interest*.

The opposite tack? Working to destroy your former spouse. I was talking to a businessman drinking beer with a colleague in the café car of an Amtrak to Boston. He'd had an acrimonious divorce, he told me, and planned to continue suing his ex-wife into poverty, filing frivolous lawsuits until she was "living under a bridge." This woman was the mother of his children, dependents he presumably loved. What caring father wants his children to have the burden and pain of a homeless mother? Also, if he succeeded in ruining her, she'd be of no help with the kids. This man had a full-time job that obviously required travel. Working toward a decent relationship with a financially fit ex-spouse would have been more high-minded, more beneficial to his children, and frankly, more practical.

You may believe you'll feel better if you exact revenge, but most of the research shows it doesn't work, according to organizational psychologist Ben Dattner, author of *The Blame Game: How the Hidden Rules of Credit and Blame Determine Our Success and Failure.* "You're still focused on them; you're looking backward. It's really not helpful. Also, it's hurting your ability to be empathic."

Or, as the Buddha said, "Holding on to anger is like grasping a hot coal with the intent of throwing it at someone else; you are the one who gets burned."

Your ex has the anger problem? You can't "teach" your ex self-worth, but you could alter your own behavior. "If you stop the way you're acting, it will change how the partner reacts to you. Because you're in an interactive loop, you can improve the interaction to some degree unilaterally," said Stosny.

I've heard again and again how one person transformed a hostile divorce, perhaps by offering appreciation, encouragement, or unexpected praise. "One thing my clients taught me is the power of one," said social worker Murray Vachon. "It only takes one person to have a pretty good divorce, unless there's alcoholism or mental illness. Even if you think it doesn't, it does."

Principle Six: Resist the Urge to Compare

Your next-door neighbor's ex-spouse slashed his tires? That has no predictive value over your divorce, even if you live in identical houses with matching wallpaper. It's important to be *self-referential* in divorce, remaining focused on your own situation, rather than comparing it to others'. This is *your* marriage that's ending. *Your* new life that's beginning. You want to stay in your own divorce.

What about the studies showing the ills of divorce? Or the friends insisting that such studies exist? Some of the scary-sounding stats and studies are true; divorced people, when taken *as a group*, have higher rates of a variety of problems. This is due to a few factors, including, for example, the higher rate of poverty among the subset of married couples who divorce, and the problems this brings. The *vast majority of people do fine*. In general, we maintain a basically stable level of well-being throughout our lives, regardless of circumstantial ups and downs. Some people become far happier after divorce. But those who continue to suffer pull down the average—and this average is what you see quoted.

Researchers are increasingly excited by new modeling methods that let them break group results into finer slices and therefore analyze with more nuance. In your own divorce, you need to keep your vision trained on your own chart.

You also don't want to compare your recuperation to that of your former spouse, particularly when it comes to asynchronous romantic re-involvement. As in, there he is, living in Alaska with his new wife, while you're raising your three children alone, as was Hollie in Colorado. Or, there she is, touring the Taj Mahal with her new soul mate, while you're ducking into bars on your way home from work, then leaving alone, having been too depressed to raise your eyes above your drink.

We all move along the route to recovery—and romance—at our own pace. Empathy for your ex may help you stay focused on your path. "I don't even know how it feels to have to stay at a job and be in love with someone in Alaska and have your kids in Colorado," said Hollie. "He says it tears him apart. I would never say it's easier on him."

Just as your ex's romantic life is no longer your concern, nor are those annoying habits you had to contend with in your home. To quote the ex-wife in the divorce comedy *Liar Liar*, "Two years ago, it was my business. But I don't have to care anymore. That's the magic of divorce."

Principle Seven: Create Positive Moments

While looking online for a divorce support group late one night, I came across the website of Amy Minkoff, a former marketing executive in New Jersey who had begun a new business offering "Joy After Divorce" coaching. I took her free consultation. Then I signed up. One of her Joy After Divorce rules: "Reframe anything negative about the divorce so that it serves you in some way."

Amy came to divorce coaching after her own marriage ended. She said the adversarial back-and-forth between the attorneys was incredibly difficult. "So I reframed it as, 'If I can handle this, I can handle anything in life.' I'd never made a budget. So I decided, 'This experience is going to put me in charge of my finances! That's great.'"

I loved this idea. All transitions bring advantages, which we usually acknowledge. We bemoan the loss of a job but then gloat about how our boss's total lack of judgment led us to find a plum position elsewhere. We miss our old friends when we move, but can't help posting photos on Facebook of what excites us now—the beach, the mountains, the great coffee shop in our new town. We know setbacks can lead to positive change, but the judgment around divorce can prevent us from embracing its upsides. We shouldn't, we may think, appreciate seeing our own strengths in action. We don't deserve, we suspect, to notice how much we're growing. But asking how something "serves" us can shift our focus from what we've lost to what we're gaining. It also generates more positive emotions.

Positive emotions are no insignificant matter. They can create an "upward spiral of positivity," said Barbara Fredrickson, a psychology professor at the University of North Carolina at Chapel Hill and author of *Love 2.0: Finding Happiness and Health in Moments of Connection*. Positive emotions help us connect to others by bouncing us out of an inward-focused survival crouch. They build "durable personal resources" such as a more expansive viewpoint, more creative problem-solving skills, and more of a "we" mind-set that facilitates cooperation.

A couple of recent studies showed that even a minor boost, such as getting free candy, can increase our capabilities. In one study, participants who received a bag of candy perceived more of the environment around them. In another study, doctors given candy made more astute diagnoses. I know it sounds as if these studies were funded by the Candy Lobby or some start-up organic chocolatier seeking funding. Researchers point not to the importance of candy, per se, but rather to how even a small reward can reroute our fleeting emotions in a positive way, with broadly beneficial consequences. Or, as Joseph Campbell said, "Find a place inside where there's joy, and the joy will burn out the pain."

Fredrickson promotes a three-to-one positivity-to-negativity ratio as a general guide for how to think about our emotional balance sheet. Negative emotions are more potent and more gripping; you need about three positive moments to counteract every negative one. "They don't need to be intense, over-the-moon positive emotions," said Fredrickson. "They could be catching a glimpse of beauty, appreciating the colors in a sunset. They tend to be so subtle that not everyone notices them."

I thought about it like this: an hour absorbed in a fast game of racquetball is one-sixteenth of your waking hours in which you are not a person bogged down by a legal fight but rather a fit, focused court contender. In my own life, I decided to try a new form of time management, or rather, "emotion management," shoehorning in more minutes of pure good feeling. Such as going dancing. My divorce mentor, Susan, said she found weekly swing dancing the best postdivorce mood-booster—the music, the jumping around, "the whole endorphin thing. Sometimes I would just go for a half hour of dancing. It was something to do that was fun and just made me feel good."

I love dancing, but I'd largely stopped doing it while married. I come from a dancing family. I've salsa danced with my dad under *palapa*-topped restaurants in Puerto Vallarta, bounded into bop clubs in Cincinnati, triple-stepped to Count Basie high atop the World Trade Center when it still rose above New York City. I danced with my grandparents, too, ballroom stylists who fox-trotted twice a week well into their eighties.

I decided to try a version of Susan's suggestion. I looked for a dance outing on Meetup.com. My friend Sara's new husband had used Meetup.com to find others on the Paleo diet. If he could locate nice, sane people who wanted to eat raw meat, surely I could find interesting, stable professionals who wanted to moonwalk to Michael Jackson? I located a group in Midtown, slipped into tight black pants with fringed bottoms and a backless fuchsia shirt from the last time I was single, and took the bus to the city.

There I found fifty embarrassed-looking strangers sweating on the sidewalk, waiting to enter a club. It's one thing to dress inappropriately for your age to go dancing by yourself. It's another to wait in line for the privilege of feeling awkward and self-conscious.

I wanted to go home. But I'd made a commitment to have fun! I hailed a cab and sat inside, debating. Go home and eat ice cream, or continue to a salsa club I'd also read about? I decided to check out the club before giving up.

Inside, the music lifted my mood immediately. A guy with construction-worker muscles invited me to dance. I was happy to follow his lead and just drift along, moving to the music. I no longer felt self-conscious. Out there on the dance floor, I was suddenly aware of the support of generations of my family behind me. I felt as if they were there, too, my father and grandparents, others before them.

We all have these moments that remind us of who we are. Your parents pass down their problems, their messed-up romances, their mistakes. But they also pass on their passions and strengths. Creating more moments of joy can reawaken parts of yourself or your heritage that may have faded in marriage.

Divorce can bring back the loneliness of being single, but in many cases, it also brings back the freedom. That freedom may not be light, but it can be exhilarating. "Sometimes we have to reconnect with a life of the possible, not the ideal," said Rabbi Mordecai Finley. The life of the possible, as Cole from the networking event showed, can be pretty great.

These days, when I'm lonely, I say to myself, *Of course I'm lonely. I'm sitting home alone on a Saturday night while my son sleeps in the next room, dreaming of fire trucks.* I could wake him up, but he'd be exhausted in the morning and I'm maxed out on discussing fire prevention techniques and making the sound of the alarm. When I felt lonely in my marriage, that was it; that was as intimate as it was going to get. Now it's circumstantial. It will change.

This is just a transition, I remind myself. *This is not the rest of my life.*

CHAPTER THREE

The Expanded Family

Break Up a Marriage, Not a Family

✪

We worry that divorce will damage our children, but the vast majority of kids do well in life and show no lasting negative effects on their behavior, grades, or well-being. The outlook continues to improve as our understanding of children and the support for co-parents increases. Some people say divorce decreased conflicts about child-rearing and improved their own parenting.

I'm a good father. Do you know why? Because I get to say goodbye to these kids every week. Are you shitting me? It's like every parent's fantasy. Who can't be a good father for half of every week? No matter how bad it gets, every Wednesday I get to go, "Goodbye, girls. Daddy's going to go upstairs and pour whiskey all over his naked body right now. I'm going to lay in my own filth until two seconds before you come back here." That's why I'm such a good dad.

—American comedian Louis C.K.

When we first discussed divorce, I balked because of my son. Sure, my own parents divorced and I'm fine. Or fine enough. I'm certainly *as fine* as most people I know. When I look around at my friends, the general level of happiness and success is evenly distributed between those whose parents divorced and the ones whose parents stayed married. The adult kids of divorce aren't wearing a scarlet *D* on their foreheads, nor radiating some nimbus of attachment anxiety, insecurity, and mistrust.

But still. While I believed my son would be fine, I also suspected he'd be *more fine* if we stayed married. Sure, research shows that 75 to 80 percent of kids with divorced parents do well. They're not derailed by ongoing psychological problems, don't bully others or fail classes. They participate in the basic job of being human—getting to school, following rules, forming close relationships, pursuing work, meaning, and connection. But about 20 to 25 percent of kids of divorce do struggle with behavioral, psychological, or academic problems, compared to about 10 percent of kids from intact families. And what about those tiny, subtle shocks that don't register on a study? Wasn't a marginal marriage a better choice, *really*, than no marriage at all?

No. For one thing, staying married was no longer an option. And the more I began reading about child development, talking to clinicians and meeting divorced parents and adult children of divorce, the more I realized I could raise a happy, healthy child in a variety of scenarios, *including not being married to his dad.*

Many factors affect a child's well-being. When kids of divorce falter, the break-up may not be the cause. Since divorce is more common among the poor, some problems linked to divorce arise from poverty, not family structure. There are other reasons kids might struggle. "One of the things that happened in the mid-nineties was the realization that a number of the kids we saw as 'troubled' were in fact troubled before the parents ever separated," said Marin County, California–based psychologist Joan B. Kelly, pointing to longitudinal studies following children for fifteen years. "The kids who were at risk, by and large, were showing a number of different kinds of symptoms before the separation. The issues were around high levels of conflict and/or violence in the married family. Also the mental health of the parents. We blamed it all on divorce back then, but we were wrong."

So what do children need? University of Cambridge psychologist Michael Lamb fields this question all the time. He's often an expert witness in custody disputes and adoption cases, and he said people constantly come up to him seeking information about childhood adjustment. "I was giving long lists of places. I couldn't find anywhere where it had actually been pulled together," he said, speaking in that crisp British accent that can make even the most banal statement sound like official policy.

He wanted one source he could cite. In 2012, Lamb decided to write it himself. He took a yearlong sabbatical. He gathered a thousand studies on child development, the bibliographies of his own five hundred scholarly articles, and dozens of books. He planned to spend the year in his comfy chair reading, and then writing the Big Book of Childhood Adjustment. He quickly realized it would be "quite a boring book." A handful of factors support a child's growth. They're obvious, essentially undisputed, and easy to explain. He needed only nine pages, plus references, to write the single most comprehensive overview of child development available today.

Nine pages. This is how consistent and simple the truth is. Children generally do well and grow up happy and healthy when they have:

- Good relationships with their parents or primary caregivers. (A "primary caregiver" is another adult, such as a grandparent, who is the main support in a family where one or both parents are absent.)
- Parents or primary caregivers who aren't embroiled in conflict with each other and who have supportive, positive relationships with *other* adults.
- Emotionally stable, attentive parents or caregivers who can set fair limits and express their love.
- Adequate resources such as food, safe housing, and social support.

Marriage isn't the critical factor for kids, but rather having a loving relationship with their parents or caregivers who create a safe and stable home, and aren't sucked under by fighting. "The mere fact that the majority of children raised in single-parent or divorced families are well-adjusted undercuts the argument that children 'need' to be raised in traditional families. These process factors, rather than family structure, affect adjustment in both traditional and nontraditional families," said Lamb.

This is not to say that divorce brings no risks. Most everyone is angry, sad, or distracted in the beginning. Routines get disrupted, families relocate. Money can be tight. Some divorced parents fight for years. Divorce is a risk factor for sure—as are many of the actions we take every day. Every time you pull out of your driveway, you risk being rear-ended by a truck. But you don't hunch over the wheel in guilty terror whenever you need groceries, or only buy food you can carry on your skateboard. Instead, you take driver's education, check your mirrors, wear a seat belt, avoid driving drunk.

Parenting during divorce is similar. We need to take precautions, and pay extra attention to our children's mental and physical state, and to our own. We don't want to be so enamored of our aspirations for a good divorce that we fail to notice when our kids need help. But nor should we consider our children lifelong victims because their parents didn't stay married.

Divorce isn't anyone's plan A. Still, it's possible to create a meaningful, fabulous plan B. We have a great deal of control over the home life we create for our kids, and the relationships around them.

I decided there were many reasons to be optimistic about my son's future and the well-being of children of divorce in general. Because we know kids crave stability, we can work to establish new routines, ones that are consistent with our own values and personal style. We can strive to reduce conflict with a former spouse, and get help doing so if we need it. Without a spouse around to blame for, well, *everything*, we can let divorce challenge us to be better parents. We can remember that we're not our children's entire world, and expand their support system by bringing in other adults. Finally, because we understand that being attentive to our children requires our own emotional recuperation, many of us need to prioritize taking care of ourselves, as I would soon see.

CREATE STABILITY IN A TIME OF CHAOS

Divorce throws changes at children, often in rapid succession. Some parents feel as if they're floundering about in disorder for months—eating dinner at a card table because they lack the time or will to buy new furniture after moving out, having no plan for getting three kids to four locations in the same afternoon. But this chaotic jumble is generally short-lived, and I met many people who ultimately found it *easier* to establish stability after divorce. Without the need for agreement from a recalcitrant spouse, they could stick to bedtimes and bath detail, meet homework deadlines, enforce rules about sugary snacks.

I have never been a paragon of predictability. I crave spontaneity. I'll always take the new route to work, choose the restaurant I've never tried. But after we split, the routines of a small child felt urgent—for him *and* for me. I wanted to firmly establish our vision of a calm, stable home in two locations. We already had a list of rules and our son's nightly schedule posted on the refrigerator. I'd point to this list as if it were a set of commandments handed down from the heavens. "After dinner, brush teeth, read two books, use the bathroom, go to bed. We have to do it. This is what it says."

My husband and I alternated nights giving our son dinner and putting him to bed, and we each watched him one full weekend day. Our routine was identical every week. I'd sit at the kitchen table with my son at the beginning of the month, helping him mark "Daddy Days" and "Mommy Days" on the calendar with an ink-stamp dolphin (Mommy) and shark (Daddy).

Our son slept in his room at my house in the beginning. While child support tables typically count overnights, this legal approach emphasizes where the children *sleep* rather than how they spend their waking hours. We focused on waking hours, on the time spent doing things with our child. Once he acclimated to two homes, he started sleeping at his dad's one weekend night, and then, later, Thursday nights, too. We had a somewhat open-door policy about whose "turn" it was; if our son was missing me on his dad's night, I could visit, and vice versa. I've spoken to other parents who said a similarly open approach helped *them* deal with the loneliness of being away from their children, and eased children's fears. The fact that we got along well facilitated this.

Many parents fixate on having *equal* time with their children, an understandable impulse but one that can lead to complicated, ever-changing schedules that confound social engagements and can confuse children. We don't want to be as dogmatic about "equal time" as we once were about the "right" family structure. Child psychologists say the ideal custody arrangement involves minimum transitions and frequent contact with both parents—but not necessarily identically matching schedules.

"There are many ways to be involved in a child's life; it doesn't have to be an equal division of parenting time," said University of Maryland legal scholar Jana Singer, who is known in divorce reform circles for borrowing the term "velvet revolution" to describe today's gentler, kinder divorce. "Even states with a preference for joint custody don't require fifty-fifty residential time. It's more about joint decision making. Joint physical custody can be sixty-forty or seventy-thirty."

Indiana-based social worker Murray Vachon asks clients to think about their careers, physical fitness, friends, and finances, and be honest about where parenting fits in. "It's shocking to say, 'Parenting is number three on my list.' But it's really helpful to know. If your kids are third on your list, you don't want to have your kids fifty-fifty. I try to work with people to say, 'What kind of parent can you be, and what do your kids need?'"

We don't worry if a married parent travels every week for work, yet we may fear that a similar absence due to divorce creates a boundless vat of emotional need. But the magic of intimate connection doesn't arise in a strict mathematical equation of "hours in = love out."

My son counts his nana, my mother, as one of his three favorite people. They don't live together. But my mother loves him unreservedly. They like to discuss engineering. I'll be driving home from the grocery store, and my son will ask to call Nana on the car's speakerphone.

I dial. My mother answers.

"Nana! Nana! How is paper made?" my son yells from the backseat.

"Well, let me think," my mother says. She takes a drag on her cigarette. "Paper starts with trees that are cut down and made into pulp. Have you seen paper pulp?"

"Um, is it like when cardboard gets wet?"

"Yes, a little bit. Paper starts with pulp."

This conversation will last until I get home, my son gripping the cell phone to keep talking while I haul in bags. They discuss punch presses, automobile manufacturing, the specific gravity of water versus lemon juice. They have their own close relationship separate from his and mine that contributes to his sense of living in a stable, loving world.

If you're worried about not seeing your kids enough, you can make an effort to ensure that your time together counts. Studies show that a nonresidential parent who is present but not engaged—just hanging out watching TV, for example—isn't as beneficial to her kids as one who participates in "authoritative forms of behavior" such as helping with homework, talking about problems, setting rules, and showing interest in her children's friends and passions.

For some residential parents, actively making it easy for an ex to stay involved goes a long way toward facilitating it. Encouraging the relationship can help smooth the way for a continuing deep and meaningful connection between your child and his other parent.

Gonzalo, a forty-something entrepreneur in Chile, said his parents had divorced when he was twenty. His father moved to Spain, and Gonzalo saw him with decreasing frequency as the years passed. Facing his own divorce as an adult, he worried that moving out of the house would similarly distance him from his young son, even though he had no intention of leaving town. A therapist helped him establish a regular schedule of alternate weekends and Wednesday nights, and encouraged him to trust the power of consistency.

When I met him, he'd stuck to this schedule for nearly a decade. "I had the biggest payoff just two weeks ago," he said. "I was supposed to pick up my son at seven thirty, and because of really bad traffic, I got there at eight. When he got in my car, he said, 'I thought you weren't coming.' I looked at him and I said, 'Dude, have I ever not been there? Have I ever failed you over these last nine years?' I could look him straight in the eye and ask him this question. He thought about it and he looked back at me and he was like, 'No.' I have never, not once, not been there. And he knows it. It was a great moment for me."

• • •

When my parents, and Gonzalo's, divorced, the notion that men are emotional beings who form important, deep connections with their children was still somewhat new, even controversial. For generations, the father's role was as constrained as the mother's—breadwinner, disciplinarian, husband. In the late 1940s, developmental psychologist Pauline Sears did groundbreaking research on children whose fathers had gone to war. She showed that these kids missed an important source of social and emotional development. This came as a shock to many. Men are emotional beings who form intimate bonds with children?! Who knew?

By the 1970s, social scientists of all types were regularly proving that infants and toddlers form attachments with their fathers. It took a few more decades for fathers to be routinely involved to the degree many are today, helping out around the house, carrying the baby in the Björn, staying home while their wives go to work—and remaining fully active as parents, postdivorce. The inclusion of the father as a full parent is one of the great improvements in divorce. Increasingly, parents assume they'll share responsibility, and many states have a presumption of joint custody.

While a huge benefit for kids, this change brings new challenges. Co-parenting requires an ongoing relationship between adults who are estranged enough to divorce. It puts a huge onus on all of us to strive toward mature, calm cooperation, and to make realistic parenting plans.

If your children move from house to house each week, you can create stability for them in two homes, though it may take extra effort. Parenting in two places can require duplicate textbooks, extra clothes, a cell phone for a child before you might otherwise get one. Some adults use a Google Doc or an online co-parenting site to coordinate classes and play dates with the other parent.

Divorced mother of two Traci Whitney created a parenting dashboard out of her own frustration with scheduling. She wanted one place to record expenses, exchange notes, and share photos and doctor's numbers with her oft-traveling ex. In 2012, she launched TwoHappy Homes.com, a perky, upbeat site that helps organize the massive production that is childhood today.

Two different parents told me their kids greeted the news of divorce with excitement because they'd finally get a second home like their friends! "It was like I said we were going to Disney World," one mother said. Some children I spoke to said having two homes quickly felt natural and even advantageous. "If I get mad at one parent, or kind of sick of them, it gives us both a break. I think it's good," one high school girl told me.

. . .

We achieved stability largely through simplicity and consistency. But there were interruptions to our routine also, which I valued. My friend Courtney would come for dinner with her daughter. The four of us would sit around the table, eating a chicken she'd roasted. Then the kids would go upstairs to jump on the bed or sing at the top of their lungs. Courtney and I would drink wine downstairs as the light faded over the back garden, and we'd all go to bed late. I want family life to be fun and social. The fact that our routine existed enabled me to indulge in the occasional late night, to relax the rules for an out-of-town guest or other welcome disruption.

During those early months, I reminded my son that nothing else was changing. I'd list the people in his life who loved him and weren't going anywhere—his parents, his nana, his other grandparents, his aunt Michelle, his cousins, my friend Courtney. I also floated the idea that I was at home, protecting the house, while Daddy was on the next street, guarding us from the outside from high up in his fifth-floor apartment. This notion of a safety net began to feel true; his dad *was* one street away, a sentinel over the city.

When we finally relocated to a new place two years after my husband moved out, people would ask how my son was handling the change. It took me a while to figure out what to say. His home life *hadn't* really changed. We'd just picked it up and relocated it. "He's doing great!" I finally said.

FOSTER COOPERATION, QUELL CONFLICT

Our son, to my surprise, seemed to get happier after his dad moved out. Certainly age contributed. The limitations of toddlerhood confounded my type A son, who yearned to be the boss. He wanted to drive the car before he could reliably cross the room on foot. He'd interrupt my attempt to teach him about vowels with an explanation of how it was done on the "Rectangle Planet," a realm he'd occupied, apparently, before he was born, and one in which he, not I, was the expert. With mastery came contentment. But I think he also was happier because his mother was no longer snapping at his father.

I worried, before the split, about small digs I'd make. I'd be unpacking groceries after my husband did the shopping, noting with rising anger the items on my list he'd failed to locate. It felt personal: the yogurt only mattered to *me*—why should he bother finding it? Opinions vary about the damage this kind of low-level friction can cause, but I didn't want my son to equate marriage with irritation and defeat.

Intense, ongoing conflict is a major stressor for children, in marriage and divorce. Putting them in the middle of fights, asking them to take sides, forcing them to listen to character assassinations of their other parent—this kind of high conflict can make children feel unmoored and unsafe.

"When you put down your child's parent, you put down her DNA. That child is drawn from that person. When you say, 'Your mom or dad is a fool,' you're saying, 'Half of you is a fool,'" said M. Gary Neuman, author of the excellent, encouraging book *Helping Your Kids Cope with Divorce the Sandcastles Way*, and creator of the Sandcastles program for children of divorce. In the worst case, parental alienation syndrome, one parent so thoroughly trashes the other that the child begins to participate in this critique.

Of course divorce sounds inherently conflictual: you failed to get along so thoroughly, you're splitting up. But co-parenting can become *more harmonious* after divorce. You're no longer bringing your hurt as a spouse into discussions about swim lessons. If you do explode in a fit of anger, you can go home, calm down, and reopen the conversation more objectively later.

Living apart also means fewer opportunities to lash out in front of your children, and more impetus for cooperation. "We have to be coordinated because we're not living under the same roof," said Gonzalo.

"We have to discuss things that, a lot of times, when you're married, you don't discuss."

Sometimes, the personality differences that rocked a marriage benefit children postdivorce. Hollie, the mother of three in Colorado, described herself as bookish and her ex as "rugged." They never wanted to do the same things in marriage. Now she's grateful that her children spend time learning sports and playing in nature with their dad, while

Custody Wars

There's one statement I think should be barred from divorce discussions or be classified as hate speech: "I will sue for sole custody!"

Certainly some parents rightfully seek and win sole custody—such as a woman I met in Hoboken who'd had a child with a drug addict who was occasionally violent. But I also met a trustworthy college professor whose ex kept suing for sole custody the way another might decide to do a juice cleanse—because she was irritable, uncomfortable, or scared. I also heard about two well-educated men who uttered this threat *in marriage* to prevent their wives from leaving. Even if it works and the wives stay, this threat now sleeps in bed between them. The wife is living with the knowledge that her spouse, ostensibly devoted to protecting her and the family, could instead pursue a path of destruction.

It's like the line in *Where the Wild Things Are*. The little boy, Max, tells the monsters he's going home: "But the wild things cried, 'Oh please don't go—we'll eat you up—we love you so!'" Or, it's as if King Solomon offers to cut the child in two, and both parents say, "Sure, as long as she doesn't get the bigger half!"

I know you would never say this, or if you accidentally did, you will now retract it. Fighting for sole custody against a decent parent is not acting in your child's best interest. It is a threat that escalates anger and damages children.

she can stay home and read a book. "We know that we each have different valuable, often opposite, things to offer the kids. We want what's best for our children, as well as for each other."

Children can appreciate our divergent strengths when they exist outside the context of an ongoing argument about whose way is right. "My mom put me in cheerleading and gymnastics at a young age, but I also wanted to play soccer, and she wouldn't take me. So my dad took

Your lawyer may encourage you to pursue sole custody as a tactic to "bargain down" for what you really want, but this is not a responsible negotiation technique. In many families, one parent is the primary caregiver, and it makes sense for the children to reside at that parent's home. But this is a decision you agree upon, not a move you make in a high-stakes gamble using your children as chips.

"Nobody fights over custody anymore, except when one of the parents is moving across the country," said Sam Margulies, a North Carolina–based legal scholar, author, and lawyer turned mediator. "When you have a two-income family, you've got to have the active participation of the other partner or you go nuts. You try maintaining a full-time job, raising three kids, and having no help. Children are not these wonderful little prizes to be won."

No loving parent should make this threat unless the other is endangering the child, which does not mean serving non-organic macaroni and cheese, skipping bath night, pursuing a barely lucrative career as a jewelry artist—or no longer loving you.

On some basic level, this threat speaks loud and clear. It says, "I don't love my children as much as I hate how I feel."

Many people in divorce feel angry, overwhelmed, or scared. I believe you can find a way to manage those feelings while still protecting your children.

me and bought me cleats," said Elizabeth, the twenty-something from small-town Texas who lived with her mother and grandparents after her parents divorced. "If he hadn't been in the picture, I wouldn't have gotten to do that. But if they'd stayed married, maybe I couldn't have, either."

If you're reading this now and feeling concerned—"Wow! I really screwed up. I guess I shouldn't have printed out a list of all the things their dad did that pissed me off and taped it to the refrigerator"—don't worry. You have plenty of time to apologize and start again. Seeing conflict resolved demonstrates that people fight and make up, and still care about and protect each other.

There's a huge amount of support for co-parenting today, including private counseling. You can find a local therapist on PsychologyToday .com, or ask a good mediator or collaborative lawyer for a suggestion. At one point, we saw a therapist who acted as a "divorce counselor" to help us make concrete decisions, such as how much time was appropriate for my almost-ex's new partner to spend with our child, and did the fact that I was angry about it matter? These were discrete issues that could be resolved, it turned out, unlike the fundamental personality overhaul we'd attempted in marriage counseling.

Nearly every state has helpful, short parenting education classes in the courts, a service that emerged in the 1980s and 1990s as a way to prevent or counteract divorce-related risk for kids. This is a public-health approach to divorce that parents tend to like, believe it or not. Bethany, a mother of one in Missouri, said the court-ordered class she and her ex took was basic, "yet tremendously helpful" in lessening her fears that joint custody would create attachment issues for their son.

Vicki, the mother of two in Oregon who said she learned what not to do from her own parents' divorce, also appreciated her state's parenting class. "There were workshops with role-playing and tests, a lot of conflict resolution and co-parenting information," she said. "The most helpful part was group discussions where people shared their stories. It was interesting to hear different points of view."

Workshops for children of divorce, also increasingly available, tend to receive rave reviews from parents and to show immediate benefits for kids in systematic evaluations.

Attorney Forrest Mosten encourages couples to impose structure to increase co-parenting harmony. Amorphous arrangements can trigger anger and strafe old wounds. "Some people don't have a parenting plan, so every time Dad is going to see the child, it's a negotiation," he said. Mosten recommends "blind transitions"—one parent dropping off a child at school and the other picking him up—rather than an in-person handoff that can lead to fights and stir loyalty conflicts.

Some judges require high-conflict couples to communicate through a website such as OurFamilyWizard.com. "At first I thought it was stupid. I'm an adult. I can handle my own conversations. But it's actually really helpful," said Lauren, a thirty-year-old stay-at-home mother of one in California who sought a temporary restraining order against her ex, and was then required to use the site by the judge. "There's a tone meter, so it makes us both really notice how we sound. It's also good to know that if I have to discuss something, like his birthday party, there's a place I can do it."

We didn't have a high-conflict split to begin with, and our relationship grew increasingly cooperative with time. I found myself actively praising my ex to our son, intentionally and reflexively. "Your daddy is really good at rock climbing," I said one morning, as we biked along the Hudson River to the climbing wall at Chelsea Piers recreation center. "He used to teach rock climbing. You'll probably be really good if you work at it, too." Later that day, I heard myself saying, "Your daddy is very responsible, and that's a good quality."

It may seem that admiring your ex would confuse your kids or fuel reunion fantasies. Praise is problematic if you're ambivalent about the divorce and are secretly "arguing" for reconciliation. But honestly letting your kids know you still care for each other helps them feel safely held within a *type* of family. "Children fear that something irreparable is going to break, that the bottom is falling out, that no one will take care of them and that they'll have to choose sides," said child psychiatrist Mark Banschick, author of the *Intelligent Divorce* book series. "If they hear that the parents still care about each other deeply, but that the marriage isn't working out, it's a transition to another form of family. It's not quite the same hard break. That's a beautiful thing to offer children."

Praising your ex sets a tone of respect within your family. It also conveys a larger truth: people can care about each other in a variety of relationships, and we need to make an effort to preserve the connection with those we love.

•   •   •

Your children may dream you'll reunite, regardless of what you say. I did. Not as a child, but as an adult.

The year after my mother's second divorce, my sister suggested we take a family vacation—as in, our *original family*, my mother *and* father, my sister and me, and all our kids. I'd traveled a great deal at that point, having spent a decade visiting five-star resorts to write about honeymoon destinations for bridal magazines. But that family reunion was the most exciting trip I'd contemplated in years.

The last time I'd traveled with my mom and dad together, I was four. We'd rented a house in Jamaica, curved like a banana around a swimming pool. I'd loved the sugarcane fields, the palm fronds, the locals playing bongos. *We should go back to Jamaica*, I thought!

No one else wanted to reconvene in Jamaica in August, it turned out. After much discussion, we finally agreed to meet in Cincinnati, my father's "turf," for that city's Labor Day fireworks.

My mom and sister and I checked into a hotel on the Kentucky side of the Ohio River, with views of downtown Cincinnati. On our second night, we had drinks at the hotel's outdoor bar. The Ohio River Valley heat, as intense as anything in the Caribbean, had finally broken. My parents started reminiscing about my dad's first foray into business; he'd started a swimming pool company after their aboveground pool split, flooding the neighbor's yard.

I knew the outlines of this tale, but I loved hearing them tell it in tandem. It brought those early years forward in a new way, somehow. It replaited them as a shared experience. I was struck by the realization *This feels totally normal.*

There was something fractured-feeling about the old-style divorce, despite my parents' best efforts to do better than the times. My dad hadn't been around enough, I could now see—for us or for him. Seeing my parents joking with each other, smiling in that lit-up way of old friends who really understand each other, made me feel more unified within myself.

At the end of that trip, my father had another vacation inspiration. "You need to come to Mexico with me," he said to my mom, referring to Puerto Vallarta, where he's had a beachfront condo since my sister worked as a time-share closer down there. My mother, still flattened by her divorce, needed a respite from her reality, my dad insisted. She agreed to go.

That fall, they set off for Vallarta. I felt like a little kid, waiting for my parents to return from vacation, eager to see what kind of unexpected wonder they'd bring home.

BE YOUR BEST PARENT

Our son also was happier, I suspected, because he was getting more attention from us, now that we were no longer distracted by our own conflicts or conversations. I started teasing him—or maybe us—that his father and I, and my now-single mother, had hours of free time to follow him around town, buying him lollipops.

Some people worry that divorced parents overcompensate out of guilt, buying too many toys, refusing to discipline. I'm sure this is true in some cases, maybe even ours. But a surfeit of love is not what spoils children, and concern about the effects of divorce can better attune you to a child, make you take the time to say, "I love you," ask how he's doing, engage. The married-with-children lifestyle can be frenzied and *fraught*, a child's needs brushed aside, not fully seen.

Many people I spoke to said divorce forced them to become better versions of themselves—and better parents. Gonzalo, in Chile, said divorce sharpened his focus. "When we were married, I'd work late and not worry about seeing my son. There was always tomorrow. I'd slack off on changing the diapers or whatever. Now, when I'm with my son, I am totally focused. I have him ten days a month, and I never take that time for granted."

Gregory, an attorney in Los Angeles who had primary physical custody of his two boys, had to develop domestic skills after divorce. "I thought I could give the kids everything they needed, until it got to be dinnertime. Then I realized, 'Oh shit. They have to eat something. What will I do?' I wanted not to let them know I was completely at a loss, dependent on their mother in regard to cooking. I learned to cook and I taught the kids to cook. Now I love to cook. We all watch cooking shows. It's incredibly empowering for children to know how to cook."

A mother of four in California told me that getting divorced, which was not her choice, made her reexamine all her relationships, including the ones she had with her children. She stopped wearing a "mask of perfection" around her kids, became more honest about her own needs, and less apt to snap at them due to frustration and fatigue. Hollie in Colorado said she felt like a better role model for her children, post-marriage, because she became more broadly competent. "I'm back in college, where I feel I've belonged my whole life. I think my kids really deserve to see their parents both doing things, like me going to college. I don't think this would have happened if I'd stayed married."

Some said the struggle of divorce provided a teaching moment itself. "You have to show your kids that your life isn't how you would have drawn it up. Things happen," said the restaurateur from a Catholic family in New Jersey, Vince. "I can let it defeat me or I can say, 'I'm going to take this situation and learn from it. I'm going to move on.' You've got to strive. I use life to show that to my kids. I was blessed with great kids, but I helped make them great."

• • •

Being your best parent also means actively creating positive moments—tilting the balance toward the good—and bringing our specific strengths to the job. Paula, a filmmaker in Manhattan's West Village, divorced in 2000, when her daughter was five. Paula had a socially demanding career, and she began taking her daughter, Clara, to networking events at art galleries and screenings.

When I met them, Clara was a happy, studious high school senior with glasses and long kinky hair, doing well at a private high school. She was excited to go to college in the Midwest to study science. Clara said her lifestyle seemed lucky. "You feel special and privileged because you get to go do cool things. Especially as an only child, I get one-on-one time with both of my parents."

I took a tally of my own interests and strengths. I like to host dinners and attend parties, travel to see family and to visit little towns, bake, do arts and crafts projects, hike, sit on the floor and tickle my son. These activities became part of my parenting plan. Many parents sign up their kids for art or sports. Stimulating, demanding activities can moderate the effects of even a contentious divorce. A child who focuses on something he loves—the gymnastics team, the math club, a church group—may fare better than a sibling without a personally engaging endeavor. As parents, we can look for activities that help our kids enter a state of *flow*—the feeling of being so absorbed that it's as if time stops, and worries fade.

• • •

We also have to accept that our children may feel sad about the divorce, and not let that fact overwhelm us, make us angry, or inspire us to "correct" them by insisting that they "shouldn't" feel bad.

All children face sadness, loss, and change. A child may lose a grandparent or parent, a best friend, the family cat after she wanders into the street. Childhood involves one uncomfortable transition after another. School itself can feel like a never-ending rejection mill for some, and a constant shifting of classrooms, teachers, courses, and routines. As parents, we're always helping our children adapt to change and learn to cope; this is today's lesson.

In some ways, we're more prepared to help a child deal with death

than with divorce, said social worker Murray Vachon. We naturally em-
pathize with loss due to death; this is the right emotion to show toward
children expressing sadness about the divorce, too. "We don't have to
fix it, but we can acknowledge it and say we're sorry. We can aim for
'accompaniment'—sitting with our children when they express difficult
feelings, not making light of them or turning it into a catastrophe. Kids
just want us to say, 'I know this sucks for you. I'm sorry this happened.'"

The divorce may come as a surprise to one child, and yet have
seemed an obvious eventuality to another. Some kids are relieved by
the news. As a college-age boy whose parents fought through high
school said, "Divorce was likely the best decision they ever made for
me and my brother."

Whatever their initial reaction, children can handle change and
even loss. They are, by and large, resilient.

One day, when my son was four, he was bounding around his bedroom like a Ping-Pong ball. I finally snapped, "You're bouncing off the
walls!"

"Bouncing off the walls? That's a great idea!" he said, jumping from
his mattress into the wall, body-slamming the plaster. This is the kind
of behavior that makes a parent need to go lie down. But he remained
unharmed, and it's a good image of the springiness of our children's
inner lives.

BRING IN OTHER ADULTS

The presence of other stable adults also has been shown to be a protective factor for children, even in a messy split. As parents, we can nurture positive relationships between our children and family members
and adult friends.

Many of us overestimate our own influence, worry that we should
save now for our kids' therapy bills because our parenting flaws will
scar them forever. This sense of our own utter significance comes in
part from a view of childhood development widely touted from the 1970s
through the mid-1990s that emphasized the direct influence of parents.

Today, developmental psychologists see growth as a dynamic process, and one in which children participate. A child's personality, skills, and interests affect who she becomes, as do her own efforts to interpret and understand her circumstances. Events do matter; they "turn on" or "off" potential neural pathways and aspects of our personalities. But a parent is not an omnipotent creator, not Geppetto fashioning Pinocchio out of wood. People grow into themselves.

Stephanie, the mother of two from a close-knit Mormon community in the Midwest, said she's seen how much her family's involvement has helped her daughters feel secure. Her mother, grandmother, ex-sister-in-law, and church friends watch her kids after school while she's at work. "I've never hired a babysitter. It's always been family or a family friend. People can hate on the Midwest, but we know how to do the community thing."

Carly, a chef who co-managed a restaurant with her husband, quit after their divorce in 2012. She and her four-year-old daughter moved in with her parents while she searched for a new career. "She thinks she's the luckiest girl in the world because she gets to spend time with her grandparents. I always had this very reserved, undemonstrative father, and now he's like, 'I can't live without her.' I think I needed the support of my parents, too."

Adult children-of-divorce told me about the importance of nonparental figures. Elizabeth in Texas said that growing up, she felt cared for by both parents, her relatives, and her mother's friends. Her mother created a strong social network that she still maintains. "I have five or six childhood friends I still see. I feel like they kind of took care of me, too," Elizabeth said. "If my mom was going to work late on the weekend, and I didn't want to stay with my grandfather, I could go stay at the Smiths'. I liked it. Having those other adults around made me feel secure. I could talk to these other people, these parents of my friends. They were like other mothers."

The benefit of social support is one reason to consider religious attendance. If you like your religious tradition, this may be a good time to get involved. In a church or synagogue or meeting hall, children think about morality and spirituality, and are wrapped in an intergenerational community of support.

Amy Ziettlow, an ordained pastor in the Evangelical Lutheran Church of America, said kids can really connect with other adults when away from home. "A lot of denominations take youth service trips. We went to Nashville after the flood in 2010 to rebuild houses. Those activities bring us out of ourselves and bond us to others. They provide us a safe place to talk. You're up at three a.m. You're four hundred miles from home. Everything is new. You're physically exhausted. Your defenses lower. You feel safe."

On one mission trip, a teen shared his worries about the new baby his father and stepmother were having. "We could say, 'I know that's hard, but we love you, and you like your stepmother, and we know you're going to be a great big brother.' It was helpful for him to have that affirmation, that this does not make you a bad person to feel angry. But let's talk about how you're going to express that."

These close friendships that feel like family can create their own legacy. A fifty-something performance artist from California named Dan was eight when his Japanese-American mother and Chinese father divorced. He and his three sisters lived with their mother. Dan saw his father on Sundays, but the relationship, already remote, grew more distant.

After the divorce, his mother began spending more time with a family friend, a young artist named Max. Dan bonded with the young man. "He played this incredibly benign, supportive role in my life. He was a former cross-country runner, so he'd take me running. He played clarinet, so I started playing clarinet. It gave me someone to look up to and admire, an adult male who liked me. Every time I would see him, he was happy to see me."

In his twenties, Dan dated a single mother with a two-year-old son, and an uninvolved father. Dan grew close to the boy. "At some point, a few years into it, I realized, 'I'm going to care about this kid for the rest of his life.' The relationship with his mother was amorphous. With him, it was very clear."

The little boy also became an artist. Now in his thirties, he crashes at Dan's when visiting L.A. "I've told him, 'You're like my son. You're my family. Don't forget you have someone in this world.'"

TAKE CARE OF THE CAREGIVER

As much as we want to prioritize our children, we also need to remember the oxygen-mask rule from the airplane—make sure we can breathe first. The "oxygen mask" in divorce might be hiring help, scheduling a weekly social outing with friends, or even getting enough sleep. We don't want to put too much responsibility on children, asking them to comfort us. A "parentified child" may grow up to stifle his own needs, overperform, take care of everybody else to his own detriment. Certainly parentified children can come from intact families, too, but in divorce, it's a risk against which we should guard.

At some point, I realized that taking care of myself meant not keeping everything quite so unchanged at home. My second single summer, I applied to be a visiting artist at the child-friendly 18th Street Arts Center in Santa Monica, eighteen blocks from the Pacific Ocean. I'd wanted to move to Los Angeles for years, but my husband couldn't imagine leaving the East Coast. Now that we were divorcing, I'd put aside my West Coast dream. I would not fight for the right to take my son away from his dad. But we could certainly go to California for a month over the summer!

Santa Monica was like a dream life. Our live-work unit had bright white walls and nothing to remind me of my former married life. The sun poured through the clerestory glass. I kept the back door open to the ocean air. I enrolled my son in day camp at a fancy school across the street. I could work and see the kids coming and going all day.

I hadn't felt that light in years, maybe since my breezy twenties, when everything still felt possible and I was never tired, irritable, or burdened by my choices. I spent the first week floating around like I was slightly buzzed on ecstasy. I wanted to stay forever. I may have voiced that desire aloud to a visitor in front of my little son.

Later, I sat out back, talking on the phone to a friend in New York. My son played on the floor beyond the open door. I wanted to stay in L.A., but I had to return, I told my friend, because my son's dad refused to leave the New York area. Which is not too hard for a small child to realize means *because of him*.

Did I do this, sit in the little plastic chair, looking up at the slowly purpling sky and state out loud, and loudly because we were not getting great reception, that I felt trapped in New York because of my child—within earshot of my child?

That night, my son climbed to the top of a stepladder we'd left out, and hurled his metal police car to the ground. He picked it up, mounted the ladder, and threw it again. Was he angry, acting out? Or just an average five-year-old boy with a tall ladder and a concrete floor? I couldn't tell. When you're divorcing, it's easy to worry that otherwise "normal" behaviors signal serious distress.

At camp the next day, the counselor asked to speak with me. My son wasn't following directions, she said. He lies down in circle time when the rule is to sit up. He sits behind the line when the rule is to sit in front. What did I think she should do?

She should find me a new husband so I could establish a new family? She should call his dad and convince him to move to L.A.? She was the professional. I was just the mom going through a divorce. The mom whose kid, it turns out, was not 100 percent comfortable.

I'd interviewed dozens of therapists about the need to provide a sense of stability, and reassure the children this is not their fault. Then I moved my son across the country for a month to live in a largely empty artist studio, sent him to camp with a bunch of strangers, and spent the entire time talking about how I never wanted to leave.

Suddenly, out there in the clear air of L.A., I was aware of how frustrated I felt back home, my life strapped in duct tape, compressed, bound—all our old furniture standing around, reinforcing my former identity. Yes, I wanted to keep my son's life stable. But I also needed to accommodate my urgent desire for change. Overfocusing on a child's well-being to the point of squelching your own can lead to acting out like a teenager denied a voice for too long.

I also would need to forgive myself for parenting mistakes. I thought about Paula, the filmmaker in Manhattan. She'd committed to staying in her apartment near her ex, in one of the most expensive neighborhoods of an already outrageously pricey city. She faced a series of career triumphs, one spectacular financial disaster, and years of economic anxiety. Throughout, she worried how it affected her daughter.

When we spoke, Paula said she wished she'd had a glimpse of how well Clara would do. "There's guilt about being divorced, which, looking at it fourteen years later, I didn't need to feel. I wish I could have been more forgiving to myself about things I did as a parent that I didn't think were perfect. Four-year-olds are four-year-olds. They're difficult. They act up. People become who they're going to become.

"I like this whole concept of the 'good-enough mother,' that if you were perfect you wouldn't be preparing your child for the real world. Maybe my shortcomings during those difficult years might be making her a better person. She's good. She's okay. We're all okay."

Many of us still secretly believe family *should* look one specific way—maybe like the old TV show *Happy Days*—a mother and father, two kids. But there is no single, correct Good Family model hovering above us in the firmament. Or rather, we may hold one in our heads, but it bears little resemblance to the reality of family life for most people in the past, present, or probably future. We get to create our own ideal family, help our children grow in it, and let it stand as the safe harbor from which they sail out into the world.

CHAPTER FOUR

The Opposite of an Engagement

Telling Others about Your Divorce

Some people are reluctant to share news of their divorce, but talking about it can create new closeness with old friends and decrease isolation. How we discuss it influences other people's reactions. We can take charge of the dialogue to help friends and family offer appropriate support.

When we argue for our limitations we get to keep them.
　　—Evelyn Waugh, twentieth-century British writer

Early on in my separation, I took a mini vacation to Cozumel, an island off Mexico's Caribbean coast. It was my first trip away from home as a single woman, post marriage. I was excited to be traveling by myself. Even sitting in the airport for a four-hour flight delay felt thrilling. I was out in the world, on my own.

I also felt a little nervous. Back home, my future ex-husband had rented his own studio apartment. We'd told a few friends about our split, but not his parents or our broader circle. How would others respond to me, an almost-divorced woman with a child? How would I feel, seeing the news reflected in their eyes? How would *men* react?

Like me, many people are anxious about breaking the news of divorce. We're entering a new state, one that isn't "happily married," yet is not quite "still single." I was glad for the chance to test-drive being a divorcée on vacation, away from my routines and home-based identity.

Hours later, I arrived in Cancún. I took a livery van down the coast to the dock where I'd catch the ferry to Cozumel. I leaned against a thick wooden pillar, exhausted, and looked out at the snaking line of tourists waiting to board. I was practically the only person traveling alone. Sunburned Americans in Señor Frog T-shirts and baseball caps drank beer from plastic cups. Squat *abuelitas* cradled baskets of avocados and pearly white onions. Little girls in frilly dresses giggled and ran after one another. A slender, vaguely Asian-looking young man in dress shorts smiled at me, then tilted his head. "Tired?" he mouthed over the crowd.

I pushed myself from the pillar and walked toward him. "Early flight," I said.

"I just jumped out of an airplane!" he responded. The line started moving, taking him with it. "I'll see you inside!"

Inside the huge, overly air-conditioned ferry, I strode through the two interior decks, glancing around for the skydiver, then found a seat on the open-air fly bridge. I turned my face up toward the warm sun. The ferry gunned its engine, sending salt spray flying.

A few minutes later, the young man from the line appeared. "Hey there!" he said, sliding into the metal bench next to me. He was not a professional skydiver, it turned out, but a dancer on one of the massive cruise ships anchored off Cozumel. He'd spent the day on the mainland with the cruise ship band, getting blitzed out of his mind on tequila.

"How long are you in Cozumel?" he asked.

"Just two nights," I said.

"Just two nights! Why?"

"Well . . ." I looked into his slightly bloodshot yet still quite beautiful almond-shaped eyes. "I'm getting divorced, and my mother thought I needed a vacation. So I left my *four-year-old son* with her so I could visit my sister who's scuba diving in Cozumel, but I'm a little nervous about being single again because now I'm *forty-five*."

There was a long pause. "That's hard," he said.

"It's okay," I said. "It seems like the right thing to do."

"Still. It has to be tough when you loved someone, and then it ends." He put his hand on my thigh. "I'm sorry."

I smiled. He *was* sorry. Also, I was pretty sure he wanted to sleep with me, which I found flattering and in no way incompatible with sincere human caring. I envisioned him back on the ship, talking to the guys in the band. "You know that chick I picked up on the ferry? She's going through a divorce, with a kid. That's rough, right? I wanted to Cheer. Her. Up. *Hard*." He'd make a hip movement to show which part of his body he'd use to help boost my mood.

A salsa band struck up a tune from a lower deck. "Do you want to dance?" he asked. *Yes! This is what you can't do when you're married and traveling with family*, I thought. *Dance an improvised fox-trot/salsa/grind with a stranger on a fast ferry slam-splashing its way across the Caribbean.*

We parted ways when we docked in Cozumel. I wasn't looking for a one-night stand but rather reassurance that I'd be okay, that my new status wouldn't send others running, which the brief encounter with the slender young dancer provided.

The next morning, the encouraging feedback continued. At a jewelry shop near the hotel, the owner asked if I was married.

I looked up from a tray of silver rings. "I'm getting divorced."

"High five!" He raised his hand for me to slap. "Twenty percent off everything in the store!" He leaned in close. "You're going to need to watch your cash."

At a cosmetics store, I told the sweet, solicitous saleswoman that I needed a new lipstick for my new, unmarried life. She grasped my hand. "I wish you good luck. I feel that good things will happen for you. I really believe this."

I loved this enthusiastic support of strangers. It reminded me of some other time in my life. When was it? Oh right, getting engaged! As a bride-to-be, I felt like the perpetual belle of the ball. Strangers acted as if my mere existence were a cause for celebration. Waiters sent over free appetizers or bottles of wine to my fiancé and me, gazing off into the distance as if glimpsing some magical Brigadoon.

A similar vicarious joy had bubbled up when I was pregnant. Women brought water, gave up their seats, shared details of their own childbirth, hour by hour. I loved the way these common rites of passage connected me to others. New moms whisper about how having a baby gives you exclusive membership into a new "club." Divorce does, too. The insta-connection with strangers can be more intense than during those other, more uniformly positive life passages, because people are still processing their own divorce, or that of a loved one, and they want to talk. Also, the cracking-open of loss conveys its own type of excitement. You are *right there*, in your life, not napping through it. Others feel this, and recall their own experiences of high-flying freedom with no net underneath. The club of divorcées may not be one you wanted to join, but membership reinforces an important truth: you are *not* alone.

The flip side of the intensely emotional nature of divorce is that nearly everyone has an opinion that they feel compelled to share, even when their thoughts are negative, hurtful, or unrelated to you. Friends

or family may strike an authoritative tone from a position of total ignorance, cast moral aspersions based on a religion they don't practice,
or unload forty years of distress about their own parents' parting—
completely disregarding *your actual situation*.

"At no other point in my life have so many people tried so hard to
convince me of how miserable I am," wrote the essayist Katie Roiphe
about her own divorce.

We may find ourselves uncharacteristically rattled by negative
feedback, or surprisingly susceptible to divisive suggestions. This discomfort and vulnerability make sense. We've just ripped up the tiles of
our home and are standing on the plywood subfloor, looking out past
the two-by-fours, genuinely unsure what comes next.

Advance conversational planning can help protect us from un-
constructive feedback. We might need a different strategy for talking
about divorce with our parents, often the hardest hit by the news. Many
people dread telling their children, convinced the wrong approach will
scar them for life. Finally, many of us need to monitor how we talk to
ourselves about our divorce, in the privacy of our own heads.

As Salman Rushdie said, "Those who do not have power over the
story that dominates their lives, the power to retell it, rethink it, decon-
struct it, joke about it, and change it as times change, truly are powerless." Taking control of our story can empower us as we move through it.

TAKING CHARGE OF THE CONVERSATION

A few months after I returned from Mexico, I went to a play with a
friend I knew through my ex, and her mother. Before the play, we'd met
an older woman-about-town, a four-time divorcée. In the lobby, we'd
joked about love and marriage, and marriage, and marriage.

At dinner after the show, my friend's mom leaned across the table
to ask why we were splitting up, *really*.

"Well, he's not emotionally present enough," I said.

"What does that mean exactly?"

I gave some examples.

"Are you sure you need to divorce?"

I gave more details about my ex's bad behavior, or at least the things I'd found hurtful.

"So why did you marry him in the first place?"

Suddenly, I couldn't remember. I shared a decade of complaints, fueled by defensiveness and also espresso. Yes, I'd made a pact not to bad-mouth my ex, but when caught off-guard, I choked. Or rather, I wish I'd choked. That would have ended the conversation. As it was, I couldn't stop talking.

Safely home alone much later, I replayed the dialogue. I'd criticized my ex to a woman who was *his friend first*? And her *mother*? Wasn't I a proponent of the considerate decoupling, the kind quit? What was I thinking?

I wasn't thinking. I was reacting. I was feeling judged and maybe pitied, both of which I hate. In my own increasing negativity, I'd helped steer the conversation in exactly the opposite direction from the one I desired.

What we say and how we say it influences other people's reactions, far more than we may expect. Emotions are contagious. We mimic each other's gestures, expressions, and even tone of voice without realizing it. Our minds then follow our bodies. You see emotional contagion in action when you're talking to someone shorter than you, and widen your stance automatically to meet her gaze, or when a coworker complains about the boss, and you begin to feel a shade of her resentment. Or when you gasp for air at a comedy club, tears of hilarity streaming down your face over a set of jokes that would not sound so funny without a nightclub full of strangers cracking up through their two-drink minimum around you.

In divorce, if we slump down in our chair, brows furrowed, shoulders hunched, and unleash our greatest fears at our darkest moments, our friends can effectively "catch" our unhappiness, and then bounce it back to us. We now feel worse, without realizing we've inhaled a contact low—and one for which *we* lit the match.

In Mexico, my news received such a positive response not only because I was in a tourist town talking to salespeople eager to warm me into profligate spending, but also because I was excited to be on vacation, free from my usual concerns. Others felt my zest, and volleyed it back to me. Back home, my enthusiasm for the end of my marriage did not continue in quite the same lubricated-by-piña-coladas way. Real life involves real worries, and these can dip-dye a discussion an inky gray, make us lose our hold on our optimistic position.

Honesty is good policy, but indiscriminately sharing only our darkest moments can lead to depressing and harmful feedback from otherwise caring friends, and certainly from those who are not intimates. Emotional *flexibility*, it turns out, is the better approach during stressful times, and a skill set some of us need to cultivate. Emotional flexibility means the ability to talk openly about your feelings, but also to *repress them when appropriate.*

I know this sounds counter to the idea of talk therapy, and to the whole notion of living an examined life. In general, expressing feelings expands self-awareness and strengthens relationships. But when we reflexively (or obsessively) vent about the negative, we blind ourselves to our own victories. We zoom in on the most distressing images, cropping out the supportive friends, the great parties, our good health. We also leave ourselves open to the judgmental opinions of unsympathetic listeners.

What I needed, I realized, was a prepared script about our divorce, something I could memorize in advance and haul out when questioned, particularly by someone I didn't know well. I needed a divorce elevator speech. A term from the business world, an elevator speech is an overview of your skills, start-up, or script idea that you can share in the time it takes to ride an elevator from an office to the lobby. You have thirty seconds, or maybe two minutes if you work on a really high floor, to pique interest and communicate the salient points, and avoid an awkward scramble for words.

A divorce elevator speech would do the same thing, I decided, though somewhat in reverse. It would encapsulate our divorce, but *end* the conversation, rather than encouraging a listener to follow me down the hall, wanting to know more. It would be a way to tell the story as I wanted it understood, reinforce our best intentions, and prevent me from saying things I'd later regret. It also would be a chance to ask for support.

The ideal divorce elevator speech has five parts, I decided: a definition of the tone of the divorce; details tailored for the audience; a call to action; a close; and updates as facts change.

Writing a Divorce Elevator Speech

Define the divorce: A guide to elevator speeches offered by Pepperdine University's Graziadio School of Business and Management poses these questions:

1. What are your key strengths?
2. What adjectives come to mind to describe you?
3. What is it you are trying to "sell" or let others know about you?

Strengths, adjectives, selling points about my divorce? I might say, "What's great is that my ex and I are on the same page. It's amicable, and we wish each other well. We think it's best for us both. Our son is happier having so much one-on-one time with each of us."

Maybe you're fighting but don't want to be. As the business gurus say, dress for the job you seek. Or, I'd say, speak for the divorce you desire. "I really want a cooperative, non-confrontational divorce, so that's what I'm working toward."

If your divorce is due to an affair that's common knowledge, address it only if you can use it to cast yourself in a positive light. Criticisms of others often stick to those who voice them, and this is your chance to focus on what *you* want. You might say, "I never would have gotten divorced if this hadn't happened. It has made me realize again how important family is to me. I want my next relationship to last forever."

Tailor details to the audience: What you share depends on who's sitting across the desk or dining table or platter of cake pops. A child's teacher may need to know about changes in the after-school routine, but not why your marriage ended. A date might want to know if you're really ready for a new relationship, and what nights you're free.

Your boss might care about how your divorce will affect your work. You might try: "My husband and I have decided to split up. It's a mutual decision and amicable. I have more free time now on nights and weekends because we're taking turns watching our children. So I will be getting more done on the job than ever."

In a social setting, such as the dinner with my friend's mother, you may need more of an explanation. In my case, my ex had already defined the divorce as due to differences in desire for emotional intimacy. I probably could have repeated this explanation and then moved on to a "call to action."

Issue a call to action: Since many people process *your* news in terms of how it affects *them*, your call to action is your chance to let them know. Identify for them what part they can play. Do you want emotional support? Help redecorating? Fix-ups? (I wanted fix-ups.) The call to action steers the conversation away from the "why" of the divorce, and toward a "what's next?"

At a child's preschool, you might say, "I have him Tuesdays, Thursdays, and Saturdays, and am always looking for play dates. Let's get together."

At dinner with my friend's super-social mother, I could have said, "*You* are so connected! Do you know any nice single men I could meet?" We then could have spent the rest of the evening talking about men *other than* the one I'd already married.

Close: As TV reporters say, "Back to you!" Your close gets you out of the conversation before saying anything you might regret. Your call to action may serve as a graceful close. If not, have a ready question that shifts the attention from you to the other person. Most people will stop talking about you if given a chance to talk about themselves. Even a clunky transition will work: "Speaking of family, how are your kids?" Or, "Thank you for asking. What's new with you?"

Update as facts change: Like a business, a divorce matures. How you talk about it should change, too.

Imagine you have a performance review three months after your split. You might say to your boss, "As you know, my husband and I decided to divorce. I've been putting in extra time with my free nights, and my department has shown record profits. I'd like to discuss the possibility of raising my compensation to reflect my contribution."

• • •

Todd, a software salesperson living in a small town in Michigan, wrote a divorce elevator speech with his wife. They e-mailed it to friends and family before he moved out, but after they told their children. "It's almost like high school, a clique-y kind of place, a rumor mill up here," Todd told me. "People tend to speculate. We didn't want people saying, 'Oh, she must have had an affair,' or, 'He must have.' We wanted to make a preemptive strike."

This is what they sent:

> We are writing this letter with heavy hearts because we need to tell you, our family and great friends, that we have decided that it would be best for the both of us if we were to continue our journey in life separately. The purpose of this letter is to assure you that this is a good thing, it is something that we both want and is necessary for both of us to continue to grow as people. THE most important thing to us is our children. We ask, for their sake, that all of you are supportive to them during this time.
>
> We know sometimes there is an awkwardness of who to befriend in a divorce situation, but we say don't worry about this!! You will still see us out doing things together and continuing to be great friends. Neither one of us will be saying bad things about each other, we love and respect each other deeply.

After the e-mail, Todd went out with a few friends. "Everyone was saying, 'How could she leave you? You do everything.' I said to them, 'You've only had a day to process this. I've had six months. I was pissed off, too, but I'm not now and I'm asking you to treat her with respect.'"

Many people told me about meeting with a similar resistance to the notion of a positive parting. Friends don't generally criticize your spouse—at least not to your face. But in divorce, they may take a community-property approach to your ex, as if she's now the villain in everyone's story. They pile on critiques, perhaps to differentiate to themselves between your (bad) choice and their good one. Maybe they want to protect you. Some seek to make your divorce conform to their expectations. Striving for a kind and balanced parting can force others to confront their own pettiness and negative assumptions, their belief in the smallness of the human spirit. You may have to remind your friends that criticizing your spouse is not the same as supporting you.

Sometimes friends rehash your old frustrations to help prevent you from crawling back toward the itchy safety of a miserable marriage. I found these reality checks useful at times. But a loving reminder of past difficulties is different from a gratuitous, zealous critique.

Hollie, the Colorado mother with three young children, could barely meet her expenses during the early stages of divorce. Both she and her ex scrimped to get by. She encouraged him to stay in the kids' room on his visits from Alaska to see them. "Oh my God, my family think it's nuts," she said. "They think it makes more sense for him to pay for a hotel for two weeks and have the kids stay there. We both decided that's ridiculous."

PARENTS SHOULD BE SEEN AND NOT HEARD

Parents can be the hardest to tell, and may need the most help understanding your vision of a decent divorce. You probably can't deliver your speech to your parents, say, "Please pass the potatoes," and consider the conversation closed. Your divorce may affect them directly, disrupting their holiday celebrations, threatening to end their weekly golf game with your wife, depriving them of the good friend they had in your husband.

Parents, especially aging ones, also are more likely to have outdated, overly negative ideas about divorce than contemporaries. I met a designer who'd immigrated to the U.S. from eastern Europe to marry when she was twenty-three. When her husband left seven years later, she couldn't bring herself to tell her parents. "I came from this place where people just don't divorce. There's an old Hungarian expression, 'Divorce isn't for poor people.' It means it's difficult to raise a kid on your own with no means, and that divorce is frivolous."

Your parents may secretly suspect that your divorce is their fault. New York City therapist Hollis Brown told me about a profound moment in her career, a lecture she gave to a group of older adults. Many of them started crying when discussing their grown children's divorces. "They felt so guilty. They thought it meant that they raised them wrong. So they had to blame somebody else. That's why they start to get intrusive. They give advice and foul things up. They say things like, 'You've got to get rid of him as fast as you can.' Or, 'He's terrible and he was all along.' It's bad versus good. Black versus white." Often the in-laws start fighting with each other: 'If only your child had done this or that, the marriage would have survived!'"

It can be tough to assert your vision over that of your parents. Some people move back home for a while, which can really feel infantilizing. But you're not a child, even if you're sleeping in your old twin bed beneath plastic stick-on stars. Telling your parents how to treat your divorce is a challenge of adulthood. I think of American author Peter De Vries's quote, "The value of marriage is not that adults produce children but that children produce adults." I'd rewrite that paean to partnership in another way: The value of *divorce* is not that marriages break down but that individuals grow up.

Or, as the eastern European designer said, "I became a better person, as far as relationships go. I don't judge people like I used to."

You might offer your parents specific details about how and why your divorce will not be a disaster *in their eyes*. Such as, "We've both agreed to keep sending our children to Sunday school." You might assure them that you're a happy, well-adjusted person (or will be one soon), and that your children will remain eager to spend time with the all-important grandparents, *them*.

You also might try a little diversionary praise, an emotional bait and switch. Encourage your parents to engage in self-affirmation. Self-affirmation theory proposes that we see our beliefs as *part of us.* We may reject new thoughts that threaten our ideological-backed sense of self. Asking a proponent of lifelong marriage at all costs to accept your divorce can feel as if you're threatening something dear. You are: you're asserting a different reality, one that directly confronts his personal identity. We derive self-worth in part from our beliefs, and from our conviction that they're *true.*

Affirming a parent's *other* beliefs may help him be more open-minded about this one. I was intrigued by a recent study in which college students listened to debaters deliver strong and weak arguments about a proposed tuition hike. The students had differing opinions about the hike. In the study, half were given a chance to affirm their values in a variety of other areas before listening to arguments for the tuition increase. This self-affirmed group was better able to objectively gauge argument quality. They rejected weak points, even when made in support of their own positions. Researchers concluded that self-affirmation "helps participants adopt an objective and unbiased perspective." In other words, strengthening a person's overall sense of self through affirmation can lessen resistance to "counter-attitudinal" information, such as, say, the idea that divorce can be the wisest, healthiest choice for everyone in the family.

I love the idea of launching your own self-affirmation experiment on your parents. You could try steering the conversation toward their other, uncontested passions. Ask them for gardening advice. Let them hold forth on politics. These people who reared you are not only the parents of a child facing divorce; they're also great grandparents, good cooks, superb croquet players, savants about JFK. Let them bask in their knowledge. Then bring up your divorce. By encouraging them to voice their other opinions, you help them remind themselves that they are stronger and more flexible than one pillar of belief.

If parents are intractable in their criticism, you may need to set boundaries. "The couple needs to tell the parents, 'We know you love us. However, we will make it very clear if and when we want you to get involved,'" said therapist Hollis Brown. This reminded me of advice marriage counselors give newlyweds with difficult parents. Establish a unified front before parental hectoring and tell them, kindly, what is tolerated in your house. The same holds true for newly unweds.

You also might try aiming for emotional non-contagion by looking away to prevent yourself from mimicking their frown. "You wouldn't want to do this all the time in your social life, but you could try this as a barrier or blockage method," said Hawaii-based social psychologist Dana Arakawa.

· · ·

I hadn't worried about telling *my* family: they were experienced with divorce, optimistic about remarriage. But I did not want to tell my in-laws. My mother-in-law in particular, a scholarly and devout Catholic, believes in the sacrament of lifelong marriage. My husband's parents had been my New York–area family for more than a decade. I didn't want to disappoint them, or sadden them. Or lose them.

My husband didn't want to tell them, either. He managed to sign a lease, move the furniture from the third floor of our house to his new studio apartment, and invite friends to see his new place—all without telling his parents. On a Sunday afternoon, he finally decided to drive to Westchester to break the news. Our son clamored to go along, and for me to come, too. Somehow, we wound up making a family outing out of sharing the news of our divorce.

When we arrived, my husband told his parents he needed to talk. I took our son to the little hilltop public library. He flipped through picture books while I stood looking out the big windows at the Palisades rising from the river, pre-nostalgic for the decade of family dinners we'd shared. Would this be my last time standing on the bluff overlooking the Hudson, my husband's idyllic childhood now part of my own stock of memories—his five siblings in their big house, his elementary school skateboarding gang, his junior high years of listening to Joni Mitchell in the woods?

As the sun began to set, we returned to my in-laws' house. I parked my car on the street. I did not want to face them. I looked at myself in the rearview mirror. "I'm not going in there," I said to myself.

"This is part of it," I replied. "Get. Out. Of. The. Car."

I got out of the car. Opened the gate to the side yard. My son went running toward the house. My husband's mother opened the screen door and waited for me on the threshold, tears in her eyes. "I just want to know that this is really mutual," she said, her voice wavering. "He'll be okay. We're worried about you."

So then I started crying, which I hadn't meant to do. I assured her that it was mutual, that he had not wronged me, and that I would be fine. *Would I be fine?* She hugged me. We both said we'd always be family.

Here's something I forgot to say over dinner with my friend's mother: I'd also married my ex because I loved his parents.

Later, my future ex-mother-in-law told me she'd talked to a few of her children and her granddaughter about our divorce. They assured her that if we weren't seeing it as a tragedy, she shouldn't, either. Her granddaughter, fifteen at the time, had more friends with divorced parents than married ones, and they were fine. "It really made me feel better to talk to them," she said.

I was grateful for my mother-in-law's effort to accommodate a reality that violated her beliefs. It's humbling to see people work hard to continue caring about you. I'm incredibly fortunate to have such open, compassionate in-laws. But even difficult, judgmental parents may find solace and wisdom by talking to others, particularly younger people or friends whose children have divorced and done well on the other side.

TALKING TO CHILDREN ABOUT DIVORCE

Now how should I put this
I've got something to say
Your mother is staying
But I'm going away
—Sonny Bono, "You Better Sit Down Kids"

This deep, throaty ballad sung by Cher was part of the soundtrack of my childhood. Released in 1967, it was Cher's second top ten hit of the '60s, popular even before the first no-fault law went into effect. I always felt so sad for these unknown kids learning that their parents were splitting up. In the incredible myopia of childhood, I didn't think this song related to me. I had no specific memory of being told my parents were separating. I was too busy and narrowly focused, in the way of five-year-olds, to notice such a huge shift happening around me. The separation and divorce folded into my life.

When telling the children, it's definitely an advantage if you happen to be a pop music duo experienced with delivering highly charged emotional material. For the rest of us, telling the kids is still a kind of performance, an elevator speech, ideally one you prepare ahead of time, perhaps with your spouse.

Tips for Telling the Kids

Tailor for their age: Tailoring your talk for their age means integrating it into the life they're leading—riffing off the characters they know or the activities you do together. It also means talking about their immediate concerns, and emphasizing how the divorce impacts them. "What school they'll go to, where they'll live, whether or not they'll still have their friends," said child psychiatrist Mark Banschick. "Kids are very self-preoccupied. The goal is that they come out knowing there's going to be a divorce and that they are going to be okay."

Today, unlike in the early 1970s, there are myriad resources to help you handle the conversation. I found a ten-part plan online that includes consulting a family therapist, crafting a script together with your spouse, and delivering it in a neutral, private setting. I think this sounds great. I have to tell you, I did not do this. My son was too young and his father too distracted for such a formal plan. I wound up telling my four-year-old that Daddy was going to live in an apartment down the street, by the firehouse. They could visit the firehouse whenever he wanted! Daddy would be over three mornings a week to take him to school, and three evenings a week to give him dinner and put him to bed. Nothing else would change.

I had trouble getting my son to focus on this conversation. He had more pressing concerns, like whether that noise outside was a police car or an ambulance, and could he get up and look? He seemed no more perturbed by the news than I was at his age.

Older children probably need more of an explanation. Teens may press for a reason or need reassurance that it isn't their fault. Focus only on what they need to know, keep it short, and find a positive way to include them in what happens next. "Since we're moving, let's paint your new bedroom walls that lilac shade you love."

I've heard various opinions about the "best" and "worst" age for children to go through their parents' divorce. Each child reacts in her own way, regardless of the age. The constants? Your divorce will affect them in *some* way, and how you talk about it can help them accept the news and adjust.

Paula, the filmmaker in Manhattan who divorced when her daughter was five, had a garden on her roof deck. She used this to help explain the divorce. "I'd put tarragon and mint together in a pot the first year. Mint is very aggressive and tarragon is more delicate. The mint will dominate and the tarragon will not thrive. It will be unhappy. But if you put tarragon in its own pot, it's happier. Clara could see that different plants have different needs. I said to my daughter, 'Your father and I are in different pots, but we're still part of the same garden.'"

I loved this explanation because it let Paula say something that was true without making a value judgment. It's no one's fault that mint takes over everything. Clara said that the metaphor made sense to her. As she grew, it framed the divorce as an organic process. "Some plants like acidic environments. Some don't. They live better in two pots," she told me.

Todd, the software salesperson in Michigan who'd written a divorce elevator e-mail with his wife, worked with her on a letter to their kids, age nine and eleven. They described their union as a fairy-tale marriage between two best friends that had a new ending. "We told them that we're not getting divorced because we hate each other. We're always going to be best friends. We said that we've all seen people who yell and fight, and we are not having that kind of divorce."

After reading the letter to his children, Todd shared the upsides, such as the fact that two houses meant they'd each have a second bedroom to decorate. "Later, they each came up to me separately and said they were glad the divorce wasn't because we didn't love each other," he said.

Tell the truth, but not the whole truth: If you hate each other, at least for now, don't lie and claim lasting familial love. Your body language and tone will belie your words. Lying can undermine your children's ability to trust their own intuition, and you.

Focus on reassuring truths instead—you're both committed to parenting, for example, or you both think you'll be happier and more attentive to them, once unwed. They don't need to know he's addicted to prescription drugs or that you caught her in your bed with another man. If they're older, and an affair or mental breakdown is obvious, acknowledge the truth, assure them that they are safe, and refrain from elaborating. You don't let them watch you have sex; hearing sordid details about adult concerns similarly disrupts their equanimity.

Parental over-sharing violates what Banschick calls the "intergenerational boundary," an information barrier between adults and children that allows kids to progress normally. "You can say, 'I'm not going to talk about this with you because my goal is your happiness, not criticizing Mommy,'" said Banschick. "They seem so mature. But they still deserve their innocence."

We are so worried that becoming unmarried will harm our children, as if our kids are as invested in our romantic bond as we are. But kids aren't generally in love with our romantic union. Older kids get grossed out thinking about what goes on behind closed doors. Kids are in love with their own lives, and with us as their parents.

Listen to what they're not saying: As adults, we often struggle to articulate serious, complicated feelings. This task is even more difficult for a child, particularly a young one whose vocabulary consists primarily of names of construction vehicles and parts of trucks. Older children may worry about hurting your feelings or getting in trouble if they tell you how they feel.

Children do reveal their inner worlds, often through stories, play, or make-believe. Teenagers express themselves in their choice of music, movies, and friends. You can help them communicate by engaging at their level. Ask why they like a song or book. Draw together, then talk about their picture. Watch a movie about divorce, such as *Mrs. Doubtfire* or *Liar Liar*. Listen to the fears or concerns they may be sharing when they discuss the plot or characters.

"I've always been about 'projective techniques,'" said Gary Neuman, author and creator of the Sandcastles program for children with divorcing parents. Projective techniques are play-based methods that encourage children to project their emotions out of themselves onto something else, rather than holding them within. Sandcastles uses art, letters, poetry, and role-playing to help children share their feelings about their parents' divorce. "We had a girl who was cutting off all the hair of her Barbie. It turned out she wanted to be strong like her brother. It was just a matter of talking to her, asking her about the hair."

You could try the Two Men Watching Baseball approach to intimate connection; bring up a delicate matter while partly focused on something else, such as a ball game or bike ride. "You never want to look your kid squarely in the eye and say, 'How's that divorce going?' It's too intense, too abrupt. They don't want you to be an investigator," said Neuman.

"Cooking is great," said Gregory, the attorney who was the primary custodial parent of his two boys. He used his newfound interest in cooking to stir conversation. "You can't talk to boys. You have to do an activity, and then while you're doing that, you can talk. Cooking is dangerous enough to be fun. You've got boiling oil, razor-sharp knives flying around. You have to pay attention. It makes conversation easier. It leads to so many places. If you ask about their friends, that can lead to information."

Making dinner together also became a way to learn about their time at their mom's. "I could ask, 'What does your mom cook? Do you like the food?' That can open the door to feelings."

Lutheran pastor Amy Ziettlow said that she tries to primarily listen when kids in her congregation's youth group talk about divorce. "I find the quieter I am when asking the questions, the better. Like, 'When have you felt this way in the past? What was helpful?' Allowing them to discover how they're going to move forward, to name it. And then just sitting, and allowing them to say it. They always say something I never would have suggested. And it's better than what I would have said."

Children may benefit from talking to other adults who aren't you. The New Jersey restaurateur, Vince, divorced when his children were eight and ten. For perspective, they turned to his brother's wife, who had grown up with divorced parents. "She's a teacher, so she knows how to communicate," he said. "She'd say, 'You know this is what happened to me, and I'm okay. You see my mom and my dad, and we're okay.' She encouraged them to ask questions."

SesameStreet.org wound up being the most helpful resource I found for talking to my little boy. I downloaded the site's divorce "tool kit," which is based partly on resilience research. I printed out the activity sheets and a picture book called *Two-Hug Day*. In the book, an only child splits his time between his parents' homes. He uses the term "two-hug day" to describe the days he switches houses. At one point, he tells his mom, a yellow-haired Muppet with glasses, that he wishes they all still lived in one house. Muppet Mom says, basically, "We're divorced, which means we don't live together. It's okay if you don't like all these changes. But also, let's look at how much remains the same, such as the fact that we both love you and will always be your parents."

I read the story to my son a few times over the course of a week, and we colored in the pictures. He seemed calmed by the tale, as if it answered a question he hadn't known he had. "On two-hug day I sometimes feel glad and sad all at once," I read, pointing to the boy Muppet in his car seat behind his mom. My son repeated this: "Glad and sad. Glad and sad."

The next morning, he came into my room and said it again, as if it were a new "in joke" we shared. He liked the rhyme of it, but I think it also introduced a new concept, the idea of holding opposing feelings. Learning new words to express internal nuance helps kids develop "emotional literacy"—a greater range of understanding about emotions in themselves and others. Emotional literacy can increase empathy, self-knowledge, and self-regulation.

"'Sad' can be distinguished from 'disappointed,' as in, 'I didn't get to see my dad today. I'm disappointed,'" said Geraldine V. Oades-Sese, a professor of pediatrics at the Robert Wood Johnson Medical School in New Brunswick, New Jersey, and an investigator/advisor for Sesame Workshop's Childhood Resilience Initiative. "These skills contribute to children's social and emotional competence. They help them better establish and maintain relationships with other children, teachers, and other adults. They also make them better at facing or resolving everyday challenges when they arise."

If you don't get your speech right the first time, don't worry. You'll be talking about it with them throughout their lives. You are living this divorce with them, so telling them well means living it well.

THE WORDS IN YOUR HEAD

I discovered that I needed one more type of elevator speech: the one I told myself. An inner elevator speech is a type of "exit story," a narrative that makes sense of the events in a way that reflects positively on you. The fact is, the facts are pretty slippery when it comes to divorce. As Rabbi Mordecai Finley said, "You can't change the facts, but the same facts can support different narratives."

Even if the reason your marriage ended seems indisputable—he's a drunk who can't manage his life!—how that relates to *you* can be interpreted in more than one way. "I got screwed by a lying alcoholic" may feel true, but that narrative casts you in a powerless position. There are other narratives that also are true. Perhaps, "I fell madly in love for the first time in my life. It was such a wonderful feeling that I overlooked some red flags. I didn't realize what a passionate person I am, how intensely and deeply I can feel." Or, "I am someone who sticks with a commitment as long as is humanly possible. I work hard at my relationships." These are other sides of the same story, and the facets that reflect you in the control seat. Recasting your narrative also evokes Principle No. 2: Take ownership of your future (and your past).

An inner elevator speech isn't a generic affirmation like that repeated by Al Franken's old *Saturday Night Live* character Stuart Smalley, who would look in the mirror and say, "I'm good enough. I'm smart enough. And doggone it, people like me!" Research shows that empty self-praise doesn't truly shift a pessimistic mind-set (though I've found it helpful in practice). But a basic tenet of cognitive behavioral therapy, which can be hugely effective, is that many of us have knee-jerk, inaccurate, negative assessments about ourselves, fueled by twisted thinking styles. By noting how we think and replacing our automatic negative stories with more realistic, balanced ones, we can make real strides toward overcoming depression or feelings of defeat.

One way to write an inner elevator story is to challenge what psychologist Martin Seligman calls your "explanatory style," how you explain to yourself your role in positive and negative occurrences. Pessimists tend to blame themselves for bad outcomes, yet not claim credit for good ones. They also see negative events as permanent, pervasive, and personal. After one disastrous date, a pessimist might think, "I ruined that date and I'll never meet someone better because nothing works for me." When a die-hard pessimist gets a much-deserved raise, he discounts his own involvement and sees it as a temporary, site-specific gain: "I got a raise, but the boss has been in a good mood lately." Pessimists tend to give in more quickly to defeat, and no wonder. A person with a negative explanatory style basically lives with a Funeral Dirge Pandora station running through his brain, with no commercial breaks.

The optimist flips both these explanatory styles. She interprets a negative experience as temporary, contained, and no reflection on her, while taking credit for good news, noting her contribution to it, and envisioning ways it might continue. This might make optimists sound like self-deluded narcissists, and in some ways, as Seligman writes, pessimists are more realistic. But optimists are happier and often more successful. When it comes to crafting your inner elevator speech, you want to rewrite your exit story with the optimist's approach.

Many people have difficulty drumming up praise for themselves. The European jeweler whose husband left her at fifty felt proud of her own recuperation. "I said to my mother, 'Don't you think I'm doing well? How I'm handling my life? I could be under the covers, crying the blues, making my children take care of me. Instead, I'm enjoying life, being with you, focusing on what there is and looking forward to the next steps.'

"My mother turns to me and says, 'I completely agree with you, but how can you say this about yourself?' For her, the idea of allowing yourself to say you're proud of yourself, even to yourself—it's not done. It's okay to receive compliments, but not to give them to yourself."

This story stuck with me, because many of us have internalized a version of her mother's humility. We'll criticize ourselves in the privacy of our own heads, but not bask in our own praise. We hush our internal whispers of pride and amplify our shortcomings.

It's natural to feel negative and discouraged in divorce, to see your flaws, or those of your ex, as highlighted in neon yellow. But we also deserve kudos for our efforts to protect our children, move forward, and face this massive change. As the jeweler said, "Where is it written that we have to wait for someone else to tell us that we're worthy and beautiful and worthy of being bejeweled? It's written everywhere. We as a society have written it. We need to rewrite the story."

It can be hard to ferret out those sparkles of personal value under the rubble of a marriage. Some people need to bring in outside assistance. I was talking to a responsible, hardworking mother I know whose husband had experienced a mental breakdown as they were on the verge of separating. Jennifer had stayed in the marriage, seen him through it. But his long-standing drug and alcohol abuse continued, increasing the risk of a relapse.

She finally decided to leave. She felt guilty about abandoning him, yet simultaneously ashamed at having stayed so long. Some friends advised cutting him off completely. She'd known this man her entire adult life, and he still relied on her for emotional support. The friends' advice *felt* wrong, but she wasn't confident about the merit of her own opinions. She felt paralyzed when faced with even minor decisions, such as what kind of plants to buy to stage the house she now had to sell. "How can I trust my judgment about anything?" she asked. "I married him. I stayed in it. I have no idea what my 'gut' tells me."

This woman had made many brilliant decisions and keen judgments throughout her life. She needed to remember these, to grasp her strengths in order to lean on them. She could have written a list of her positive qualities. Actually, she couldn't write it at that moment, but *I* could have written it for her:

- ◆ She always gets herself to work and earns a living, no matter how bad she feels.
- ◆ She always protects her children and tries to shield them from distress.
- ◆ She generally remains calm and compassionate, even when someone around her acts crazy.
- ◆ She volunteers in the community in addition to working full-time.

In divorce, you may need to ask others to remind you of your strengths and accomplishments. Or, if that idea makes you squirm, try spending time with friends and family who reflect your gifts back to you in a way you can see. You also could offer honest praise to others. Complimenting another elevates the praise-giver. It also can begin a cycle of admiration, inspiring others to comment on something they appreciate about you. Or, as it says in the Proverbs, "He who waters shall himself be watered."

• • •

For my mom, spending a week with my father in Mexico helped her remember parts of herself she'd lost in her second marriage. She returned from that trip sounding buoyant and energized, more elevated than she'd been in a couple of years. "He was so nice and protective and complimentary," my mother said of my father. "He knew me really well and wanted to have meaningful conversations. I'd forgotten that somebody could be that nice to me. I had forgotten what it's like when somebody really wants to hear what you think."

My mom felt better not only because my dad was a good listener, but also because he'd known her so long. I think a connection forged when we're young touches us so deeply because those early years are woven into the fabric of who we've become. The people we know contributed threads.

In Mexico, my mom and dad sat on his balcony talking for a week straight. They also went dancing, my father encouraging her to get back on the floor to cha-cha, something she hadn't done in nearly forty years. Spending a week with her first husband helped my mom process her second divorce in a new way. She'd struggled for two years with the question of where to "put" it, how to accept her husband's defection into her worldview. "It's so out of my frame of reference for what could possibly happen to me in my life," she'd said, more than once.

When she returned from Mexico, she said, "I finally figured out where to put the divorce."

"Where?" I asked.

"In the past. You put it in the past."

She'd been so stuck, trying to figure out what had destroyed her second marriage, how it could possibly have ended. But after that week, she was able to see her second divorce as something that *had* happened, was receding, could be gotten through, if not now, at some point. By reminding her of who she'd once been, my father had helped her step forward.

A couple of weeks after my parents' Mexican vacation, my whole family assembled again. It was Thanksgiving, and we convened at my sister's house in Austin. My sister's own ex-husband was there, too.

I watched my parents talking. *Was there a new charge between them?* My mother and father definitely seemed protective of each other, *influenced* by the other.

How far would this reconnection go?

• • •

At the end of my first solo vacation, to Cozumel, I walked past a restaurant I'd gone to years ago with my then boyfriend/now future ex-husband. I'd decided on that previous trip that *yes*, I could envision my life with him as my husband, his physical vitality propelling us out of the house, his slowly tanning, buttery skin luring me back in. His view of a more independent way of uniting, his non-merge ideal, wasn't mine, but maybe it was another style of couplehood to which I could adapt. Maybe it could work.

There I was, back on this North American fantasy coast alone, because it hadn't.

Later that night, I was twirling in the balmy air under the stars at the resort with my sister, feeling free and loose and rangy, like an old, pre-marriage version of myself. I felt deep within me that other dreams would surface. There would be a new love, a new future. It was out there, somewhere. I couldn't say what it looked like, but I knew it would arise.

In every divorce, there are these moments when a new life path seems ascendant and shines silver in the moonlight. There are plenty of dark and scary times that feel more like being stuck in a cave with no exit. It's important to build a reserve of positive moments and supportive memories, stories we can retell ourselves to talk us back out of those dark days.

CHAPTER FIVE

Friends . . . and Lack Thereof

Loneliness and How Divorce Affects Non-Romantic Relationships

✦

Some people feel lonely or socially adrift during divorce. Though painful, a social shake-up also can be a great opportunity to update our roster of friends. Recreating a social life may require retooling our skills. Some of us need to regain appreciation of ourselves.

I t's Saturday night, and I'm putting my son to sleep. We're snuggled under his blue and white gingham comforter, reading a picture book, *In a People House*. His room looks like the one in *Goodnight Moon*. He has a fireplace and cushy chair, a wooden bed, and big brown bear. In twenty minutes he'll be asleep, flat on his stomach, legs akimbo over the sheets. I'm thinking about the long night ahead, the only adult in my house. A new rhyme starts in my head:

> *Come inside, Mr. Bird,*
> *said the mouse*
> *I'll show what there is*
> *in a Spouseless House.*
> *A Spouseless House*
> *has empty . . .*
> *. . . rooms*
> *quiet nights*
> *too much gloom.*
> *No one to watch TV*
> *With me.*
> *I'm all alone. Just me and me.*

I list into Dr. Seuss:

> *A fish in a tree? How can that be?*
> *My spouse, my friends, all gone . . . kersplat.*
> *The Cat in the Hat knows a lot about that.*

Now I'm Barry Gibb from the Bee Gees:

> *Lonely days, lonely nights, where would I be*
> *without my woman?*

I'm striding downstage in tight white pants, my shirt open to my navel. My hair streams behind me like a mane. Chase lights flash at my boots. I throw back my head and let loose that long, high-pitched vibrato: "Where would I be without my woooommmmaaaannnnn!"

My son grabs at my leg. "Mommy. Read. Reeeaaaaddd!"

• • •

My entire first year alone, I'd find myself swept by loneliness. It would disperse, then gather anew, building up outside the house, pressing in the walls, bowing the windows. Loneliness is like an emotional barometric pressure rising, rising. Or, as Paul Simon sang, "Losing love is like a window in your heart. Everybody sees you're blown apart."

At various points during my first year alone, I wondered: could I get *too* lonely? Was this loneliness dangerous?

Not really, it turns out. *Chronic* loneliness is a risk factor for a host of ills: high blood pressure, a weakened immune system, even cognitive decline. But the common, postdivorce loneliness I experienced— let's call it the sense of being sucked into a sinkhole of despair—tends to be short-term and therefore not likely to cause lasting damage.

Loneliness *feels* so risky, so steel-fanged, in part because of our evolutionary history. In our deep, ancestral past, being alone meant you'd lost the protection of the group. You were vulnerable to attack by predators. Researchers talk about loneliness as a historic warning signal that we need to rejoin our group immediately.

In today's world, when you can order chicken soup from a diner if you have the flu, or call 911 in an emergency, loneliness isn't deadly. The dire feeling it generates will pass. But it's still a reminder—in case you somehow forgot—that your world is inadequately populated.

"Marriage fills us in a very big way, psychologically and physically. Divorce takes those two things away very abruptly," said social worker MJ Murray Vachon, when I called her to complain about my endless-seeming nights at home. "I would be nervous if you weren't lonely."

Not only was I lonely, but what was going on with my friends? I'd had so many when married, including the two hundred or so acquaintanceships my husband consistently tended. We were always rushing off to parties or dinners or readings, sometimes with people I'd completely forgotten we knew. I didn't love every outing, but I liked the social whirl in general, and the fact that I didn't have to do much to keep it spinning.

After we split, I wasn't sure all those people I knew actually liked me, now that I was circulating without my spouse. I had my own close friends, too, and some stepped forward with acts of real kindness. But the two people I'd been speaking to daily suddenly disappeared—one completely absorbed by a new girlfriend and new job, and the other . . . who even knew what was going on with her? Coincidence of timing? Worry that her own strained marriage might domino down by contact with mine? Neither was bringing me cupcakes and conversation after my son went to sleep.

In divorce, we turn to friends and family to fill roles vacated by our spouse. Relying on others is part of Principle No. 4: Build a tool kit. But while we need more from them, we may discover that they've structured their days largely without the newly single us. Others may seem to be pulling away.

I felt reluctant to reach out, strangely insecure about my social allure. I was suffering from Divorce Onset Social Insecurity, I realized, another common ailment, it turns out. Divorce Onset Social Insecurity reminded me of an earlier period of eviscerating social decline: eighth grade. In eighth grade, in suburban Detroit where I lived, being popular was a basic need, up there with food and shelter, inextricable from clothing. But the route to popularity was treacherous and unlit. You had to wear the same sweaters and purple nail polish the "in" girls flaunted. Then they'd change colors between classes, and you'd be left out, plum-fingernailed, *insecure*.

Adolescence is a time of insecurity, in part, because so many things are changing at once. Boys' voices. Girls' bodies. Our sense of ourselves as burgeoning teens. We fear our weaknesses and don't know our strengths. It's a lot like getting divorced. Only this time, your best friend has left the building, leaving you to face the phalanx of mean girls without a comrade in your corner.

Divorce Onset Social Insecurity also may have an evolutionary basis. "When we depended on friends for survival, we needed to be number one on someone's list. Now we've lost that one person who values us above all else," said Carlin Flora, author of *Friendfluence: The Surprising Ways Friends Make Us Who We Are*. "We're very motivated to be sensitive to where we stand in the hierarchy of our friends."

I expected to be scared ending my marriage, but I was totally unprepared for how lonely I'd feel, or how much time I'd spend worrying about, being mad at, and reassessing my friendships.

On that night of reading to my son, I called my satisfied, single friend Abby for advice. "How do you *do* this?" I asked. "How do you handle being alone?"

"Your task is to learn to navigate the world as a single person, *temporarily*," she said. *Temporarily*. That felt important, prophetic. I wrote it down and taped it to the wall above my desk.

In the meantime, dealing with the painful mix of loneliness and shifting friendships would take real effort. Many of us need to identify what type of loneliness we're feeling in order to address it. We also have to take action—make new friends, and keep *some* of the old, exercise discretion about who we see. Finally, feeling fulfilled can mean rebuilding an alliance with ourselves.

THE HUNDRED NAMES FOR LONELINESS

Many people come to divorce pre-lonely. Living with an estranged spouse can feel like having a window left open to the Arctic tundra. You're leaning on the sill, gazing into the sleeting wind, aching for your partner's return. Your dog shivers under the table and ice sheets are forming on the floor.

Some people told me they'd been sleeping on the couch, or in a different room, long before the divorce. As University of Arizona behavioral scientist Chris Segrin put it, "Loneliness is the end of the line for marriage, the caboose in the train. You're not free to go out and develop new relationships, yet the one you have is completely unfulfilling. I would argue that the majority of people headed for divorce are lonely."

Even if you feel better the minute you separate, most people face moments of stark isolation in divorce, what researchers call "episodic loneliness." Episodic loneliness is that chafing sense of deep *wrongness* that arises when doing something alone that formerly involved another person. Such as, in my case, being home after putting my son to bed. For others, it might be taking the kids to an amusement park, wrapping holiday presents, making dinner. Episodic loneliness is different from *trait loneliness*, a persistent feeling of painful isolation.

My mother got walloped by episodic loneliness at Home Depot the first year after her divorce. She'd taken my son to buy giant candy canes to decorate the lawn. The Christmas carols blaring from the sound system yanked her back to the early years of her marriage to my stepfather, when we four kids lived at home in our blended family. "Hearing the music, it just hit me that all of those things we did as a family of six, and then with grandchildren, it was all gone," she said. "Not loneliness for the past, but for the future, that continuation of family. That's what was lost."

With time, we'll create new celebrations, other families. But during the early months of separation, the possibility of future additions can feel as fanciful as Santa Claus.

In divorce, many people add to the emotional loneliness of an empty marriage a new state of unpleasantness called "social loneliness," the longing for basic human companionship. Social loneliness is the unmet desire for a tennis buddy, a dinner partner, someone to watch TV with you. Social loneliness might seem like a trivial discomfort that should be easy to address, but it seriously pains many people. Judging yourself for it—"I shouldn't *care* that I'm seeing another movie alone!" or, "Why is it so hard to find someone to go jogging with me?"—can make it last longer, and lead to depression and anxiety.

There seemed to be a hundred words for loneliness. Scientists have created a lexicon of loneliness—a robust taxonomy that reflects its prevalence in our world. Understanding which kind of loneliness you face can help you lessen it. Loneliness is the discrepancy between your *desired* level of social contact and how many people you actually see. We don't all need two hundred friends, but we do all feel pain if there's a gap between our desire for society and our reality. Here are some suggestions for closing the gap:

Lessening Loneliness

Restructure your time (and your space): For episodic loneliness that seizes you at specific moments, *avoid those moments*. Don't go gambling in Aruba over the holidays alone, if that's what you always did with your spouse; take a ski trip with friends instead. Swap out your Sunday coffee-shop-and-newspaper routine for a spinning class. Instead of laundry and a movie night, try volunteering at a homeless shelter.

You can also try "environmental restructuring," changing the environment to reduce pangs of loneliness. Avoid settings that recall your loss—at least temporarily—and update your home or office in ways that make you feel more connected. Merely hanging photos of friends and family can remind you that you live in a world filled with others.

You also can look at your photos and talk back to loneliness. Muffle its haunting voice by listing all the people in your life you love, and who love you. They're there, even if they're not in your house at the moment.

View distraction as a friend: If you're stuck in the house with a sleeping child, as I was, or facing another form of episodic loneliness, distraction can be a great aid. Watch TV, call a confidant, surf the Web—find an activity that takes your mind off your loneliness until it passes. And it will pass. Episodic loneliness is a feeling, a wave; it rolls out much as it rushes in.

Your distraction of choice might yield surprising gains. A friend of mine spent the months after his divorce sanding and staining the wood trim in his old apartment in Brooklyn. A few years later, happily remarried and the father of a small child, he rented out his now mint-condition three-bedroom on the park for top dollar, and used the monthly income to fund a romantic, canal-view place in Venice, Italy.

Be with the ones you love: For emotional loneliness, you might try spending more time with people who love you and know you well. Go visit out-of-town family or college friends. Don't wait for the holidays; make an impromptu trip when loneliness starts to creep in.

Connection with non-human animals also can be surprisingly soothing. Consider getting a dog, taking up horseback riding, or volunteering at an animal shelter.

Give others (and yourself) the benefit of the doubt: How you think about your loneliness can have a terrific impact on how long it lasts. Loneliness can create hypervigilance for social snubs, a radar for ways we're being left out, real or imagined. But we have to ward off *negative assumptions* about how others view us, because these thoughts give loneliness the upper hand.

A recent meta-analysis by John Cacioppo and Christopher Masi of the University of Chicago looked at forty years of research on loneliness and social isolation. They found that while concrete actions to mitigate loneliness do work, those that addressed people's negative habits of thinking, or "maladaptive social cognition," were more effective. Of the twenty best randomized studies on loneliness interventions, those teaching participants new ways of thinking (such as through cognitive behavioral therapy) reduced loneliness even more than those that helped people develop better social skills, increased social support, or upped their opportunities for interaction.

My Divorce Onset Social Insecurity is the kind of negative thinking that can increase feelings of isolation. A longer-lasting example? An attractive, well-traveled, forty-something told me she remained suspicious of others, eight years postdivorce—because her husband's pals had "dropped" her summarily after their split. They may have merely bumbled about in a confusion of loyalty and weak social skills. By assuming their behavior was intentional rather than incompetent, she let an unfortunate experience from a wobbly time compromise her connections nearly a decade later. She continued to doubt other people's interest in her as a friend, to not reach out, and to question others' honesty.

Lean into loneliness: Another way to lessen the grip of loneliness is to accept it as part of the human condition. Sit with it. Or sand the trim with it. "All human beings, at some point in time, have to develop a comfort level with solitude," said Segrin. "One of our major life tasks is how we handle solitude and even savor it."

MAKE NEW FRIENDS, KEEP (SOME) OF THE OLD

One big fear of those divorcing—that your social circle will shatter, or your friends will pick a side and it won't be yours—can happen, even if you insist there are no bad guys in this split. There's some evidence of divorce contagion, a way that divorce can spread through social groups. Friends in an unhappy marriage don't need a study to tell them that your divorce has introduced a new option. Someone who shuns you in a misguided effort to preserve her own marriage is making a statement about the vulnerability of her union, not your worth as a friend. Still, it hurts when it occurs.

In many weddings, the officiant charges the guests with the task of supporting the new couple, a tradition that reflects how much others are involved in our marriages. An Indian-American man told me that he'd been going to couples' counseling with his wife for five years, loath to divorce in part because he worried it would end their weekly get-togethers with other young families from their community.

He might be right. We foster many of our connections as part of a pair. Sometimes friendship circles formed in marriage fail to contain us outside of it. Other times, close friendships falter. Two married couples might "date," as Nora Ephron wrote about in *Heartburn*, the novelized tale of her own divorce. "We saw each other every Saturday night and every Sunday night, and we had a standing engagement for New Year's Eve. Our marriages were tied together." Once her marriage ended, the foursome unraveled, too.

In fact, we change friends during all major life transitions; this is not unique to divorce. We go away to college and let some of our high school buddies slide. We quit our first real job and no longer want to dis the boss with our former colleagues. We marry and have kids, and the dating dilemmas of our single pals seem tedious and inconsequential. Divorce is no different; your priorities and interests may genuinely shift. You may *feel* rejected, but you may be the one dumping *them*.

While painful, a social shake-up also can be a great opportunity to seek out people who better support you and your new life. Our friends have a profound impact on us. They expose us to new ideas, encourage our aspirations, motivate us to get to the gym or send out our résumé. They connect us to opportunities, introduce us to new partners. They can be tremendous cheerleaders and clear-eyed voices of reason.

But friends also can reinforce negative tendencies, undermine our confidence, or thwart our self-improvement goals. As adults, we don't usually have the opportunity to switch up all our friends, "but in a big transition you can do that," said *Friendfluence* author Carlin Flora. "You can choose with intention. You can say, 'Who do I want to be influenced by?' If you think about what your goals are and get yourself around other people whose goals are similar, it lifts you up."

I loved the idea of being lifted up without having to do all the hauling myself. But restructuring a social circle can take work. For many of us, it's a two-part process involving first pruning back thorny connections, exercising discernment about who we see.

If you're in a marriage that's chronically itchy, after a while others see you as that irritable, constantly scratching person. Moving on may require sloughing off those who maintain that image. Lisa, a forty-something sales representative for a telecommunications company, said that some formerly mutual friends seemed determined to keep her bound in an outdated identity.

I met Lisa while on a flight to Phoenix. With her thick red hair and freckles across her nose, she looked like the grown-up version of girls I'd jumped rope with as a kid, though she was wearing a pin-striped suit and heels rather than Keds. She ordered the cheese-and-fruit plate from the flight attendant, pushed the black plastic plate across her tray table toward me, and said, "Help yourself."

So now we were two professionals chatting over hors d'oeuvres. Lisa had married at twenty-seven, she told me, and moved out the day before turning thirty. She needed to divorce not only her husband, but also their group. "Anything I said, they'd tell my ex. I felt they were being nosy and gossipy. I didn't want to look vulnerable or weak. I wanted to be a stronger, better person. I had my own life now. I'd moved on." She moved to a new apartment complex an hour away. Some of those friends faded away due to the drive.

Stephanie, the mother of two from a Mormon community in the Midwest, said that she and her husband had enjoyed a standing get-together with a few former high school classmates. After divorce, these friends blamed her ex, constantly bringing up his indiscretions. They derided him at parties and refused to speak to him in public, even in front of the children.

She, meanwhile, was dedicated to building a positive co-parenting relationship. "I had to step away from those friendships. I clearly was aware of what he did, but I didn't want to be reminded of it, and I certainly didn't want the girls around anyone who was saying bad things about their dad," she said. "I honestly feel that they got annoyed that I wasn't mad. They can't get past it."

She also left her church. Its intense focus on marriage for life, *and afterlife*, left her daughters distraught after Sunday school. Congregants spoke to her with pity. It was well meant, but it felt awful. She joined a Presbyterian church more open to differing family styles, and found a new community there. Switching churches is a great example of resilience. Church had been the axis of her spiritual and social life since childhood. By adopting a flexible attitude about *which* church she'd attend, she maintained a connection to an institution that anchored her, but in a way that better accommodated her new reality.

• • •

The second part of rebuilding a better social life is bringing in new people. This can be harder than you might think. In marriage, many people turn inward, toward each other. They stop initiating new friendships. Social skills are like muscles—you have to use them to keep them strong.

Not only might our social skills have grown slack, but most of us never had to make friends from scratch, not really. Friends came pre-packaged throughout childhood. We're in school with hundreds of kids our age from our hometown. We see them in Spanish class, pile together on the bus. In college, we live in dorms, eat in the cafeteria, travel for spring break. In our early twenties, we take internships together, hang out in groups with other recent grads after work.

As we continue into adulthood, friends don't drop from the sky or show up at our locker as they once did. We may work with people nothing like ourselves, or spend days alone before a screen. We may relocate for a career, a spouse, or a cheaper house. We may find ourselves more alone than we want to be, and unsure how to change that state. This is not a personal flaw, but rather a feature of adulthood.

"We're overly proactive about dating, but are not proactive about seeking friends," said Carlin Flora. "If you meet a guy at a coffee shop and he asks you out, that seems normal. But if you see a woman at a coffee shop you might want to be friends with, and ask her to get together, you worry that might seem weird. When you're single, a friend will say, 'Let me fix you up!' But if I say, 'I feel like I need some friends,' people don't say, 'I know someone you might like!' We rarely talk about how to find friends proactively, but it does work."

And so, in a reprise of my efforts in eighth grade, here are my updated, revised notes on How to Be Popular:

How to Be Popular: The Adult Version

Start with your interests: One of the easiest ways to feel surrounded by like-minded individuals is to join a group doing something you love. A century of research on social networks shows that both depth and *breadth* of connection influences our happiness. We gain security and joy from feeling part of something larger than ourselves. That sense of affiliation can improve your health, increase the pleasure you gain from leisure activities, and inspire you to take more social initiative.

Even casual surface interaction, such as hiking with strangers, can lessen some of the negative effects of isolation. After a day on the trail—or the courts, or in the volleyball pit—you'll probably sleep more soundly and awaken with more zest for the day.

Despite the books and articles lamenting today's epidemic of isolation, there are more single-person households today than at any time in recent history, meaning that restaurants, grocery stores, coffee shops, family resorts, and consumer product manufacturers cater to single adults and single parents. "Cities have booming subcultures of people who live alone. Suburbs are becoming more urban, too," said New York University sociology professor Eric Klinenberg, author of *Going Solo: The Extraordinary Rise and Surprising Appeal of Living Alone.* "These cities are playgrounds for urban people. We're always joking about how much more fun the single people seem to be having." You also can find activity groups easily online, as well as divorced-parent meet-ups and single-parent getaways. The popularity of Internet dating has normalized the idea of "shopping" for friends.

It can take time to develop real friendships from activities. Be patient, advised University of Arizona's Segrin. "Your marriage didn't happen overnight. Realize you'll go down a lot of culs-de-sac. Sometimes the best relationships in our lives start out with little baby steps."

Ritualize a favorite activity: By creating a routine around an enjoyable activity, you harness the power of habit. Many of us need a routine to get ourselves to activities we love. Lisa, the telecommunications salesperson I met flying to Phoenix, joined a gym near her postdivorce apartment complex. She committed to hitting the treadmill at the same time every night, as a way to run into those on a similar schedule. "You start by saying hi to people, just casually, like, 'Oh, I like your shirt!' Or, 'Oh, you're not coming tomorrow? See you next week!' It makes you feel like you belong to something. I had a 'gym club.' It felt like its own little community."

Go against your gut: When you have a case of Divorce Onset Insecurity, the natural reaction may be to hide out at home, to assume others are bad-mouthing you.

A better approach? Do the opposite. Extend yourself. When you're home alone and the phone isn't ringing, pick it up and dial out. The insecurity of divorce can make you fixate on being left out yet unaware of your friends' own preoccupations and of how much less *you* may be giving to *them*.

Our friends may have no idea how to act or what we'd find helpful in divorce, even if it seems painfully obvious to us. We may have to tell them what we need, while first assessing what they can easily give. Think realistically about their capabilities and limitations, their free time and other commitments. As if divorce weren't hard enough, we have to help our friends through it, too.

Susan, my divorce mentor, refused to entertain the notion that anyone might be avoiding her, unless it became an indisputable fact. She kept lists of friends, and made a point of going out with single friends of both genders, and with couples. She maintains all these activities today—and has the active social life she wants. "I'm a reacher-outer. I never say, 'I called them last time, now I have to wait for them to call me.' I need it, so I don't hesitate."

Use your strengths: Airplane Lisa, outgoing and comfortable with strangers, hosted a cocktail hour in her new apartment complex to meet the neighbors. "I made it very time-bound, with a couple bottles of wine, some beer, and some appetizers. It was just two hours, so people are like, 'What's two hours? You stop by, you have a drink, and you go home.'" Today she counts some of the people she met in her apartment among her closest friends.

Dave Cervini, a radio personality and event planner in New York, lost his job around the same time he separated from his wife, who had been his high school sweetheart. He said he felt as if his identity had been washed away. He spent a few months lost and alone. One night he was lying on his living room floor, lamenting the state of his life. "I looked up and there was this ray of light coming through the window, a lamppost shining extra bright. I felt like I heard that angels-singing sound. I remembered Lucy saying to Charlie Brown, 'You need involvement. You need a director.' I realized I had to do something to get out of this rut."

Dave remembered that he'd enjoyed church activity groups in high school. He decided to volunteer at a church near his apartment. On his second visit, he saw a flyer announcing an evening get-together. He went to the bar and met some people he liked.

Then he remembered: *he was a social director himself!* He tapped his professional event-planning background to start a Catholic singles social network. He ran this group for a few years, eventually expanding it into a business called the New York Social Network. When I spoke to him, he'd grown it into a company with thousands of members, about two hundred of whom he considered close friends.

Even if you're not a professional party planner, it can be far easier to rustle up a crowd than you might think. Many people are milling about, waiting for someone to invite them to *anything*. Chloe, the mom who was traveling to France with her ex, formed a solo moms group as an offshoot of a parenting website she'd helped found. She quickly met other divorced and single moms eager to join.

Embrace your weaknesses: "I could never throw a party!" you might say. Or, "I'm a full-time parent with no childcare, living in a hamlet of five thousand people, including the guy who drives the snowplow over from the next town." You may be able to utilize your limitations to your advantage, something I realized when talking to Catherine, an environmental educator and mother of one.

Catherine moved from her hometown in Canada to upstate New York to marry a man who'd long been a good friend. After the birth of their daughter, he wanted out of the marriage. Catherine found herself alone with a newborn, far from family, without a car, in a snowy, exurban area.

Then a new job took her to Beacon, population fifteen thousand, a former factory town turned arty enclave on the Hudson River, about two hours north of Manhattan. All the action happens on Beacon's Main Street, a long, store-lined road ambling down to the river. Without a car, Catherine shopped and spent her free time on Main Street. "I'd walk everywhere, so people would see me a lot. I made a lot of friends just like that, through grabbing a beer after work or going to the coffee shop. You do that enough, the people who work there become your friends and then you meet their friends."

She felt quickly welcomed into this new community, insisting that her self-described dorkiness helped. "I think people feel sorry for me because I'm so awkward. They try to make me feel better. But then I think I'm kind of cool when I'm not awkward and we wind up being friends."

I suspect Catherine's positive attitude attracted people more than some universally evident awkwardness. But, like Catherine, we all have perceived deficits upon which we can draw.

Single parenthood can be a "weakness" that generates connection. While we may lament today's overscheduled childhood, all those organized play dates and extracurricular activities are opportunities for us to meet other adults. Going where others congregate, such as your child's soccer game, puts you in contact with potential friends.

But you may have to unfriend your phone to meet them. There's a classic book on mindfulness meditation by Jon Kabat-Zinn called *Wherever You Go, There You Are*. I always think of this title when I see people walking down the street, staring at their cell phones. They're not where they are; they're buying shoes on eBay. If you sit with the discomfort of being alone, rather than filling it with technology, you open yourself to meeting other people also seeking society.

For Susan, the painful reality of being home alone while her ex had their children served as a social motivator. "If I knew the kids were going to him, I would go stay with my friends in New York. I would just go when they go." The New York trips led to reconnection with old friends, and a new boyfriend. She also capitalized on her ability to connect with family. "I'm vastly lucky to be able to spend time with my parents in Florida. I was able to visit them more often and stay longer because of our custody arrangement."

All of this is to say, we're not in eighth grade anymore. While we may have to work to rebuild a social life, there's every reason to believe our efforts will succeed.

ONE IS NOT THE LONELIEST NUMBER

Loneliness is a negative state. Aloneness is the presence of oneself.
—The loneliness card from the Osho Zen tarot deck

In mid-July of my first single summer, I was standing in the middle of Greenwich Village in old yoga pants and a stretched-out tank top, eating a Vietnamese catfish sandwich slathered in mayonnaise, and scrolling through the contact list on my iPhone. I wanted a friend to join me at yoga, or blow it off and grab a drink, but I didn't have anyone to call. I know single moms are purportedly the busiest people on the planet, but I had more free nights than I knew what to do with, and no one to help me fill them.

The heat of the day rose from the pavement. Women floated by in flirty dresses and strappy sandals, shiny hair freshly styled. They were meeting friends, or maybe going on dates. I was standing alone, mayonnaise oozing over my fingers. It formed a milky patina over my screen, like a scrim between me and some earlier, more connected era.

A handsome young man in a crisp shirt walked by, also alone. I smiled, wiping mayonnaise off my cheek.

He kept walking.

I was out in the city, heading to an activity that doesn't require a partner. But I wasn't enjoying it. I felt incomplete.

I'd begun to be aware of another relationship that had suffered in my marriage: the one with myself. On some critical level, I no longer saw myself as good company. I had in the past, in my twenties. I'd go places alone, sometimes invite others to join me. But for the entire first year of being separated and on into the second, I felt an impatience with myself, a boredom, an unstated accusation that I was inadequate company, not *fun enough* on my own.

Part of this feeling came from my marriage. In a bad relationship, we can lose awareness of our own charms, even stop manifesting them. After separation, we may be too focused on getting un-single to nurture our strengths.

Discomfort with being single can be part of the problem. Michael Cobb, a professor of English at the University of Toronto, and author of *Single: Arguments for the Uncoupled*, thinks we unfairly malign the single state. Viewing singleness as inferior reduces our enjoyment of alone time, he said. "We live in such a couples-obsessed society that there really are no 'singles' out there—everyone is pre- or post-coupled. They're either in the wings waiting or they're past their prime and are no longer allowed to be part of this central way people not only organize their intimate lives but attain social legitimacy."

I talked about being alone, post-marriage, with Airplane Mandrake, the Midwestern professor who'd bought a house on his own as a step toward divorce. We were discussing his adjustment to living alone in a big house that made strange noises at night and put him on edge.

"Well, it's short-term," I said, trying to be encouraging. "You won't be alone forever, right?"

"I feel like that's mean to being alone," he answered, in his thoughtful, quirky way. "Like, if Being Alone were a person, it would hurt its feelings to talk about it that way. As if it were something bad that you hoped would end quickly."

I did think Being Alone was something bad, requiring an exterminator to bomb it, preferably with old-fashioned, highly toxic pesticide long banned from use in the States. But I hated the idea of being mean, even if only to a concept. Mean as in unappreciative, inattentive to its positive qualities. Would being "nicer" to Being Alone help me handle it better?

"Yes," said my friend Abby, insisting that there's a lot to like about lacking a lover, such as being able to do whatever you want, without having to accommodate another person's schedule or "issues." Divorce coach Amy agreed, objecting to the idea that we're incomplete without a spouse. She said some friends wouldn't invite her for dinner after her divorce unless she brought a date, as if she were a second-rate guest when arriving alone. "But after a divorce, you're not broken. I reject that idea. For me, it was the beginning of viewing myself as whole exactly as I am, and not a split part of something."

Amy encourages clients to "fall in love with themselves." I hated this suggestion, the trite phraseology of it. It sounded like something a greeting card writer might conceive of, then dismiss once fleshing it out:

> *How do I love me? Let me count the ways.*
> *I love me with a handheld, battery-operated device,*
> *And massage oil that smells so nice . . .*

Well. You can imagine the accompanying illustration. But Amy was right in principle. Ending this loneliness would require regaining a connection with myself.

Almost a year later, a friend canceled dinner plans, citing back pain. I was thirteen months into having no husband, and still, all day, the empty night ahead loomed.

In the late afternoon, I wound up in a bookstore near Columbia University. There was an open-mike night that evening. I'd loved going to readings on my own in my twenties, I remembered. I decided to stay, and sat in a folding chair among the poetry students. A woman named Moira T. Smith stood up to read. Decades out of college, she was thin and lithe, dressed in a rock 'n' roll T-shirt and low-riding jeans. She looked like she didn't *give a shit* what anyone else thought. Her poems were quips of defiance. "If I didn't enjoy my own company so much, I might be compelled to make more friends," she read in a confrontational, deadpan style.

Yes! I thought. *That's how I want to feel!*

And then, slowly, I started to.

The next month, I had plans to visit Sara, my old friend whose beachfront wedding had inspired our divorce discussion. I'd seen her infrequently since then, largely because our lives had diverged. Sara is eight years younger than I, and when we met, she was living with her mother in Queens, while I had my own apartment and a fast-paced life as a freelancer in Manhattan. I was something of a mentor.

Then, just as quickly, I became an anti-mentor, as she noted the downsides of my insecure, insufficiently remunerative career. She went back to school for a master's degree in journalism, landed a stable staff job, and eventually earned enough money to buy an investment property in Manhattan. That spring, she had a new, coveted position at a major newspaper, her marriage to her ideal man, and a new baby. I was feeling priced out of New York, facing divorce, and still wanting a second child of my own.

I dropped by to see the baby. As I was getting ready to leave, I sat on the floor in her long front hall, strapping on my sandals. She asked if I had Memorial Day plans.

I did have Memorial Day plans! Spooked by my vacationless first summer without a spouse, I'd made plans three months in advance for my second single summer—starting with Memorial Day, when I was going to the Catskills with Chloe's solo moms group and all our kids. One of the mothers owned a sprawling, historic guesthouse backed by a plashing waterfall. We were carpooling there and had arranged a yoga class, elaborate dinners, and a potter to bring clay for the kids. It was the kind of mommy-bonding weekend I might have fantasized about, but never planned, while married.

"Wait a minute!" Sara said. "Are you going to the Waterfall House?"

Yes, I realized, I was. The guesthouse had its own name, and that was it.

A good friend of Sara's was going, too, it turned out, a stylish woman who lived in a chic apartment in Greenwich Village. "I heard about this trip!" Sara said. "That's where you're going? I want to go!"

You can't go because you're married. Nahnahnahnahnahnah! (How much I've matured since middle school really takes my breath away.) In her exclamation, I heard the tiniest bit of what we newly single, spouseless individuals sometimes fear we'll never hear again—envy.

I don't really want to inspire envy. It's a negative feeling, and I don't want it sloshing in either direction, toward me or away. But that flash of desire from my hyper-enviable friend illuminated a critical fact: I needed to challenge my sense of being limited due to divorce. There are all kinds of activities I might do—alone or with others. Much of what we enjoy is actually marriage-optional.

• • •

At the end of June, I flew to Los Angeles for a month with my son to be a visiting artist at the 18th Street Arts Center. It was my first-ever residency of this sort. Out there in a city known for atomization, a place where everyone is sealed off in his own hybrid vehicle, where I knew almost no one, my recurring, painful loneliness finally receded. It bleached out under the sun, dried up in the desert-like air, and blew away.

Certainly part of my more solid sense of self had to do with the weather; I perk up from sunshine the way others respond to Prozac. I'd also inadvertently staged the loneliness intervention of environmental restructuring—removing myself from the daily reminders of the life we'd once led. But I also felt more content because I wasn't comparing my situation to some imagined "better" state. I wasn't hearing about some party I hadn't been invited to, or some opening or lecture I couldn't attend. I didn't have two hundred "friends" in L.A., so I didn't know what fabulous outings I was missing. Without that comparison between what I was doing and what I thought I *should* be doing, I didn't feel lonely.

I'd loved the nonstop socializing that characterizes life in Lower Manhattan, but in the waning years of my marriage, it had taken a negative turn. I'd often commuted an hour to see an acquaintance whose company I hadn't enjoyed the time before. In divorce, I'd been so careful not to jump into a romantic relationship merely to fill the void. But back home, I'd grown used to doing the friendship version of sleeping around. I was dining around. Going to theater around. Meeting for coffee around. I was so afraid of being alone that I'd tried to fill my time with anyone, even those who, in retrospect, made me feel worse due to our lack of real affection.

There'd been something procrustean about my marriage, both of us trying to squeeze ourselves into a relationship that didn't quite fit. For all of us, living a "life extraordinary," to quote the Carbon Leaf song, means engaging in activities of our choosing with friends we truly value—and counting ourselves among our staunchest supporters.

It took me more than a year to regain this level of calmness and contentment with myself. Things got a lot harder in my divorce first.

THE TUNNEL OF DARKNESS

PART THREE

THE TUNNEL OF DARKNESS

CHAPTER SIX

Hurricane

When Crisis Hits

✦

Some of us find that the stress of divorce compounds upon itself, leading to emotional and physical problems. Even in crisis, we can focus on taking charge of our attitude and approach.

Why must a man go out and take strange things
so much upon himself as might the porter
from stall to stall of some large market basket
strangely filled more and more, who, laden, follows
and cannot say: Lord, what's the banquet for?

Why must a man just stand there like a shepherd,
so much exposed to more than he can bear . . .

—Rainer Maria Rilke, nineteenth- and early-
twentieth-century German-language poet

A CRISIS IN THREE MONTHS

January 2013. Ten months since separation: I'm sitting in the bathroom, peering into an empty blue box that once held feminine hygiene products. My son, up past his bedtime, is swinging on the bathroom door, asking me something, maybe how hinges work. "Stop coming in here!" I say.

More swinging. "If you're going to hang out, then help me figure out who I can call to bring over supplies!" There's no way I can get myself to the drugstore in this condition—flooding blood; no supplies.

My son stops to think. "Sophia?"

Sophia! The five-year-old who lives next door, with her *parents*. "That's a great idea!" Sophia's mother is out of town, but I reach her father on his cell phone. He happens to be at the CVS. Ten minutes later, in a moment of embarrassing stoop-front intimacy, I greet my tall, dark, and handsome neighbor and receive a shopping bag of maxi-pads.

This happens to a lot of women, I tell myself. *Heavy flow.*

It's never happened to me, but I'm in my mid-forties now. Bodies change.

The next morning, I ask my friend Courtney to take my son to school. I remember a family friend who, in her late forties, was felled each month by hormonal hyperbole. *So I stay home from work one day? So what?*

146

I stay home that night, too. My almost-ex watches our son, even though it's my turn. He's unworried about this menstrual anomaly, assuming, I suspect, that I'm exaggerating. I assume he's right. My self-image remains affected by his perception of me, or my sense of it: *Complainer, overly reactive, lacking grit.*

The third morning, I wake up exhausted. I have an appointment at the gynecologist scheduled already, and I get myself to it, mention the heavy flow. But I've adjusted to it by then, the way we acclimate to many troubles—a bad marriage, a deadening job. *Maybe this is just some new normal.* The doctor offers to do a biopsy, to see if it's something "sinister," like uterine cancer or hyperplasia. I do not have uterine cancer or hyperplasia, I know, because I've had a variety of health exams over the past few months. "Call if it gets worse," the doctor says. "I'll be in the hospital all night."

That afternoon, walking to get my son from school, I feel woozy. I have to rest on a neighbor's stoop. Then another stoop. The next morning, I wake up dizzy. The nurse at my doctor's office tells me to go to the hospital. I reach my future ex-husband on the phone. He agrees to take our son to school, then drive me to the hospital in the next town.

At the hospital, we sit together in a waiting room teeming with flu victims. I feel guilty, taking up my husband's workday. We wait for hours. I'm growing increasingly exhausted. I finally pull myself up and tell an orderly that I've been bleeding for four days and need a private room and my doctor *now*. He manages to locate both.

The doctor orders a hemoglobin test. The test comes back low. Too low. Heavy flow can happen if the uterine lining sheds in patches, the doctor says, not unusual with aging. But in my case, it has gone on too long. I've lost too much blood. My heart could stop working if we don't do a transfusion.

My heart could stop working? We've been sitting the waiting room for four hours, and my heart could stop working?

Actually, this doesn't send me into the panic you might expect. Partly because I'm in a state-of-the-art hospital in New Jersey rather than, say, a refugee camp in a war-torn desert where, I suddenly realize, I would bleed out and die. But also, it's hard to get a rise when your blood pressure is dangerously low. The day has assumed a slow-motion, molasses feel. I'm slightly dazed. My ears are ringing. The blue veins normally prominent on the backs of my hands have flattened, disappeared.

I'll also need a D&C, the doctor says, a dilation and curettage, to scrape the uterine lining to stop the flow. I'll need to be knocked out for this procedure, and stay overnight in the hospital. Maybe two nights. As an orderly wheels me to the OR, I gaze at the backs of my hands. *I could be a hand model*, I think, absently.

Many people get sick, have medical emergencies, lose too much weight due to the stress of divorce, a fact I hadn't fully noted in my optimism about life after marriage. I'd been growing increasingly anxious, ever since October. As I lay on a cot, waiting for the anesthesiologist to arrive, I began to suspect that this weird uterine bleeding was a physical reaction to my own mounting stress.

October 2012. Three months earlier: My anxiety had started back in the fall. My husband invited me over for a talk. He lit a few candles, poured wine. *Does he want to reconcile?* I'd begun to fantasize, on some of those long, lonely nights, that perhaps this trial separation could end in recommitment. I was so tired of being alone. Also, I still wanted a second child. I'd always planned to have two children, assumed I would.

"I'm seeing someone," my husband said, a secretive smile curling the corners of his mouth. It was a woman we'd met together at a party on the evening we'd announced to our group our plans to split. She'd hosted the party at her apartment for a mutual friend. Now they were in a committed, exclusive relationship.

The candles flickered, casting a yellow light against his tweedy couch. There was more, he said. He took a sip of his wine. After seven months of cooperative co-parenting, he finally agreed with what I'd felt all along: one child between two parents wasn't enough.

We'd spent a huge amount of time and money trying to have our son. After a couple of miscarriages and a round of minor fertility interventions, we'd resorted to in vitro fertilization in 2007, a high-tech, expensive procedure with slim odds of success, particularly for women my age. We'd been lucky; it had worked the first time. We had our healthy, bouncy son—no complications.

But we also had frozen embryos remaining, eleven of them, at the time of our separation. There was only a 30 percent chance of one of those embryos being good, actually developing into a live baby. I'd been forty when we created them, and IVF was still new and somewhat mysterious. But 30 percent isn't zero.

As much as I'd wanted out of my marriage, I felt waves of loss whenever I thought about my unborn baby. I'd begun having nightmares of a little girl frozen in ice, crying to be thawed out to play. *Couldn't we just use the embryos anyway?* I'd started to wonder. Would we really destroy them, and the possible life within, just because our marriage didn't adhere? I'd finally decided that—married or not—if we *tried*, at least I wouldn't wonder my entire life if our son could have had a sibling.

My almost-ex hadn't agreed. He'd felt overwhelmed by the end of our marriage, by the expenses of one child, two apartments. But over the months, he'd come around to seeing how it could work, he told me that night in October, taking a sip of his wine. He realized we *could* handle two children in our two homes. He was heartened by how well we were doing. Our lives were so orderly, calm. There was room for another child. He was willing to use our embryos, to co-parent a baby with me, if I was game. The girlfriend, age fifty, wasn't objecting—at least not in any way forceful enough to deter him.

At first, all I could think about was the possibility of having another baby. I could be out of my marriage and still have our second child! Or at least try.

Sure, it would be hard to be pregnant alone, to live by myself with my young son and a nursing infant. But I could handle a few more difficult years. And five years from now, what difference would it make that we'd gotten the order wrong, had our second child after divorce, rather than before? I was so excited! He was willing to try, to co-parent a sibling for our son.

But the next day, the idea of the other woman wormed its way into my brain. My husband had established an exclusive relationship with another woman within a few months of our split, during our *trial* separation? Why did we work so hard on our marriage if another woman could so easily do? How connected could he have been to *me* if I was so easy to replace? I felt terrified, sickened to think of her place, to know the contours of her face.

I also felt like a cowering hypocrite. I *had* been feeling better since he moved out, and yet I didn't want him to find someone else? I'd spent months touting, promoting, *bragging* about our positive parting. Now I was crawling out of my skin, wracked by a crazed kind of jealousy I'd never experienced before.

"Of course you're upset," everyone said. "I'd be worried if you weren't. You know men. They can't be alone."

Everyone said this: "Of course you're upset." And, "Men can't be alone."

Any armchair evolutionary biologist could have cited at least one good reason for this reaction: the resources I needed for my proposed baby were being diverted to the father's new mate. But to not use the embryos? That seemed out of the question. Time was running out for me to build my family, and for my son to have a sibling close in age.

I gave myself two weeks to adjust to the news, to sit with the jealousy rather than assuming it meant I genuinely wanted to reunite. *If I'm still freaking out after two weeks, I'll say something to him.*

Two weeks passed, and then the biggest storm in local recorded history threatened to slam into Manhattan. Hurricane Sandy tossed my plans, all of ours, to the wind.

The storm churned up the East Coast. New York City's mayor shut down the subways. Hoboken's mayor declared a mandatory evacuation of all ground-floor apartments. Schools were closed. By nightfall, seventy-mile-an-hour winds split trees, flattened houses.

My future ex came to my house to stay. Divorce or no, he was still the dad, and his little boy's home was about to be whacked by gale-force winds. I was swooning with relief at not being alone.

My almost ex-husband played with our son upstairs while I cleaned the kitchen, brought the basil and rosemary plants in from out back. The kitchen smelled homey with the wet earth and dewy herbs. I baked chocolate chip cookies. The impending disaster outside made our home feel extra-safe, *married*, in the way I'd wanted it to be—snug inside, regardless of threats from without.

My husband made a pot of chili. It gurgled on the stove, reminding me of the good parts of our country days, when I was pregnant, and the excitement of our coming son pulled us together. After dinner, he put our son to bed while I did the dishes. Then we sat for a second dinner ourselves, the silk chandelier casting a circle of light over us. The wind rattled the windows. A rivulet of rain snaked in through the front sash. He opened a bottle of champagne I had in the refrigerator. We drank a whole bottle—perhaps both a little grateful for the respite from our split.

The next day, news of devastation filtered in. Water had flooded the subways, short-circuited power, turned walls to paste, left dead in its wake. Half of Hoboken was underwater. Our bulwark of a house stood high and dry. We put a power strip on our stoop for low-lying neighbors to charge their cell phones, welcomed friends to use the shower, the stove. We took turns watching our son and working. Later, my husband made dinner again, pasta with herbs. I looked across the table at this man I'd married. Had he always been so cute?

He set up the old DVD player. We sat together, watching a video, the romance of being safe in the midst of disaster seeping in with the tiny water leak in the front room. I thought of a line from the Michael Blumenthal poem "A Marriage":

"You are holding up a ceiling with both arms. It is very heavy."

Then "something wonderful happens." Someone walks into the room and holds up the ceiling with you. You get married.

I had been holding up the ceiling with both arms and my head. God, I wanted a husband! I was worn out by the constant effort to fill, fill, fill my time, to manage every detail.

I remembered a conversation I'd had a week earlier while waiting for the ferry from Hoboken to Manhattan. The ferry had been late. A guy about my age wearing an ironic felt hat grumbled about the wait. I complained, too. Then, to add to the general air of dissatisfaction on the dock, I said, "My husband got a girlfriend, like, two weeks after we split."

"Ah!" said the man in the homburg, gazing north, up the Hudson River. "After my divorce, I was like a tiny little flower in a dried-up pot of dirt. Parched. This other woman comes along and thinks everything I do is wonderful. I was being watered again, blooming. Then she dumps me. Don't tell your husband this, but the first woman who comes along and is nice to you seems like a fairy princess. Then she breaks up, and you think you'll die."

How significant was his new relationship, *really*? We'd been together a dozen years; he'd known her what, six months? I moved a little closer to him on the couch, pulled the blanket over us.

Later, we turned in for the night, in the house that we still called *our* home, together.

The next morning, my husband decided to take a break from caring for us to go care for his girlfriend. She was alone without power, but "she has lots of candles," he said on his way out. I envisioned him at her apartment, filled with a hundred candles, like in some romantic movie. He promised to come back the next morning to help with our son.

He returned the next day around noon. "I overslept," he told me, a notion I found sickening.

"How'd you feel, being with her, after being at home with me?"

"I was happy to see her," he said with that sweet, sappy look of new love, that sickening, simpering expression you want to slap off someone's face if he's your husband, smiling about someone else. "Besides, she's another pair of hands on deck. She's there in an emergency. She could help out with childcare."

I was going to throw up. I could feel it. I never throw up when upset. I just eat and eat, adding girth to grief. I went into the bathroom, splashed water on my face, did some deep yoga breathing. I was considering having a child with this man, and he was offering his girlfriend as a second "pair of hands." I was willing to endure the hormonal roller coaster of pregnancy, the pain of childbirth, all the risks doctors constantly warn you about when you get pregnant after the age of thirty-five. And my husband, who always lands on his feet, whose toast, if it drops, falls buttered side up, was telling me I should be glad he'd found someone else to love. Yes, he was technically within his rights to move on, but that did not make it feel better.

This is not the right man for me, I remembered, once again. People have trouble in divorce, but they bounce back. My own resilience made its perky reappearance. *I'm fine. I'll be fine.*

November 2012: Two weeks later, my son showed me a goody bag from a children's party he'd attended with his dad and the new girlfriend while I'd been out of town. This was how I discovered that my husband was including his new girlfriend in his weekends with our son, even though we'd agreed to discuss introducing new partners first.

Later that week, we headed to his parents' house for a family party for our son. He was turning five! While I was unloading the dishwasher with my mother-in-law, she told me she'd met the girlfriend when they'd come up together for a large family dinner, along with our son. "She had a nice way with him," my mother-in-law said, in a reassuring voice.

My hand shook on the cup I was holding. What else was he doing that he wasn't telling me? The crazy anxiety and jealousy returned. I felt like I was standing on quicksand. Or peering over the edge of a cliff, digging my toes into the dirt. Clods of black earth loosened, plummeting downward, turning dirt over sod. Where was the bottom? How low would it go?

I was heading for a crisis. I could feel it coming on. I thought about people I'd spoken to who'd had real breakdowns. A man in Ohio had told me about a crushing depression after his wife left. His dog of sixteen years died the following week. He was living apart from his son half the time, far away from his own parents and siblings. He couldn't sleep, couldn't rise in the morning. "I'd think, 'This feels low.' Then it'd get lower again. It felt like rock bottom. It lasted a solid six months," he'd said.

Finally, a therapist prescribed an antidepressant, and group therapy. He found the group dynamic incredibly helpful.

Group therapy sounded so Esalen Institute/lava lamp/1970s heyday of divorce. It sounded so *social*. *I'm doing it*, I decided. I logged on to PsychologyToday.com and found a therapy group in my old Manhattan neighborhood.

A week later, I sat on a leather couch, gripping a box of tissues, and told six experienced denizens of self-reflection about my separation, my reaction to the girlfriend, my desire for a second child. You can't pay for that kind of focus group! Well, I was paying, but not that much.

Two of the women talked about their own bad breakups, their great new marriages. They gave me hope, a peek at life on the other side.

But soon, the quicksand feeling returned. Our childcare exchange perforated me. Every time my husband dropped off our son, I knew he was heading to a romantic date in the city, perhaps to take her to another party with our mutual friends, then return to her place to have sex, sleep in. He'd bring her coffee as he'd once brought it to me.

I felt like one of the hairier, more aggressive primates, like an orangutan perhaps—raging, free-ranging fury. I went down to the pier to lope through the grass like an orangutan, thinking maybe that would exorcise my anger, this ripped-to-shreds feeling, this desire to rip something else apart. It was Orangutan Therapy I'd just invented, a version of scream therapy.

It didn't work. I felt like an orangutan who needed a nap.

December 2012: My therapy group got into a fight about my embryos. "You can't handle the girlfriend, and now you want to have a child with this man?" half said. "No offense, but this is crazy."

"She obviously knows it will be hard," the other half countered. "This is her only chance to have her own biological second child. Who says family has to look any one way?"

I watched the conversation volley, the future of my maybe-baby bouncing from yes to no and back again. I wasn't sure which side I was on.

I called Chloe, the mom who'd traveled to France with her ex. She was pushing forty, and single. "I totally understand how you feel," she said. "I don't think you're crazy. I think you're lucky to have those embryos." She told me that she'd tried to get her ex-husband to have a second child with her, *the natural way*, even after divorce. He wouldn't oblige.

I could not shake the anxiety, the nauseating feeling of being replaced. I made an appointment to see a psychologist. "You need to see a lawyer," he said. "The legal has a way of impacting the emotional."

I'm sure he was right. I did not go see a lawyer. I was hardly in a position to think calmly about finances and infant custody when I felt like an orangutan. I'd be too easily riled into a fury of retaliatory position staking. I suggested to my husband that we go see a divorce counselor, together, instead. He agreed.

While marriage counseling often felt like a patch, divorce counseling helped immediately. The therapist concluded that my husband wouldn't do what I wanted (break up with the girlfriend) but was willing to make discrete commitments to help me feel more secure. She advised him to go slowly when including a new partner, for the sake of our son and himself.

We crafted a plan; he could include his girlfriend on his days with our son once a month for the next three months. If he was still committed to her after that, we'd reassess. We decided to move forward with the embryos after the winter holidays.

I believed I could do it, be a Solo Pregnant Mom by Choice. I'd never had a mental breakdown, and I wouldn't now. My mind would not throw in the towel.

I didn't know then that my body might.

• • •

A few weeks later, ten days before our proposed embryo transfer, there I was in the hospital bed, an IV line dripping someone else's blood into my veins. I couldn't help but see this bleeding as some wiser, more cautious side of myself hitting the brakes on this pending pregnancy. I hadn't taken any IVF hormones; I couldn't blame them.

I wanted to be able to handle it, but my body staged an intervention. My uterus, actually, the site of all this proposed baby making. It said, "You will not take this action you are considering." It was too much of a coincidence, too obvious a metaphor to be a mere side effect of age.

STRESS AND ILLNESS

Later, people would share stories of divorce-related health problems such as sleeplessness, racing heart. Two women said they were diagnosed with breast cancer, an illness they believed was linked to the stress they felt in divorce.

"Almost one hundred percent of my clients have some sort of physical ailment," said Washington, DC–based family lawyer Regina DeMeo. "Not to the point of needing to be hospitalized, but they'll have panic attacks, an immune system disorder, constant sinus infections, a bout of depression. I'll say, 'You've got to take care of yourself.' I feel like a nurse sometimes, but it no longer surprises me."

While stress can make you sick, grief can make you wild, turn you into an orangutan, or those wily minions, Thing One and Thing Two, who destroy the house in *The Cat and the Hat*. They're a hurricane of chaos, vicious or maybe just crazed. "Most people don't even realize they're grieving," said psychiatrist Mark Banschick. "That alone is crazy-making. You're grieving, but it's not like your husband died and your whole community is supporting you. You're grieving by yourself."

Psychiatrist Elisabeth Kübler-Ross, author of *On Death and Dying*, popularized her observation that many people pass through five stages of grief—denial, anger, bargaining, depression, and finally acceptance. While a helpful model for some, she was working with terminal patients, not divorcees, and hers is not a scientific truth about loss. "Many people have been harmed by this idea because they don't go through these stages and think there's something wrong with them," said Columbia University psychology professor George Bonanno, author of *The Other Side of Sadness: What the New Science of Bereavement Tells Us about Life after Loss.*

I went up to Columbia University to talk to Bonanno shortly after my brief hospital stay. A leading bereavement researcher, he looks like the movie version of Your Favorite Professor—tall and slender, with salt-and-pepper hair. He was wearing jeans and bright red tennis shoes, a jacket over a T-shirt. A core-building balance ball sat before his sit/stand desk. I sat on his couch, listening to the jazz on his sound system. In that setting, my own recent experience with grief felt less personal, more *academic*, safe.

Most people bounce back from loss, Bonanno said. Resilience is part of our makeup; even clinically diagnosable depression persists only from about three to twelve months, in 90 percent of all cases. Grief, while it lasts, doesn't wrap itself around us without relief, like a bad case of poison oak. Grief oscillates. You feel fine, then terrible. Then fine again.

The fact that we recuperate from grief matters. An unquestioned assumption that the pain of divorce must be long-lasting and existentially damaging can hinder our ability to move past it. How fast we recover has to do with our natural resilience, and the actions we take.

I hadn't expected to suffer in my divorce, not really. I'd wanted out so clearly; I had no hint of the coming onslaught of second thoughts, jealousy, and nostalgia for the "good times" I hadn't always enjoyed. I never believed Nietzsche's famous truism "That which doesn't kill us makes us stronger." I thought suffering built suspicion, resignation, fear—a petty-minded clinging to what one still has. Nor had I suspected that pulling myself together in the aftermath of my marriage would make me feel stronger, wiser—*better*—in some lasting ways.

THE UPSIDE OF FEELING DOWN

Our emotions evolved along with us and are part of our survival package. Sadness, for example, turns our attention inward, helping us take stock and adjust. In studies of people shown sad movies, they become more detail-oriented and accurate. Sadness can make us remember past events more correctly, better assess our own abilities, become more thoughtful and less biased. Sadness also generates intimacy. When we're sad, we show it. Our slack posture and furrowed brows increase the likelihood of altruistic behavior from others. In this way, visible sadness is a coping skill; it motivates others to step in and offer comfort.

As new insights from the field of bereavement studies show, loss can bring gains. Loss or crisis can be the path to insights and skills, the discovery of hidden strengths, the formation of stronger connections, more confidence, deeper spirituality—and even greater happiness.

While we often think of happiness as synonymous with *fun*, this is an incomplete understanding. The Greek word *hedonic*, from which we get "hedonism," characterizes this side of happiness—enjoyment, pleasure, a tailgate party with all our friends. But there's another side of happiness that comes from having a sense of *meaning and purpose*. This is the side that loss can activate. It's the emotion I heard in the voice of people who blew me away with their strength, people able to accept a seriously negative turn of events, and thrive in the righting of their lives. People like the former radio personality, Dave Cervini, whose debilitating divorce led him to start the New York Social Network, and retool his life as a social entrepreneur.

Or the young mother of three in rural Colorado, Hollie, sideswiped by her husband's infidelity, but remarkably clear-eyed about her priorities, able to raise three babies essentially alone while pursuing a college degree at night. "I can change the oil in my car now," she said, in a tone of amazement. "I can repair my disposal in the kitchen sink. I'm a better parent because I'm calmer. I used to think that you turn into this magical adult. Like all of a sudden, you're the person you want to be. But I wasn't the person I wanted to be in my marriage. I've experienced more growth in the past two years than at any time in my life, from being on my own and wanting more for myself. I feel like a whole person."

It's not a rip-roaring good time to stay up late studying. It's not fun, like ice cream with sprinkles, or a new boyfriend buying you a sapphire ring. But people like Hollie speak in this openhearted, internally fortified way about their own newly discovered abilities, and their conviction that they finally know what really matters.

Psychologist Mavis Hetherington at the University of Virginia has written about how some women become like "superwomen" after divorce, succeeding at work and parenthood while also being active in the community, church, or philanthropic endeavors. This is where hard times can get you. And it is, in some iteration of the word, *fun*.

Or, as family lawyer DeMeo said, "I keep in touch with my clients, and it's amazing to see some people a year later. They look like an entirely different person. You can see that this was a bad part of their life but it's not the end of their life. They bounce back and then they thrive. They go on to do amazing things. It's really inspiring."

• • •

Some people experience divorce as a trauma. For novelist Gabriel Cohen, the day his wife walked out on him in 2005 shattered his belief that things would generally turn out well, that he was somehow "cosmically" protected from harm. "My idea was that any marriage has ups and downs. I wasn't expecting smooth sailing, upbeat all the time. I felt like I'd waited all this time and I'd found the perfect person. And then to not have that work out was a profound shock. It rent the fabric, the sense that the universe is a safe place," he said.

He started attending lectures, looking for company and insight. At a talk on Buddhism, he became intrigued by the idea that our reaction to events and our thoughts about them can spur happiness or misery as much as the events themselves. He went on to write a book about using Buddhist insights and practices to deal with his grief: *Storms Can't Hurt the Sky: A Buddhist Path through Divorce.* As he wrote, "What I learned astonished me: that change and loss are inevitable, but that the suffering we derive from them is not."

We aren't all going to find mind-expanding new insight from an

Eastern religion. But some kind of philosophical rebooting is the major work of dealing with traumatic loss, said Stephen Joseph, a psychology professor at the University of Nottingham, England, and the author of the surprisingly uplifting book on trauma *What Doesn't Kill Us: The New Psychology of Posttraumatic Growth*.

Joseph uses the metaphor of the "fractured vase" to describe post-traumatic growth. Say you accidentally knock a treasured vase from its shelf, shattering it. If you try to gather together every shard and glue the vase back together exactly as it was, it won't be precisely the same, yet it will be more vulnerable to cracking every time a truck drives by and rattles the shelf. In divorce, "gluing together the vase" would mean desperately trying to salvage a belief that has been proven false and doesn't serve you—such as "I'll never be happy unless my spouse returns," or, "Winners never fail."

People who grow from trauma and loss don't cling to false stories. But nor do they jettison all of their prior values in a storm of jaded negativity, becoming cynical or defeated. Instead, they fish out the fundamental underpinnings of their beliefs, their *axiology*, and incorporate these essential pieces into a new, more mature worldview. They "pick up the beautiful pieces and use them to make something new—such as a colorful mosaic," Joseph notes. Growth comes from this struggle to identify and recommit to your *core moral values*, to update your operating system of beliefs.

We update our beliefs all the time, but the process is usually more gradual. As a child, it dawns on us that a fairy probably does not hover above our town with a bag full of dollars, waiting for us to lose a tooth. Our mommy put the money under our pillow! This new belief is truer, and more truly reassuring. Our parents love us so much, they'll celebrate our most banal accomplishments, even ones over which we have no control. Our parents' love is a broader, more tightly woven safety net than the existence of an ethereal fairy focused solely on dental development.

With adult-size disillusionment such as divorce, equally solid truths may surface. Novelist Gabriel Cohen maintained his belief in passionate love and the value of marriage, yet tempered it with the acceptance that we can't control another's actions. He added the new, empowering belief that our own happiness derives more from attitude than circumstances. This "mosaic" let him accept his wife's defection without dismissing love and commitment wholesale, or doubting the integrity of every other person on the planet.

The European jeweler whose husband left her arrived at a different constellation of conclusions. "I was coming from a world where everything had to be a certain way. When something really turns your life upside down, you realize that your greatest plans might be turned around in a split second. It made me see that I don't have to be so careful because I'm not secure and protected anyway. It was the opening to a whole new life that I didn't even know was behind that door. Flash-forward two years. My life really expanded. At fifty-two, it felt like a big positive. I had not expected that to happen."

Or, as Nobel and Pulitzer Prize–winning divorced author Pearl S. Buck said, "Growth itself contains the germ of happiness."

The shattered-vase metaphor can be empowering in concrete ways, too. What aspects of your married identity do you want to preserve? What shards are worth claiming as your own? Was I still someone who cooked, a skill I developed as a wife? I decided that I was still a mother, even though not a wife, and the ability to make a meal was now mine. I also could use this skill to host parties, and invoke Principle No. 7: Create positive moments, for myself and my son.

Fishing out the fragments of a jointly created identity, polishing them off, and claiming them as your own lets you honor the good parts of your marriage and your own growth in it.

COPING LIKE A CHAMPION

For some, getting divorced feels like entering the Personal Growth Olympics, competing in a sport for which you haven't trained. Psychologist Terry Orlick, author of *Embracing Your Potential*, coaches Olympic athletes on the mental side of elite performance. He has said that the difference between a really *good* athlete and an Olympian often comes down to a person's mental game, including *how well she uses setbacks to her advantage.*

A world-class player capitalizes on time laid up in bed with an injury, for example, to mentally "practice" her moves, reflect on her life, and even reexamine her goals without the distraction of daily obligations. Here are some steps we all can take:

World-Class Coping

Set mini goals for recuperation: Olympians stay in the game mentally, even when injured. They "accept responsibility for their own healing by setting daily goals for rehabilitation and improvement, by imagining themselves healing, and by persisting in doing anything that might help," Orlick notes.

I find these sports metaphors incredibly helpful when it comes to coping with *internal* slaloms. After I consulted Orlick's book, I decided to set daily goals for my own recuperation, as if I were recovering from a collision with a pine tree. I could look back at the week and ask myself, "What did I do to help with my own healing?" Then I could answer that question. I made dinner plans with a friend. (Gold medal for social support!) I went hiking during the weekend. (Gold medal for endorphin-upping activity!) I avoided coffee after 3 p.m. and turned off the phone's ringer at bedtime. (Gold medal for sleeping through the night!) Getting enough sleep is so critical to mental clarity and calmness, one researcher I spoke to thought "Get enough sleep" should be a principle of parting.

Psycho-oncologists—therapists who help people deal with the emotional side of cancer—stress the importance of attitude even when one is facing a terminal illness. Memorial Sloan Kettering Cancer Center in New York City offers patients and their families "meaning-centered psychotherapy," an intervention based on the work of Austrian psychiatrist and Holocaust survivor Viktor Frankl, author of *Man's Search for Meaning.* "A principle that was highlighted by Frankl is that when all else is taken from a person, they have the ability to choose their attitude in the face of their suffering," said Wendy Lichtenthal, a clinical psychologist with Memorial Sloan Kettering. "That attitude in and of itself, the way I respond to a situation, can be a source of meaning."

Visualize victory: Superior athletes laid up in bed visualize themselves going through the motions of their sport. Mental imagery also can help when you're hiding under the covers from your divorce. You could envision yourself living your desirable future—being on vacation with your next love, signing the note for a mortgage on a new house you bought yourself, getting a raise at work. You feel as if you've actually done that thing, and the imagined success gives you energy.

Projecting backward can be surprisingly effective, too. Recall an instance when you felt joyful or powerful. Remember what you wore, what the room smelled like, what you saw around you.

My mother said that at one of her lowest points in divorce, she began checking her blood pressure at the machine in the grocery store. When it was high, she'd visualize a recent experience with my son running to greet her at the airport. He'd been so excited to see her that he'd barreled right into her legs, knocking her down in his rush. After concentrating on that moment of pure little-kid love, she'd check her blood pressure again. "It lowered it like twenty points," she said. "You wouldn't expect that thinking about something totally happy would make your whole body feel better, but it really worked."

We can court victory by noticing signs of it, even exaggerating them. A suspicion that you're stronger and wiser, even with no confirming evidence, can help you act in line with this ideal.

Some of us have trouble seeing our own signs of growth. This is one reason I found my divorce coach so helpful. I'd rant about whatever was bothering me. She'd listen, then point out a goal I'd met. "I want to congratulate you for the progress you've made on figuring out where you want to live, since our last call," she'd say. I'd stop and think about it. She was right! I had made progress.

Indulge (a little) indolence: As much as we want to remain active at
all times and get through this dark tunnel *now*, sometimes the unpro-
ductive behaviors that make us feel lazy and less than our best help
us recharge. "Approach-oriented" coping—actively seeking meaning
and solutions—is a faster, more successful route toward serenity than
"avoidance" coping, such as drowning your troubles in milkshakes or
staying up all night watching bad TV. But avoidance coping can be useful in small doses; it's a way to take a needed break from the effort to
rebuild. Playful, juvenile, somewhat mindless activities reconnect us to
the lighter, pleasurable aspects of life that are not about divorce. Indul-
gences can be positive moments, if we let ourselves enjoy them, relax
into them, and use the break to regain energy and strength.

• • •

For me, spending those two days in the hospital felt like a two-week
time-out, a mini vacation from my life. I loved the super-comfortable
hospital bed with its snow-white, matelasse coverlet and reassuring
safety sides. My own king-size bed back home suddenly seemed too
big, too weighed down with the history of my marriage. The nurses
came and went, bringing me lunch, checking on my blood volume. I
had no meals to cook or dog to let out. I lay there with nothing to do but
text friends, note who called, and think.

What I thought was: I'd felt anxious in my marriage. I needed to
stop accepting anxiety as "normal," now that I was out of that union. I
needed to flag anxiety as an aberration, and restructure my work and
relationships to lessen it.

I thought: I'd wanted to be able to handle a pregnancy alone, but I
was not going to try to have a baby with my future ex-husband while he
had a girlfriend and I had no one and was not feeling fine about these
facts.

We did try with our embryos again later, the following summer,
when I felt far stronger and more in control of my life. The process
didn't work; no baby girl developed out of the thaw. But there was some
comfort in knowing we'd tried.

I spoke to my father about my sense that this crisis was connected to my continued awareness of my ex's current life. "I think you can do one of three things," he said. "You can move out of your house. You can get a boyfriend. Or you can set up better boundaries. Which is going to be easiest?"

None of these sounded easiest, but he was right: I had to take some concrete steps to create more distance. Alone in that twin bed, I could see a vision of myself as a single person, in my own space, having set parameters to keep anxiety-making situations at bay.

These hospital-inspired epiphanies may seem small, but they allowed me to begin the process of thinking more seriously about how I was taking care of myself. I didn't completely change the landscape of my life, but the crisis helped define the territory to address.

CHAPTER SEVEN

I Love You, You're Perfect (Now That You're Gone)

The Need for Boundaries

✦

Some former spouses remain too connected for their own good. Setting boundaries can help both people move on. Others find that distance makes the problems fade, perhaps even leading to recommitment. Some turn nostalgia for the past into greater appreciation for today.

"I meant to let you go, Hildy, but you know how it is. You never miss the water till the well runs dry."

—Cary Grant, to Rosalind Russell in the
1940 comedy *His Girl Friday*

My divorce started out so pleasant and peaceful. We established a clear co-parenting schedule, and we stuck to it. True, if a stranger had dropped by on any random morning, our divorce would not have looked a whole lot different from a marriage. But I liked how not-totally-separate my separation was. It was great.

Until it wasn't. Until it felt kind of sickening.

I was on a flight to Atlanta, seated next to a large, ruddy-faced man with sparkling, ice-blue eyes. He had the eyes of a teenager, one who's just jumped from a rock while gripping a rope wrapped to a tree, then swung out, wide and high, to drop with a splash into the all-possibility of a swim hole in Georgia. Now, however, his body sagged in defeat. Everyone grows up, settles down. But this salesman sitting next to me looked as if the air had been let out of his spirit.

Carl, as I'll call him, said he'd married at nineteen, had children, then divorced when the kids were in elementary school. But he and his ex-wife got along so well, they decided to continue living together as a family, just without the husband-and-wife part. "Neither of us wanted to be a weekend parent," he said. "Our differences didn't have anything to do with the children. We were both committed to this, and at the time we thought that was the best chance for them to be around both of us."

Lately, though, he'd begun to question the wisdom of staying so connected. He and his ex-wife still traveled together for the kids' sporting events. They were in the process of buying a bigger house to give more privacy to the kids, and both parents. They'd struck up these barely-there boundaries, whisper-thin, lingerie-sheer walls, and never fortified them. "If we all went together somewhere today, we'd stay in different rooms. I think my kids would expect that, and that's a little bit troublesome to me. I may have made a mistake," he said. "I want our kids to have a good example of a good relationship between parents. I hope we haven't given them the wrong message."

He enjoyed his career and said romance wasn't a priority right now. But he also said he wasn't happier than when he was married. I wanted to say, "No, no! You *are* happier!"

Because what did this say about me, my chances for joy, given the intimate style of my own unmarrying?

Are there downsides to liking your ex? Of course. There are downsides to everything, even a kid's birthday party (chocolate frosting; white furniture). I was so focused on not fighting with my ex, on appreciating his good qualities, that I didn't realize a decent divorce has other risks, such as staying too close. Airplane Carl's story stuck with me, and during the next two years, I began to notice different versions of it.

Moving on after divorce requires establishing boundaries between ourselves and a former spouse, an action that may take conscious effort for some of us. We may need to create emotional rather than physical distance, to actively quit our former job as a caring primary partner. Sometimes one person must uphold a boundary for both. Some people—let's face it—hope a separation becomes a "marriage sabbatical" rather than a permanent state. Boundaries that aid good behavior can help preserve a decent relationship in separation, allowing a former couple to examine the wisdom of this dream. For the rest of us, backward-looking longing can be transformed into an increased reverence for today.

GOOD FENCES MAKE GOOD EXES

While we enlightened, peace-loving divorcées are avoiding the explosive mistakes of generations before us, many struggle with the opposite test—extricating ourselves enough to build independent, full lives on the other side. Wanting divorce to be one big pajama party, I began to realize, isn't a fully functional approach to ending a marriage. Those of us in amicable partings may inadvertently remain too enmeshed for our own good, while co-parents still roiling in anger may create an overly interactive schedule that incites fighting.

Los Angeles–based attorney Forrest Mosten stresses the importance of clearly defined roles and interactions. "It takes very special, low-conflict people to not have clear boundaries. People have high expectations for themselves: 'We're going to do this better than the way most people do it.' They put tremendous pressure on each other and on themselves to be far better than they can be, and then they get major disappointments and fail. I'd rather have people limit the trouble than try to maximize the perfect divorce."

Mosten told me a story of what he calls the "one-hundred-thousand-dollar light bulb." A separated woman needs help replacing a high ceiling bulb. Rather than spend the money to call a handyman, she asks her almost-ex to change it. While he's on the ladder, she raises a festering complaint, which leads to a fight. "They leave mediation, lawyer up, and then have a round of expensive and painful court hearings." What would have been a seventy-five-dollar service call becomes one hundred thousand dollars in legal fees.

Boundaries also can shield us from having to witness an ex's infuriating personal growth. "Here's a story that drives people nuts," said clinical psychologist Barry McCarthy, a certified sex and marital therapist in Washington, DC. "The person gets divorced, and in the next marriage he becomes a better person. One spouse always wanted the other to go to Broadway plays, and in the second marriage, he does it. It's just easy to look at that and say, 'What's wrong with me? Why couldn't I inspire that behavior?'" Distance can protect you from self-critical comparison; meanwhile, his growth may contribute to a calmer, more considerate interaction.

One physical boundary that would seem obvious but isn't necessarily? Sex. As in, with your ex. "The best estimate is that about one-third of folks have sex with each other after they get divorced," said

McCarthy. "This is bad science, but that's our best estimate. That usually fuels the fire of the bad divorce. In good divorces, people stay out of each other's dramas, emotional issues, and sexual issues."

I can think of many reasons to have sex with an ex, such as, just because you can't be married doesn't mean he isn't cute. Also, the illicit nature of sleeping with an ex can reignite an old attraction. Plus, everyone knows sex releases endorphins; who among the recently divorced couldn't use a trip to the all-you-need endorphin buffet? Isn't sex with your ex better than having random encounters with strangers, or diving into another wrong relationship because you crave intimacy?

"When I talk about a good divorce, I mean that the emotion that most governs the couple is acceptance and sadness. Conviction that this is the best decision, and sadness that this didn't work," said McCarthy. "Then they focus only on being good co-parents, and stay out of each other's lives. Does having sex allow you to move on with your lives relationally, emotionally, and sexually? Or does it keep you in that limbo phase?"

I'll raise my hand for that one, Professor: "Limbo phase!"

COURTING A COOLER HEART

After winding up in the emergency room for a crisis I believed was tied to anxiety and over-closeness, I made a list of twenty-three actions, divided into five categories, that I could take to create more distance. Among these were:

1. Crash at a friend's place in the city Friday nights to avoid spending Saturday mornings hanging out with my ex while he plays with our son at my house, where all the toys still live.
2. Remove my American Express card from our shared online budgeting program so I can use it to subscribe to a dating site without worrying about his judgment or hurt feelings.

I didn't actually implement these changes—at least not at first. But I *thought* about them, which felt like a giant step.

The bigger trial for me was gaining emotional distance. While openness is key to a good marriage, divorce calls for being closed in new ways. Adequate space requires a non-porousness, an ability to remain considerate of your ex without absorbing his problems or values as your own. Some people so thoroughly vilify a former spouse that they're never plagued with concern for his well-being, but those of us who like our exes must still prioritize *our own needs*, which can be a difficult shift.

I needed more of a "shields up!" attitude. I could envision two gun-metal sides unfolding, accordion-style, around me, like high-tech armor in a space-age Armageddon flick. I needed to build a shell around myself, to exist *not* in relation to him.

Many people need a barrier between themselves and their former partner's negative judgments, to be released from a damaging self-image that was cultured in the medium of bad marriage. "It's hard to get their words out of your head. I see this all the time with clients," said my divorce coach, Amy. "If I'm not paying attention, even I can slip into judging myself according to my ex-husband's point of view, and we've been divorced for nearly ten years. It's very easy to do."

A new partner serves as a formidable boundary, but we don't all fall in love immediately after leaving a marriage. Nor do we want to choose the wrong person merely to stand as a wall between us and our ex.

One approach to erecting internal boundaries? Actively remember the bad times. This approach works only in the short term; the goal of divorce is not anger but something more like benign disinterest.

If, like me, you lack both anger and the will to impose more distance merely because you know you *should*, you can try another tack—re-volumize yourself. Squeeze your ex into the margins of your life by taking up more space yourself. Let your own interests and pursuits balloon ever larger. Crowd her out of your internal room by filling it up with you.

My son came home from kindergarten one day and showed me the "personal bubble" he'd learned about in school. We each have an invisible bubble of air around us that others should not puncture with their hands or feet, apparently. While I couldn't make myself tell my ex not to come over when, in fact, I wanted the company, I could build a bigger bubble. I could start by reconnecting with friends and family, and reinvesting myself in activities I loved. I could go back to school, take a new dance class, take on more work, even stroll the malls as I'd once done for fun, back before my husband's disdain of recreational shopping sapped the joy. The more you can reclaim your strengths and quirks, the more your own essential existence will create a boundary for you.

It can be hard, admittedly, to identify your passions and tastes, coming out of a long marriage. You're trying to construct an updated version of your pre-married self, the person you were before you spent so much time merging your life with someone else's. You're older. You may have children now. Your children may have grown and left the house. My mother attempted bridge, mah-jongg, and volunteering in the courts. None of these hobbies stuck; she didn't know what she liked to do, nearing seventy, her kids all grown, after spending thirty-five years accommodating the preferences of a spouse.

I found myself unable to choose a car when our old, shared one died, unsure what make or model suited the new me. Was I a mom who needed a minivan? A sporty single who should zip around in a coupe? While married, I'd driven a hatchback Subaru that my husband had bought from his dad. We'd needed four-wheel drive because we had a house in the country with a steep dirt road. Our car made a statement. It said, "We may look like effete urbanites, but in our other lives, we're hardy adventurers."

I finally decided to lease a compact Hyundai. Which said what? "Budget is job one!" Or, "I care about the environment but not enough to buy a Prius." Or actually, "I am too distracted by my own life to pay attention to what kind of stupid car I drive."

As with making new friends, finding new interests may take time. But every failed attempt is still one big exhale, helping in the attempt to re-volumize yourself.

HOLD THE LINE, UNILATERALLY

If you want the divorce and your ex doesn't? You may need to hold the line for both of you. Roald, a fifty-something aviation entrepreneur originally from Norway, met his first wife while in college in Wisconsin. They married in 1983, had three children, then separated in 1990. "She didn't want the relationship to end, and I did. It was up to me to uphold that, to be very consistent," he said. "I felt I had to be almost brutal in my honesty that we'll never get back together. I'd see other divorced parents who would give each other a hug or kiss. I was very careful not to do that, because you can say whatever you want, but if your actions can be interpreted differently, that is what she's going to look at."

Roald also limited conversation to parenting issues. "If she tried to ask, 'How is your mom?' or 'How are you doing?' I would not engage. In our phone calls, I was short. At one point, one of my kids said, 'You're rude to Mom.' I said, 'No. I'm to the point.' I was upset about it, but I tried to explain it from my perspective without explaining the reason. This was only for the first year, or maybe two. Then she moved on."

For Roald, maintaining distance in the beginning allowed a friendship to develop later. "She came back a few years later and thanked me for making it very clear there was no hope, so she could move on with her life. Now we're great friends. We have Thanksgiving together. She gets along great with my girlfriend. When we see each other, I give her a hug. Now it's natural to do that. She's my kids' mother, a family member."

If you're hoping to reunite, it may seem as if your ex is sending you mixed messages. She's flirtatious, then remote. Then warm again. This can feel like inconsideration or manipulation, but it may be a sign that she is struggling. She doesn't know how to be unmarried to you.

Some people fail to set limits because they're compensating for past mistakes. "My parents' divorce was epically awful, everything you're never supposed to do," said Theresa, a separated mother of one who runs a restaurant on a small island off the coast of Maine. "My parents wouldn't talk. Couldn't talk. When they talked, they argued. His parents, the same thing. We said, 'We're not going to do it like that.

We've screwed up enough. We are going to try to do this in a way that is good for our daughter.' By and large, we have done that for her. We just haven't done it very well for ourselves."

Three years into their separation, Theresa and her ex still haven't established a clear child-support amount or visitation schedule, sought legal advice—or even changed the dynamic that drove them apart. He moved a few hours away with his new girlfriend, but continues to call and complain about his financial struggles. "I said to him, 'You have to send me a little money every month toward her food and clothing and shelter.' He says he wants to. I believe he means he wants to. But he tells me about the other struggles and pressures he has, and how he hopes he can get to it," said Theresa, admitting that knowledge of his problems makes her feel too guilty to insist he contribute his share. "I don't want to be his mom or his boss. It's how we did it in the marriage. Everyone says you have the same relationship in divorce that you have in marriage. We've certainly proven that to be true."

Talking to Theresa made me sad, hearing how much the effort to protect her daughter from an ugly divorce was prolonging instability and financial uncertainty. But the negative dynamic of marriage need *not* dictate the tone of the divorce. Divorce is an entirely new relationship. Your old interactions do not have to carry over like frequent-flier miles from your former fights. You can change the terms, even if you have to rewrite them largely on your own.

IS THIS A DIVORCE OR A MARRIAGE SABBATICAL?

About two and a half years after my husband moved out, I got a note from Anne in Colorado, the self-proclaimed "happiest divorced woman on the planet." "Jay and I are currently discussing the possibility of getting back together, but living apart," she wrote. "I got a wake-up call when he started dating some *bee-otch* who was very clear that our relationship wasn't okay with her. Plus, after dating for four years, it is starting to seem totally impossible to meet a 'one' that's better than him, flaws and all."

Sometimes when I'd hear a story like this, I'd think, *Could that be us?* I was different than I'd been. I'd continued to work, if not on my marriage, on who I was in marriage, in *that* marriage in particular. I went on dates, but slept with no one. My heart wasn't in it. I was unilaterally still engaged in a trial separation.

My husband was doing nothing of the sort. He was never going back to our marriage, one in which he felt like the Designated Disappointing Spouse. But I still considered it. *What if it was all my problem, and now that I've changed, our marriage could work?*

Many people I spoke to admitted that, for a while, one person was still asking that age-old question, "Can this marriage be saved?" For some couples, a positive separation does lead to calling the whole (divorce) thing off. I met several people who had recommitted post-separation or even post-divorce. This possibility is another argument for parting kindly: if there's any chance your marriage could be saved, taking a respectful break may allow it to surface.

Boundaries provide a chance to regain your own confidence and equanimity, and then to assess your relationship from that calm internal state. They also give you time to become a person your spouse might desire to see.

Sometimes *relaxing* a boundary can show you if things have really changed. We're all susceptible to the allure of the "off-limits." Feeling that you're not allowed to spend any time together can make you want it more. If you're seriously questioning your split, loosening the chokehold of total separation can ease the urgency, and let you clarify your feelings. Don't go on a date (or a sex date), but propose a casual afternoon bike ride, or meet for coffee. Doing an activity you once enjoyed may provide the confirmation you need—whether that means realizing that you do want to try again or remembering why you left.

There's a lot of support out there for recommitment, if you do want to try that route. Indiana-based social worker MJ Murray Vachon said she helps people notice how much the stress of work, family, and personal commitments contribute to marital strife. "In the past, people would fight over gender issues. Today, it's about being too busy. Most people are overcommitted time-wise and financially. They're really mean to each other because of these over-commitments. I have them write down on three-by-five cards all their activities, everything they're trying to do. When they see that, they're shocked. They say, 'No wonder we're fighting.'" Ratcheting back other obligations helps some salvage their initial love.

William Doherty, author of *Take Back Your Marriage: Sticking Together in a World That Pulls Us Apart*, believes divorce can be caused by unrealistic expectations of romance, and a consumerist attitude. He worries that our instant-gratification, consumer culture convinces people they should upgrade spouses, too, swap out an old one for a better model coming down the line. If we can accept a partner's flaws and our own, he writes, we can avoid exchanging a perfectly decent spouse for the ever-alluring notion of a new one.

I'd certainly manifested some of the intolerance Doherty cites. But when I stopped, our incompatibilities persisted. Our problems were not the result of a consumerist quest for The Ideal Husband: Version II. Nor did my second thoughts derive from a resounding sense of the rightness of our union. They came from how much I missed being married, and disliked being single. They also stemmed from a deep amnesia regarding my own recent past. With each month that I felt better, post-separation, my memory of how bad we'd been together faded. I could not have been that person so deeply troubled by her own marriage. Who was that person? That wasn't me. I simply stopped believing my own dozen years of experience.

This is a common psychological reaction; we tend to recolor our story with the brightest crayons in the box. Research on memory shows that we have a "positivity bias," a tendency to remember the good times and let the bad fade away, in part because this helps us maintain our self-image.

Like me, many people are not pursuing a materialistic dream of a better life with someone else. Instead, they're entertaining airbrushed fantasies about what they once had. The technology activist in Washington, DC, Alex, spoke so highly of his ex-wife that I had to ask if he'd hoped to reunite. "No," he said. "I mean, there's the fantastic element—in an alternate universe, were she a different person than she actually is, would I want to get back together? And then you bring yourself back to this reality, and you're like, 'Oh no. Definitely not.' I think that's more like daydreaming. If you really sit down and think, 'So here's the reasons why things didn't work. Have those things changed?' Usually the answer is no. You're just looking at an alternative that seems bleaker, or you're having a bad day."

Those of us with questioning natures or a heady faith in the power of self-improvement may always wonder if there could have been *some way* to make the marriage work. "You look back on it later, and you can't be completely sure it had to end," said a happily remarried father of two in California. "Of course, you're looking at that from the perspective of who you are now, in your new marriage, given all the ways you've changed. There's no control group. No way to see if you would have changed in the marriage, and if those changes would have made it work."

• • •

My parents did get a chance to see if they could live happily together, both of them remade by divorce, perhaps improved with the years. After our Labor Day reunion, their trip to Mexico, and our first all-family Thanksgiving in Austin, they decided to take another trip together. This time, they met near Tampa to visit my father's sister, Lois, whom my mother hadn't seen in years.

The trip turned out to be a great reunion opportunity for the two *women*, who had grown distant after my parents' divorce. On a day trip to St. Petersburg, my mother and aunt strolled the Dalí Museum together, reminiscing. "I always liked Lois," my mom said. "I admired her when I was in high school. She had this super-cool husband, and an apartment. As a teenager, I just thought her life was the most ideal thing in the world. She didn't know I felt that way. It was very nice to be able to compliment someone, to be completely honest, and have that make them feel good."

The parental reunification fantasy I harbored? That didn't go quite as smoothly. The problem seemed to be, well, *reality*. Such as politics. My mother has remained a left-leaning liberal; my father has grown increasingly right-aligned. Becoming Facebook friends shoved this stark divide into the light. They had to agree not to discuss political issues. Their opinions also diverged when it came to child-rearing and grand-parenting.

There was even some friction around travel. My mother wanted to consult an old-fashioned paper map and her own sense of direction; my dad preferred to rely on his voice-activated GPS. The discrepancy between the routes these alternate methods suggested created conflict.

These are all minor differences, maybe. But while the specific disagreements between them were new, they also seemed to represent a maturation of personal characteristics that had driven them apart in the first place. They'd gotten divorced for real reasons.

Of course, every married couple has incompatibilities. Were theirs the kind that could be easily tolerated, even humored, with age? I wasn't sure.

COMMIT TO THE *NOW*

One Sunday, at the end of my second single summer, my former spouse and I were sitting at the table on the back deck of my town house. Our son was between us, giggling, just plain glad to have his two parents together. He looked warm and soft, flanked like the filling between two slices of bread.

Twilight was falling. A candle flickered in a glass jar on the table; yellow Gerber daisies sprang from a vase. We were having dinner. I looked at this life we'd built together and not enjoyed. I was finally enjoying it. *Did I make a mistake ending this marriage?* I wondered one more time.

No, I had to say. *No*. There is no way I could have gotten here from there. I'd felt constantly at error in my marriage, running a marathon in the wrong direction, applying myself to the wrong task. If we'd stayed married, I wouldn't have felt that pang of sadness as my son described a tunnel he wanted to dig between my home and his father's so our dog could traverse at will. I wouldn't have had to worry about how new partners might change our co-parenting routine or affect our child. But since we'd split, I hadn't felt like I'd made one mistake. Not really. I'd been erratic, emotional, mad at friends, and crazed by my ex-husband's new relationship. But I hadn't taken any steps that felt against my own inner truth.

I thought about my friend George who'd lived in Jerusalem as a young father, with his then-wife. After a dozen years, the city changed for him. He couldn't find work, wouldn't commit to life in Israel any longer. He moved his family back to the U.S. But he remained enamored of that old dream of life on the Mediterranean. "Part of me will always be nostalgic for Israel," he'd said to me, years ago.

That phrase stuck with me. Part of me will always be nostalgic for my marriage that didn't work. For the sweet, Hudson River–bred, Joni Mitchell–listening sureness of my first husband. The fantasy we strove for, and even aspects of the reality we made.

What do we do with old dreams that still move us, even after we've left them behind? One thing we can try is to train our wistfulness on today. We can develop a pre-nostalgia for the present, a more active reverence for what's before us now. Because we know that it may not remain forever—at least not precisely in this form.

CHAPTER EIGHT

Don't Buy Your Lawyer a Country House

Making It Legal

New legal options such as mediation, collaborative divorce, and an assisted DIY approach move divorce beyond the old adversarial model. Today, the legal process itself can help you transition from a bad marriage into a positive postdivorce partnership.

He who fights with monsters should look to it that he himself does not become a monster. And when you gaze long into an abyss the abyss also gazes into you.

—Friedrich Nietzsche, nineteenth-century
German philosopher

Nearly three years after we separated, we were finally ready to file. I'd read so much about divorce by then, I figured we could manage the legal details ourselves. New technology makes it easy for all of us to log on and learn our state's laws without hiring a lawyer, or even leaving the house. You can find child- and spousal-support guidelines online, download reams of advice from law firms, and get emotional support from bloggers with names like The Divorce Diva. County courts have changed, too, increasingly offering staffed self-help centers to guide you through the process.

My still-husband offered to find an online processing company and do the paperwork. We planned to file the minimum amount necessary with the court and also create our own, more detailed private plan to serve as a blueprint for our intentions as co-parents. I was excited about this second part, sitting down and talking about our goals for our son, such as where he might go to camp and, later, college. I liked the idea of imaging our futures and establishing clear direction.

But first, we needed to formally divorce. A month passed and my almost-ex hadn't finished the forms. I'd developed the superstition that finding my next partner hinged upon being officially "single." After all that waiting, now I wanted to hurry up and divorce. My mom, who had gone to law school in her fifties and was well-versed in legal jargon, was visiting for Valentine's Day. I posited her trip as a deadline. Could he forward what he'd done, so she could clarify any legalese?

I printed out pages and pages of forms. My all-but-ex had made half a dozen mistakes, many of which I decided to take personally. He was planning to come over that night after our son went to bed to finalize the paperwork. I went out to pick up a pizza and called him as I walked. "There are a lot of errors here," I said. "It hurts my feelings that you seem to think we were only married for four years."

He laughed. "I realize that I wrote in my birthday instead of our marriage date. I somehow got the days confused."

"Well, there were other errors." He'd misstated both our incomes and how many nights our son slept at his place in a way that made him look like the hardworking, long-suffering giver, and me the layabout, deadweight spouse. I listed these gaffes. Then, since I was worked up anyway, I went ahead and reminded him of half a dozen other insensitive comments he'd made over the past few years, my voice rising with each rehash.

"I think you are overreacting to some typos," he said.

I stopped and took a breath. He was right. Or, if his sloppiness did reflect a persistently critical view of me and a minimizing of the significance of our union, well . . . those were reasons we were divorcing.

I remembered speaking to a newspaper editor who'd been separated for ten years. "We're finally filing, and I cannot believe how much stuff this is bringing up," she'd told me over the phone, whispering from her office cubicle. "I am so angry at him and we haven't fought in years. What is this about?"

It's about the reality of it, maybe. Or the disappointment, now documented permanently in court. Or the fact that legal forms force you to corral your life into little "either/or" boxes that diminish your very existence.

Before no-fault divorce, you had little choice about the *how* of your divorce—you had to mount a case against your spouse, testifying about his evildoing before witnesses, in court. The process itself created antagonism. Focusing on the negative magnifies it, trapping you in anger-inciting recrimination. Highlighting the negatives of your marriage while ignoring the positives—a type of distorted thinking essentially mandated by court before no-fault—can lead to depression, hostility, and aggression.

Many people still believe they need to prove their spouse is at fault, but no-fault law doesn't require this. Nor will accusing your ex of bad behavior get you more money in most cases. Under no-fault, acceptable grounds for divorce include "irreconcilable differences," or "irreparable breakdown of the marriage," depending on the wording in your state. No-fault law positions divorce more as a reorganization of family than as a punishment for a crime. It's almost like a relationship bankruptcy—the marriage has gone bankrupt and the family needs to be restructured. In about half the states, you still *can* seek a fault-based divorce. But the vast majority of divorces today are no-fault.

Still, as I saw, even without the law pillorying your marriage, your spouse, and your choices, making it legal can stir up long-buried emotions. Fortunately, new forms of "alternative dispute resolution" have evolved that can help protect us from the old-style divorce and our own worst impulses.

Mediation and collaborative divorce are the most widely available forms of cooperative un-marrying today, examples of the trend in family law away from an adversarial model toward a kinder, gentler problem-solving approach. For those of us intent on doing it ourselves, a DIY divorce is easier and more realistic now than even five years ago. It's like the IKEA version of dissolving your marriage: you can get a great divorce for a fraction of the usual price, but you have to build it yourself. Some reformers are working to move uncontested divorce out of court; I visited the utopia of out-of-court divorce—the Resource Center for Separating and Divorcing Families at the University of Denver—a model of the kind of support I hope we'll soon see in every state.

THE RISE OF MEDIATION: SAVE MONEY, BE HAPPY

Mediation has been around for thousands of years. Think of an elder sitting cross-legged before two fighting villagers and helping them reach resolution. In family law, mediation really took off after the passage of no-fault divorce. "The way that divorce was being done was a disaster. People were getting torn up," said Sam Margulies, one of the first lawyers to switch to mediation full-time. He's mediated more than four thousand divorces since 1980. "A bunch of us started thinking, 'Wait a minute. There's got to be a better way.'"

In divorce, a mediator is a neutral third party, often a lawyer or therapist who has taken mediation training and will help you decide and divide, *together*. In private divorce mediation (as distinct from court-sponsored mediation), your mediator spends about one full workday, often spread out over a few sessions, helping you talk through your concerns, resolve conflicts, and hammer out details. Your mediator can write up your agreement into a "memorandum of understanding." If she's not a lawyer, you can then hire one to vet your agreement before you sign it.

In mediation, you talk to each other, rather than paying a lawyer to draft a letter or make a phone call in your stead. "With a lawyer, a client is passive. A mediator is a coach," said Margulies. "You say, 'Fred, explain to me how calling her a bitch is going to lead to her cooperating better?'" The process lets you establish a new, improved communication style and recast your roles; you're no longer angry spouses but rather two people developing a professional partnership, perhaps "parental co-workers" dedicated to raising healthy children.

Couples like mediation because of its high success rate and low sticker price. "I take a divorce that would cost fifty thousand dollars in legal fees and I resolve it in eight hours and charge two thousand bucks. When I'm done, I feel like I've done something good for people. I've helped them design a system that will work," said Margulies.

Mediated agreements tend to last, whereas those concocted in a poisonous cloud of seething resentment can look unfair or downright crazy when that fog lifts. In one twelve-year study, couples who took part in mediation settled their disputes in half the time of those who used litigation. They were more likely to consult with each other after the divorce about child-rearing, and were generally happier in their new, unmarried state. Divorced couples and professionals I spoke to corroborated these findings.

"In the traditional approach, a lawyer is trained to play the game, to argue and get the best outcomes," said former "pit bull" lawyer Regina

DeMeo, "but what one person may see as the best outcome is not best for others. Scorched earth is not in the family's interest."

When it comes to cost, divorce flips that old axiom on its head: the more you spend, the less you get.

I sat in on a mediation session in Denver that stood out as a stellar example of how mediation can lead to better agreements. The mood in the conference room was relaxed, though serious. The mediator, Colorado "Super Lawyer" Beth Henson, had a calm, reassuring attitude and was dressed casually in a crocheted sweater-vest and leather boots. The clients, a divorcing couple with four children, sat side by side at the large table. The wife, Jane, had her laptop open, her hair pulled back. She looked ready to remodel the house. Her husband looked sad; she, determined.

They were working on their parenting plan. Roberto, a firefighter, was worried about money. He'd previously requested more overnights with the kids, motivated, it turned out, by his desire to reduce the amount of child support he paid. His lifestyle didn't actually accommodate half-time residential parenting. In the traditional adversarial model, he might have continued pushing for it anyway, hoping to "bargain down" Jane into accepting less money. Even if he'd won, the tactic would easily have created lasting resentment and a cockamamie parenting plan that worked for no one.

Here, with help from the mediator, both parents decided that Roberto's desire to reduce his child support was not a good reason to create a harried, unrealistic schedule for the kids. Jane leaned forward and told the mediator that they both wanted Roberto to pay less child support than the state's mandated amount. They'd come up with the solution of having him offer more "in-kind" support, such as picking up the kids after school and making them dinner. This plan felt fair to both, protected Roberto from economic duress, and allowed him to see his children more frequently during the daytime than he otherwise would have.

I found this whole exchange heartening, both of them recognizing that a fair and logical plan was more important than "winning" a battle against the other.

Jane was worrying about expenses, too. The kids' birthday parties, haircuts, homecoming attire—it added up and constantly changed. How would they divide these costs? Henson suggested using catchall language, establishing an amount each would pay for "incidentals," rather than trying to anticipate the ever-evolving social and recreational wants of growing children. She also presented her "Own Time/Own Dime" mantra. When you make a unilateral decision to enroll a child in a class or take her out for a special dinner on your time, you pick up the tab.

Throughout the session, Henson flagged potential areas of future friction and pushed for specificity. In my own life, I've tended to keep financial matters fuzzy, maybe on the theory that this will make them warm? Here, the attention to detail felt reassuring. These adults would know exactly how much money they had, and what they could expect to spend.

The mediation format can make you want to prove just how calm and rational you can be. It evokes your higher self. Mediation is like couples counseling with a spreadsheet. Or self-affirmation theory in action; you affirm your values as you formalize details. "Yes, I do want my children to go to college, but no, I don't want to be obligated to pay for a college that costs as much as Stanford."

One caveat: Mediation requires a basic level of honesty, openness, and sanity on the part of both spouses. If you married a bully and cannot stand up for yourself in the relationship, if your spouse is abusive, hiding assets, mentally ill, or genuinely unable to consider differing opinions, you probably need a strong lawyer to advocate for you. Not a "shark," but someone able to handle a shark.

Still, it may be worth trying mediation first. The chef and mother of one I spoke to who'd moved in with her parents after divorce, Carly, was ending a marriage to a recovering alcoholic whose anger had turned to bullying. They wanted to try mediation, but had trouble even agreeing on a person to hire. They wound up working with two mediators simultaneously—a man he knew and trusted through AA, and a woman.

The team approach worked. "They were amazing. They read us like a book," said Carly. "When he'd kick into his bullying, the man would recognize it before it even started. He knew how to defuse it.

Destination Divorce

The most creative and luxurious approach to mediation may be DivorceHotel, a Dutch company offering three-day mediation "vacations" at hotels in the Netherlands and a historic inn in upstate New York. The company aims to remove couples from the negative, divisive input of well-meaning friends and family, and let them work with a skilled mediator in a serene setting. "Everyone is advising you because they love you and want the best for you, but they're blind to the fact that they're not impartial," said Jim Halfens, DivorceHotel CEO. So far, the DivorceHotel concept is getting rave reviews from couples, and the company is expanding, seeking to offer destination mediation in more locations.

Sometimes he'd say, 'Hey, let's take a minute. Why don't you show me a picture of your daughter, because that's why we're here?' That softened me, too, because we'd made her together."

Carly said the process was exhausting, partly because it pushed her toward personal growth. "A lot of times, you're sitting there, going back and forth, and you're like, 'I can't do this anymore.' The female mediator would step in. She'd say, 'This is your time. Are you sure you can support yourself on that amount of money? You have to put your foot down, and say what you want without being afraid.' It was a really big emotional process for me, realizing that I had to step up for what I needed and wanted."

I've heard stories of mediation gone awry. As with all professionals, the skill and experience varies, and mediation training and credentialing are inconsistent. Interview a potential mediator before hiring her, and make sure you trust her intelligence and approach.

There's also court-mandated mediation, part of a nationwide effort to improve outcomes in divorce court by encouraging people to find their own solutions. But ideally you mediate first, rather than being sent to a mediator by a judge after communication has collapsed in court.

COLLABORATIVE DIVORCE

Say you love the idea of a cooperative divorce, but really want a lawyer on your side? In the even newer form of alternative dispute resolution, "collaborative divorce," you each hire your own attorney, but they've each signed a contract to work out the details without resorting to court. If they can't help you come to a settlement without a lawsuit, you're still free to try going to court, but they have to give up the case.

Minnesota-based family lawyer Stuart Webb created the core idea of collaborative law in the 1980s. After practicing law for about fifteen years, he decided he would no longer go to court for his clients. He'd rather step aside and let them hire a different attorney than engage in the war that divorce court can become.

Webb's refusal to usher a divorcing family into the courtroom evolved into the idea of lawyers signing contracts to resolve the case out of court. This might sound like a trivial detail, but it profoundly changed the legal process. Without the specter of court looming, divorcing couples could speak honestly and openly about their real fears without worrying that their words would be used against them later.

Bay Area–based family lawyer Pauline Tesler heard Webb speak, and described it as a "lightbulb" moment. "What I realized was, out of that could come an entirely new concept of what a lawyer is for, and what it means to take on the responsibility of helping a family to restructure," she said.

Working with several Bay Area psychologists, Tesler helped merge the collaborative law model with other services, creating the interdisciplinary team approach that characterizes it today. A collaborative lawyer will help connect you to other experts you may need, such as a therapist for yourself or your spouse, a psychologist for a struggling child, perhaps a financial consultant. You all work together to solve real problems and create a mutually beneficial plan.

Tesler can talk for forty minutes straight about collaborative divorce, seemingly without taking a breath—that's how passionate she is about protecting families from adversarial divorce proceedings.

"We are taught in school to be a lawyer in ways that run contrary to human biology, to what it's like to be in conflict, what's required to resolve it," she said. "Decision making is fundamentally an emotion-driven process."

Many family lawyers aim to take a friendly, problem-solving approach without calling themselves collaborative counselors. If you have a lawyer you like, you can ask if she'll engage in the collaborative process. Going one step further by having both lawyers sign a "collaborative law participation agreement" helps to smooth communication, keep the focus on constructive conversation, and assure each lawyer that the other is committed to resolution.

Collaborative divorce can be a good choice if you have complicated finances, businesses, children, and houses, or emotional land mines just under the surface, not yet defused. You'll be shelling out money for a small team of professionals charging the going rate in your city, but this costs less than an ongoing court battle. As with mediation, you may come out with new skills, a better relationship, and an agreement that is far more likely to stick.

Collaborative divorce is a great shield to hold up in front of family or friends who insist that you "lawyer up" and "fight for what you deserve." The language of "just deserts" captivates, but it can send a decent divorce careening out of control. Collaborative divorce reassures everyone that yes, you have a strong lawyer on your side. *Your* side just happens to be your spouse's side, as well.

As with mediation, the cooperative nature of collaborative divorce requires participation and a will to move past negative emotions. Not everyone can do it. Collaborative divorce also carries the risk of failure; if you can't reach agreement without going to court, you'll have to find new lawyers. But, as Tesler pointed out, failure is uncommon, and if you wind up in court, the work you've done solving problems may make the process go more smoothly.

You and your spouse may be far more capable of collaborating than you think. "I've been incredibly inspired by clients around my table, in mediation and collaborative counsel," said lawyer and mediator

What's So Bad about Going to Court, Anyway?

All divorces must be *filed* in court—formally approved and registered. But this is a question of paperwork, not a request for a judge to resolve a fight. The court is a critical part of our democracy and it plays a crucial role in dire situations. It is the place where the weak or disenfranchised go to seek justice. The court is there to provide protection if your spouse is abusive, you lack money for legal aid, or you need a restraining order.

Using the court to vent rage, however, is a different matter. It may sound appealing, the notion that an Official Smart Person will decide what's best—presumably in your favor—making your spouse pay literally and figuratively for all your unhappiness. But the court can be exactly the wrong place to go in divorce.

Filing lawsuits against a decent ex can take over your life like an invasive plant species. What starts as a small introduction of a judicial authority takes root, spreads shoots like giant hogweed, tunneling under and cracking your foundation. You now find yourself with an alcoholic, court-appointed guardian accompanying you to parties with your children and making lewd comments to coworkers, as happened to a friend of mine whose wife continued suing him three years after their divorce was finalized. She meant no harm, but she unwittingly established a precedent of treating their relationship as a "case," their children collateral damage in the war she'd waged.

The court can harden bad feelings into hate. "The courtroom makes you want to punch your way out of it, not talk your way out of it," said Robert Hyatt, Denver's former district court chief justice.

With so many courts understaffed today, even the best-intentioned judges can't always adequately prepare. "You wind up saying to yourself, 'Is this the one where they waived spousal maintenance or where they didn't?'" said Judge Hyatt. This inundated judge will now decide when your children should spend time with you, where your transition location will be, or even whether you're fit to be a parent. Why not just ask any random shopper in line at Walgreens? She might have more time to consider the details.

Using the court to collect back child support carries other risks. In many states, the noncustodial parent can be incarcerated for contempt of court if he falls behind on child support, *even if the lag is due to unemployment*. If you turn to the court to collect rather than attempt to work out a plan yourselves, your former spouse could wind up behind bars. He now has no ability to help you. Your kids, meanwhile, are living with the psychological burden of having one parent in jail, sent there in part by the other.

If you're seeking government assistance, the law can force you to pursue child support from your co-parent, even if you have reasons not to. Legal scholars around the country are working to help those divorcing avoid this de facto debtor's prison and to find ways to help poor parents gain employment rather than jail time. But even in families where there is enough money to go around, threatening to use the court to collect can destroy a decent divorce.

I met a highly educated, successful father who fully believed that his equally high-functioning former wife wanted him incarcerated because she'd turned to the court to collect back child support. She wanted his financial help, it seemed to me. But by using the court instead of, say, the telephone, she'd helped push their relationship into bitter enmity—which the kids had to deal with a decade after the divorce.

It's up to us to use discretion, and to resort to the court only as a last resort.

Forrest Mosten. "It takes a lot of courage to sit around this table. I've watched most people be the very best they can be."

THE DIY DIVORCE

We were determined to have a DIY divorce. I liked the idea of saving money on legal fees, and I loved the suggestion that here was one more life passage calling for arts and crafts.

I would run down to the bookstore and pick up a copy of *The Crafter's Guide to the Good Divorce*. It would be a spiral-bound book, I imagined, with step-by-step, illustrated instructions for personalizing the process. There would be tips, such as: "How to print your own legal forms on hand-made paper of birch bark and string!" Or, "Letterpress 'Just Divorced!' announcement cards to send to friends!" Or, "Wire-wrap your own 'Forever Family' divorce rings!" I would make divorce rings for all three of us, using occluded diamonds to represent, I don't know, the imperfection of all love. My ex-husband and son would lose theirs in the back of the closet, but I'd wear mine. I'd show it off at our divorce party, where I'd serve my very own craft cocktail—a tart, fizzy potion called "Love on the Rocks."

You *can* do a DIY divorce without reaching for a glue stick and glitter. The New Jersey hairdresser, Carmen, looked up child support tables on NJChildSupport.org; she entered "two children," the percentage of time each parent would have them, and their gross taxable weekly income. Her husband was working as an exterminator at the time, while she stayed home with the girls. The computer crunched the numbers and displayed a child-support amount, to which her husband agreed.

They didn't file at first, but rather began living in accordance with these guidelines, in separate homes. Then her husband got drunk and belligerent one night and shoved her laptop while she was holding it against her chest. Her father urged her to go to the courthouse for a restraining order. While there, she sought legal advice about the divorce. "I kind of asked the people what would be the best thing to do. They said I should file our child support agreement, because if I didn't, and he stopped paying, there was nothing I could do."

Carmen filed the support agreement in court, an important legal step for co-parents to take. You want your agreement on file *in case* you need official intervention later. Not that you'll pursue it. Carmen's husband did lose his job at one point, and stopped paying. But she'd started working again by then, and didn't threaten a suit. "I just thought, 'What would be the point?' It's not like he had the money and wasn't paying it. How is that going to help my girls to take him to court?" This restraint preserved and maybe improved their relationship. When he found a new job, he began paying his child support again.

I was impressed with Carmen's "cognitive richness," an intellectual or emotional abundance that I've seen again and again when talking to people in decent divorces. It's an inner wealth that enables a person to take a broad, humanistic view of temporal frustrations rather than react aggressively to them. It's also an asset we all can work to build.

Later, when Carmen became involved with a serious new boyfriend, he encouraged her to finalize the divorce, and he helped with the process. She filled out the paperwork at the courthouse. Her ex signed it. Total cost of this divorce, including filing fees? "Between three hundred and four hundred dollars."

The DIY divorce was feasible for Carmen, in part because she and her husband had no complicated financial entanglements or assets to divide. But even with substantial holdings, you may be able to do much of it yourself.

After twenty-two years of marriage, a dental professional in New York, Adam, found himself facing divorce. He fought for the marriage, but it soon became clear that his wife was determined to end it.

While married, he and his marketing entrepreneur wife had amassed two homes, stocks, bonds, and savings. They looked up the value of their investments and agreed on a fair market value for their New York apartment and their vacation property in Florida. Then they divided everything into two piles and flipped a coin.

"We knew the law. In New York, everything is split, unless there are extenuating circumstances," said Adam. "You wind up paying forty thousand dollars to a lawyer, and that comes out of your money. But it wasn't really about the forty thousand dollars. It was trying to say, 'Okay, the decision is made. Let's do it efficiently and effectively.'"

Adam won the coin toss. He chose Pile A, which had the New York apartment. They traded each other for other items, then hired a lawyer to draw up the contract, a discrete legal service that cost $1,500. "I grew up in a military family," said Adam. "You focus on the goal, on getting it done. No one was trying to hurt anyone. It's about being able to close the door and move forward. Look to the future, not the past."

Family lawyers increasingly offer guidance on an hourly basis, such as drawing up a contract, as in Adam's case. You also can hire a lawyer to give legal advice, conduct research, negotiate a specific issue, or represent you in court for a single hearing. These "unbundled" services are important because, as divorce laws have gotten fairer, they've also grown more complex, particularly if you own homes and businesses. "I get a lot of people who come for a one-hour consultation and an explanation of the law and process," said attorney Regina DeMeo. "I let them vent for thirty minutes about their situation, and then I say, 'I'm going to make it very simple,' and I break it down. They give me a hug at the end and say, 'Oh my God, I was so scared. You really helped me.'"

My husband and I didn't start out with a lawyer-by-the-hour, but it became clear that we probably should have. I corrected the facts he'd misstated on our forms, and together we brought them to the courthouse. We had the details right, but the forms were wrong; the online service had sold us a few outdated items. Also, we'd neglected to *staple* the sheets together, the clerk barked at us, and to use the correct two-hole punch along the top. We'd have to get the right forms from the court, school ourselves on the precise assembling method, and begin again.

This is exactly what happens to people who don't hire help, said Petra Castillo, a paralegal and notary at The Document People in Los Angeles. The Document People is a group of drop-in, storefront processing centers staffed by paralegals or Legal Document Assistants—people who have been trained in asking questions and filling out forms. The storefront divorce is another option between hiring a lawyer and doing it all alone.

I'd seen these drop-in divorce shops in Manhattan, depressing hole-in-the-wall places, usually under scaffolding, that looked like the end of the line for a marriage begun in a hotel-room-by-the-hour. But Petra's office in L.A. was on a street lined with palm trees, across from a Whole Foods. How unsavory could it be? A sign in the window read: "Divorce: $399." The price certainly sounded fiscally healthy.

Inside the spare, empty office, the atmosphere felt benignly impersonal: flat gray carpet, new black desks, a giant map of the world on the wall. It looked like an H&R Block. There was an H&R Block two doors down. Castillo said she sees rich and poor; the common denominator is a lack of desire to fight. A storefront divorce doesn't make the decisions any easier—you still have to decide yourself—but it lets you leave the onerous task of filing to someone else.

"You absolutely can't file alone," she insisted in a sweet, calm manner. "You make one mistake and then they send the whole thing back. You correct that mistake, and then they find another mistake two pages later."

This is a major consideration when it comes to doing your own divorce, whether you use an online service, the courthouse staff, a lawyer-by-the-hour, or a divorce storefront: you can easily miss out on valuable help. Even if you're in total agreement, as we were, you might benefit from taking a parenting class for divorcing families, meeting with a financial planner, having a therapist talk to your children—or hiring someone like Castillo to fill in the forms. The support is out there, but it's up to those of us going it alone to find it.

THE UTOPIA OF DIVORCE IS IN DENVER

What I really wanted to do, when it came to making it legal, was divorce in Denver. Unfortunately, we were not residents of Colorado, and neither of us planned to relocate for the state's three-month minimum residency requirement. The nonprofit Resource Center for Separating and Divorcing Families (since evolved into the off-campus, Center for Out-of-Court Divorce) is the physical embodiment of the best new thinking about divorce. It's a holistic, assisted, inexpensive approach to helping families disentangle the threads of marriage.

When you arrive at the resource center, you meet with a small intake team. They ask about your marriage and its breakdown, your children, and any financial or emotional concerns. The team then creates a "service plan" for your divorce, which might include therapy, a meeting with a financial planner, budgeting help, legal education, and/or communication training. They might recommend a divorce workshop for your children, or a meeting with a therapist who can teach them coping skills and define some of the legal terms they'll likely hear. When you're ready, a mediator will help you work through your separation agreement and parenting plan—and write it all down correctly, on the right forms.

All services take place at the center, which, when I visited, was housed in a modular building in a parking lot across the street from the University of Denver's grand, light-filled, Victorian mansion-turned-law-school offices. Former Denver district court chief justice Robert Hyatt comes to the center once a month to grant divorces. The cost for all this? From $20 to $95 per hour, depending on your budget.

Many people at the resource center had no intention of talking about their feelings. "Lots of parents think they just want the mediation. But through the meeting, they often realize they want more," said executive director Melinda Taylor.

Nor do they all arrive with an optimistic, "let's be friends" attitude. I met the Flores family at the end of their process. When they'd first approached the center a year earlier, their relationship had been openly antagonistic. At one point, they'd given up on the holistic process altogether and stormed out. But the idea of working cooperatively stuck with them. They returned and managed to craft a fair agreement. I was there at the granting of their final divorce decree—the official sluicing that formally washes away the legal marriage.

Judge Hyatt stood in the conference room–cum–courthouse at the center, waiting for the couple to arrive. The judge's chamber, the first such off-site courtroom for divorce in the nation, felt like a cross between a college seminar room and overflow office space. The atmosphere was convivial, chatty. Judge Hyatt wore his long, black judicial robes over a blue oxford shirt and crimson tie. He exuded the earned portentousness of thirty years on the bench. He also seemed relaxed, satisfied to be overseeing a divorce at the forward-thinking, earnest resource center. Actually, with his ruddy cheeks, upturned nose, and eyes that crinkled at the corners when he smiled, Judge Hyatt seemed like Santa Claus, if that particular beneficent being lived near hiking trails in an outdoorsy state with an equally health-conscious wife.

Mr. and Mrs. Flores finally arrived. They entered together, both dressed in jeans and plaid shirts. Mrs. Flores had two pink friendship bracelets circling her wrist, the telltale sign of daughters back home. They took chairs on either side of the judge. They both seemed a little nervous, solemn. Hopeful, too. Eager to get on with the rest of their day—which is probably exactly how you want to feel in divorce court, ready to move forward to new adventures.

"I will be asking you some questions about your separation agreement and parenting plan," Judge Hyatt said. His goal, he explained, was to ensure that they were genuinely in agreement, and that he believed their plans were in the best interest of all members of the family. He had a calm, kind voice, and used none of that legal jargon that can send your heart racing. He asked them to raise their right hands and swear that the facts in this petition were the truth. Then he read over the agreements they'd spent months creating. Mrs. Flores was keeping the house, and refinancing it. She owed her husband for his half, which she'd pay by forgoing child support until it was met. Both parents seemed comfortable with these details.

Judge Hyatt read aloud the parenting plan. The children would live primarily with their mother. Their father would see them every day. They had set a goal of having the children stay at his place more frequently once they were older and had acclimated to their parents living in separate homes. The judge praised this plan, one that allowed the kids to see both parents daily without complicated scheduling and constant transitions. The fact that they'd managed to rebuild a cooperative relationship allowed for this routine.

I was struck, once again, by how comforting the specificity felt. It neutralized worry, defanged fears. I wished my future ex and I had assembled a team of professionals to help us plan our *marriage*. We could have agreed upon what, exactly, we each were responsible for, examined our views on parenting and work, discussed the feasibility of our expectations for each other and ourselves. At a wedding, it's all hopes and dreams, tableware and linens, and a lot of lip service given to building a life together.

In divorce, this couple had clarified their roles and mapped out a strategy for meeting their aims. A judge with thirty years of experience then vetted their vision. This divorce had more chance of succeeding than many marriages.

Judge Hyatt summarized the findings of the court. He read the date of their marriage and of the births of their two children. In his recitation, I could feel these acts as the achievements they were. These two people had grown up, finished their schooling, landed good jobs, married, birthed two babies, ushered them into early childhood. They'd been successful to date, and would surely continue to flourish.

"Do you believe the plan you've reached is fair, equitable, and not unconscionable?" Judge Hyatt asked. "Do you believe the parenting plan is in the best interest of your children?"

"Yes, I do," Mrs. Flores said.

"Yes, I do," Mr. Flores agreed.

"The court finds that the marriage is irretrievably broken, that the separation agreement and parenting plan are fair, equitable, and not unconscionable. The court declares that this marriage is dissolved."

Then I was tearing up, as I do at every wedding, overcome with the significance of the moment, the awesomeness and fragility of our lives. We throw ourselves into our attempts to love one another, to marry, to raise families. We face disappointments. We fall. Then we pick ourselves up and create new dreams, and pursue them wholeheartedly, once again.

PART FOUR

SIGNS OF LIGHT

CHAPTER NINE

Transformative Acts

Making It Feel Real

✸

While the final decree makes a divorce legal, many people need something more. We have ceremonies and rituals to mark all major life passages, increasingly including divorce.

When we trade in a loveless life for a love-created life, we are reborn. Our sense of purpose and our core values are reignited.

—Instructor's words during a class at
Jivamukti Yoga studio in Manhattan

Yes! I thought, sitting cross-legged on the yoga mat as the instructor riffed on the Bhagavad Gita and the studio's theme of the month, "renaissance." *Divorce is not just a closing-down of one life but also an opening of another.*

I believed this, but I didn't always *feel* it. Which is why I did so much yoga in those early months, to remind myself to breathe, to relax, and to accept that sometimes we have to struggle as we move toward a better, more love-filled life.

With time, however, I realized I wanted something *more*, a grander, more official announcement that I was moving on to a new stage, some formal way to acknowledge this transition.

We have ceremonies and rituals to honor nearly all major life passages. We hold a baby naming or baptism or bris on one side of life, a funeral on the other. There's the First Communion, the bar mitzvah, the high school graduation with the caps and gowns and dinner afterward at the Japanese steak house. The birthday party. The *wedding*. But there's no official rite of passage after divorce. For many of us, signing a paper in a lawyer's office lacks the pomp and significance we need. Simply watching our marriage sputter out over the months—or explode, shrapnel flying—fails to fully capture its value in our lives, or the momentousness of moving on.

"To really bring closure, as humans, we go back and look at what happened. What have we learned, what have we gotten out of our experience?" said Renee Beck, a licensed marriage and family therapist in Oakland, California, who does divorce ceremonies as part of her client work. "Marriage is initiated with a very special energy. For a relationship that started that way to end without any formal marking is sad, and can make it really difficult. It's wonderful to acknowledge how important it has been, how much we have learned, what we have given to each other."

Or, as Carl Jung said, "Only the symbolic life can express the need of the soul."

A divorce ceremony may sound hokey; after all, part of a tradition's power is the history to which it connects us. But while institutional rites link us to generations past, we launch new customs all the time, and they imbue our lives with meaning. We make French toast for breakfast one Sunday and eat it in bed in a tumble of sheets. By the following week, Sunday French Toast in Bed has become a venerable family practice.

Since there isn't any codified divorce ritual—at least, not yet—we can devise the event of our choosing. Some people plan a public ceremony or reception, hosted alone or with their ex. Others want a private moment. Many people say taking a trip out of town was the act that let them head in a new direction when they returned home.

THE DIVORCE CEREMONY

After finalizing her divorce, a painful, two-and-a-half-year process, Charlotte Eulette still felt bereft. She'd lost twenty pounds, wasn't sleeping, couldn't bring herself to date. She'd begun working as the director of the Celebrant Foundation & Institute, a nonprofit that trains people to officiate at life-cycle events such as weddings, civil unions, funerals—and, increasingly, divorces. Founded in 2001 and based on a decades-old Australian model, the Celebrant Foundation teaches would-be officiants the art of ritual, world and faith traditions, ceremonial writing, public speaking, and presenting. ("Officiant" was recently listed as a hot "encore career.") The foundation's founder, Gail Sarma, offered Charlotte a divorce ceremony of her own to help move her past ongoing unhappiness.

Charlotte jumped at the chance. She held her divorce ceremony at the Diva Lounge in New Jersey. Nearly a hundred guests came, some flying in from as far away as Chicago. Charlotte wore a silver sequined dress. The ceremony included poetry, readings, and a drum circle of her closest female friends. The divorce ceremony was the most significant public event of her adulthood, she said later, in some ways more so than her wedding. "You expect people to come around for your wedding, but who comes around for your divorce? When I realized the support I had, that these people came in for this, it blew me away. It gave me a feeling of strength and confidence, and the awareness that I would not be reduced by the divorce."

In her role at the Celebrant Foundation, she advises people planning their own divorce ceremonies. She suggested waiting until the final papers are signed to allow the ceremony to serve as a closing note and healing ritual. "It's not about bashing your ex. You don't want to be looking back in anger. You're going forward."

For some divorcing couples, a ceremony isn't complete unless it's done together. Natalie and Mike run the organic vegan restaurant Café Gratitude in Kansas City, Missouri. The café is something of a community hub, promoting a philosophy of business and life that includes honoring your word, taking responsibility, and not gossiping. When Natalie and Mike decided to divorce in 2015, they felt an obligation to uphold these ideals in divorce, and assure their employees that the café and its community would remain. "It was a way to celebrate our marriage and our lives together, to honor what we had created in the world, and then create, with the community present, the next phase of our relationship," Natalie said.

They hosted a casual un-wedding ceremony at the café for about seventy people, including their forty employees, friends, family members, and a handful of regulars. Natalie wore her wedding dress and reread her vows, replacing the word "wife" with "partner." Here's an excerpt:

I vow to you, Mike George, to experience life with you.

As we sit back and reflect on our 50 years together,

our hearts will be filled with love,

our faces will have wrinkles from all the laughs we've shared,

our eyes will be filled with tears from

the memories we've made, friendships we've formed and the lives we have touched and been touched by.

Our souls will be singing praises of gratitude because we not only found each other, but we made the most of it.

We encouraged and stood for each other to pursue our dreams,

always reminding the other that life is an adventure and we're a part of the adventure together.

We honored and cherished who we truly are and who we wanted to be in life.

Natalie said that the idea of a ceremony confused some people, conflicting with their view of divorce. But she and Mike wanted to express their continued love for each other, their sense that they'd grown up while married, and were now taking different paths. "We wanted to paint a picture: we're taking the marriage out of our relationship, but the love remains. We also asked if anyone wanted to share how our marriage had made a difference to them. We knew that people would want to say something, that it would make them feel more complete."

For her, the act of planning the ceremony helped her come to terms with the divorce. She said she worried she'd cry the entire time, but during the hectic and tearful two-week planning period, she worked through some of her grief about ending her marriage.

• • •

Unlike with marriage, with divorce you can skip the ceremony altogether and go right to the reception. "Divorce party planner" is another growing profession; in many cities you can find a professional planner to help you untie the knot with style.

If you threw an Elvis-themed wedding in Las Vegas (or wish you had), for example, you might hire party planners Glynda Rhodes and Mari-Rene Alu to plan your themed divorce party. Rhodes, a corporate event planner in Vegas, transitioned into the divorce party planning business after going through her second divorce. The aim of their company, Rhodes said, is to get people together with their friends and family, and help them feel good about themselves. For this duo, a divorce celebration might involve skydiving, golfing, and getting drinks at a strip club (men); having a sexy photo shoot, pole-dancing lesson, and drinks at a strip club (women), with a ritual burning of the wedding dress.

I find this negative humor unhelpful and potentially damaging, but for some people, it lightens the divorce, making it something to joke about and move past.

Joelle Caputa, author of the self-published book *Trash the Dress: Stories of Celebrating Divorce in Your 20s*, sees value in a public purging of the adornments of the wedding. In her vision of the "Seven Stages of Divorce," the final step is a celebration. "That's when the rituals come into play, hosting a divorce party, trashing the dress, getting a tattoo. It helps people put the past behind them and move on. The trash-the-dress photo shoot is definitely the most popular. These women are trashing the dress and everything it represents as they declare commitment only to themselves."

My divorce mentor, Susan, decided to host a divorce party for herself, using the celebration to help her create a new future. "It happened to occur on the very week my divorce papers were final. I started by asking everyone I knew, 'Who do you know who's single?' I capped it when I had twenty men and twenty women." A couple of dates came from her first party, and it was such a success that she hosted two more.

A CEREMONY FOR ONE

Of course, you can mark the end of your marriage without inviting guests. Some people do so by bringing a heightened awareness to the details of divorce, or creating a personal mini ritual. People told me about walking through the rooms of their marital home, saying a formal goodbye. Others went down to the ocean to symbolically toss the old marriage out to sea. My mother said the time-consuming process of changing her name felt ceremonial, in ways. "Changing your name after thirty-five years is a pretty big deal emotionally. You have to go to the social security office, then the department of motor vehicles and the bank. Sign all these things." For her, driving all around town and filling out forms helped seal the transition.

Steven Rogat, a licensed professional counselor and cofounder of the Creative Thought Center in Chapel Hill, North Carolina, offers a "soul retrieval" ceremony. Based on a shamanistic healing ritual, the ceremony helps people take back parts of themselves given away in marriage, and return other aspects to their former spouse. "Two people get together, and they balance each other out. My wife handles the social engagements; I handle the business details," Rogat said. "Psychologically speaking, I have given my wife the social part that I might need to develop myself. Spiritually speaking, we often give our partner a piece of our spirit or soul."

With his glasses, shaggy beard, and husky frame, Rogat looks like a traditional therapist, or maybe a high school biology teacher. He starts the two-hour soul retrieval as a traditional counseling session, asking about the marriage, the divorce, the negative emotions that persist. Then he turns on a tape of Native American drumming music, perhaps lights a smudge mixture of sage and sweet grass. He might do hands-on healing; he's trained in a dozen healing modalities, including energy and breath work.

Rogat said the ritual aspect and sensory additions help people sit in a positive, loving state. From there, they can explore difficult emotions ordinarily blocked. He may ask a client to channel love and light to her ex and to find some part of him she can love unconditionally. In exchange, she can ask him to return parts she gave away. "She can come to a realization about how much she's given, or how much she's been relying on her partner to fulfill her. Then she has a better shot at fulfilling that herself," said Rogat. The process also helps him enter into a healing "trance state," he explained, in which he is guided to the areas a person needs to address.

I'm wary of the whole communing-with-spirits thing. I think of Noël Coward's play *Blithe Spirit*, in which a medium brings back the main character's dead-yet-still-ravishing first wife for cocktail hour. Jealousy and antics ensue. Entertaining? Yes. Likely to happen? Not in my experience. Still, after talking to Rogat, I *believed* a sensory, full-body healing ritual could help me reclaim my playfulness, dismiss the judgment of my spouse, and return to him anything I took. I wanted to do it. I had to ask, though: Can you retrieve your soul if you're, you know, *skeptical* about the process?

"Truthfully, I don't see a lot of clients like that," Rogat admitted. "It can still work, but it might not be so tangible, and they might not get a whole lot out of it."

Another way to think about a soul retrieval? Grief counseling on hyperdrive. "If I can bring someone through that experience, help them let go, feel more whole, and support the other person in feeling whole, we've just done three months of healing in an hour," said Rogat.

THE TRANSFORMATIVE JOURNEY

Elizabeth Gilbert's memoir *Eat, Pray, Love* has come to serve as the Platonic ideal of the postdivorce transformative journey, in part because we believe the premise intuitively. We know that some part of our emotional life hinges on our habits, is limned within the walls of our house. Our environments hold our routines and attitudes in place—this bookcase and that drive to work, the Thursday-night poker game or Sundays at the gym.

In marriage, we adapt to our partner and to the wedded state, as we must. Upon parting, we may retain habits that worked within that union, but are unnecessary or even destructive on our own. Traveling lets us step away from expectations or limitations so established as to be invisible, and can help us see what we need to release.

Not everyone can take off a year to travel the globe; I, for one, had a small child and spontaneously generating piles of laundry needing to be addressed. But even a more modest vacation can help us redirect. "A lot of people are stuck, they can't move emotionally or physically. Travel is literally moving forward," said Karen Schaler, author of *Travel Therapy: Where Do You Need to Go?* "Just by leaving behind what didn't work, you're starting that movement, getting out of your head, off the couch, away from your comfort zone. It can be the thing that helps you reboot, reenergize, and start over."

Or, as the ancient Chinese philosopher poet Lao-Tzu said, "A journey of a thousand miles must begin with a single step."

Katie, a social worker turned art advisor, decided to take a three-month Spanish immersion course in Mexico after her divorce. She'd just finished her social work degree and had no immediate job prospects keeping her home. She went down for the course, and then extended her stay to work with kids in a school in San Miguel de Allende, a Colonial-era town in central Mexico. She also saw a therapist. "Going to Mexico was really helpful in terms of removing my patterns, daily attachments, and the identity I'd created for myself," she said. "When you strip away all that stuff you can say, 'Who am I really? What really matters to me? What do I want from this life?'"

When she returned, she transitioned into a new job in the arts, and eventually found a healthy relationship that led to a new, good marriage. For her, getting away was key to moving into a new phase. "I think a lot of people need to reset their levels in some way."

Travel-aided transformation occurs not only because of habits you leave behind, but also wonders you see before you. Some people gain inspiration and insight from cities, from witnessing the greatest works of art and architecture humans have created. Immersing themselves in the pinnacle of human accomplishment opens a deeply felt awareness of their own range of options, our innate capacity to create. Gilbert taps into this inspiring font of human excellence in many places in her book, such as when she describes the healing power of eating her way through the greatest pasta meals in Italy.

For others, spending time in nature is most healing—a trip to the mountains or beach, a volunteer vacation rearing lion cubs on an animal reserve in South Africa, a month alone in the woods with a copy of *Walden*. A nature-based trip can be transformative because both Big Nature and small fluffy animals activate our internal joy system.

"Being with animals and being in nature may lower your heart rate and help balance your serotonin levels, which play an important role in stabilizing mood and overall health," said Linda Lloyd Nebbe, author of *Nature as a Guide: Nature in Counseling, Therapy, and Education*. Nebbe has spent her career investigating nature therapy and animal-assisted therapy—two forms of interacting with the natural world that can bring us closer to ourselves. "Hugging a loved one stimulates the hormone oxytocin, but so does nurturing an animal. It doesn't matter if you're depressed or just want your life to be more full and have more energy. For someone who has gone through divorce, it can be life-changing," said Nebbe.

Some people crave serious downtime, a chance to lounge by the pool at a spa, get a therapeutic massage, and take twilight hikes in the hills. Rancho La Puerta in Tecate, Mexico, is one of the oldest and most famous destination spas in the Western Hemisphere, a postdivorce retreat for those who can afford it. But pampering is only part of the healing equation. "Sometimes in unhealthy relationships, we lose sight of who we are, what is important to us, and what we like to do. By starting to treat your body well, the mind and spirit move in the same direction," said Barry Shingle, director of guest relations and programming at Rancho La Puerta. "It works best when paired with physical activity. People feel empowered when they take care of themselves."

But don't go to a spa unless you're prepared to spend time alone with your thoughts, advised travel expert Karen Schaler, who also tends to steer the newly separated away from trips organized specifically for single parents. She encourages a more customized, forward-looking vacation. "If you're sad and feel like you have nothing in your life, you can go volunteer and remember all you have to be grateful for. If you're lacking self-worth, go do something out of your comfort zone that's challenging, like shark diving. If you were cheated on, try something that empowers you, like traveling alone, opening yourself up to new experiences and people. No matter what happens on your trip, it's not about being perfect. It's about going for it, and trying something new."

You might think traveling sounds indulgent, especially at this time. *Who am I to spend a week learning to hula dance in Hawaii?* But indulgence is part of the point. "Travel is like a reward—this is *your* time, something you're doing for yourself to help you heal and have the confidence to handle whatever happens down the road," said Schaler.

• • •

For me, the time I spent at the 18th Street Arts Center in Santa Monica during my second single summer was its own form of travel therapy. It let me shed another layer of my marriage, live exactly as the person I wanted to be. I wasn't living under the weight of a hometown that felt wrong, or seeing myself as existing in relation to my former spouse. I was simply *being*. Alone, in an empty room, away from everything we'd accumulated together, I felt my own worldview begin to reassert itself.

CHAPTER TEN

Does This Couch Match My Personality?

Creating a Home, Alone

❂

While many people feel displaced after divorce, making a home alone is a chance to create a personally expressive, supportive space. For some, divorce opens the way for a relocation that significantly improves their lives. My husband and I consider moving away, together.

> If I stay there will be trouble.
> If I go it will be double . . .
>
> —The Clash, British punk rock band

Should I stay or should I go? I wasn't thinking about my marriage. I was thinking about my town house in Hoboken. Everything inside reminded me of our union—the furniture we'd chosen together, the paint on the walls. My husband's presence vibrated on the stairs, reverberated in the halls. His was a negative space, a couch cushion indented where someone once sat.

The town outside also felt wrong. Two of the kindest women I've ever met lived in Hoboken, but everyone else I knew and everything I wanted to do was across the river in Manhattan, or two rivers away in Brooklyn. There were a total of two divorced men my age in town, and I'd already dated them both.

I needed to move. I'd tour apartments in New York City, but I couldn't find a new place that felt right. Every space I considered was invariably too expensive. Or it was too small, too far from good schools, or too short on closets, windows, and *private* bathrooms. I'd settle back into my house, decide it was fine, *fine*. Then I'd have another late-night, hour-long wait for the bus home from Port Authority, stepping around the vomit spewed by some late-night partier also heading back to Jersey. I'd decide I had to get out of Hoboken *now*. The New York City apartment hunt would begin again.

I didn't want to stay, yet felt unable to leave. I was stuck in tar, yearning to pull free.

This ambivalence and discomfort at home is pretty typical in divorce. Our marriages are based in our space. Marriage shoots roots through the floors, wraps tendrils around pillars, proclaims itself on the doorposts and on the gates. We use the term "home" interchangeably with "marriage," as in, "How are things at home?" Or, "All's good on the home front." Airplane Mandrake, who told his wife he was moving out only after he'd bought a new house, had to physically remove himself to make the divorce happen. His story stuck with me as an example of how much our homes contain our unions.

In the middle of this search, I received an e-mail from Chris, a young man I'd been a virtual mentor for back when I was in my thirties, and he'd just entered college. Like me, Chris wanted to be a writer. He, too, had assumed this vocation mainly involved sitting around in a bathrobe, sipping espresso. We'd begun a weekly e-mail correspondence that had blossomed into a friendship.

The fall after my husband moved out, Chris, now in his thirties, was getting married in Texas. I stood under the orange and pink paper lanterns hanging from the live oak trees and felt proud that, just as I'd been an anti–career mentor for my friend Sara, I'd apparently modeled how not to choose a spouse for Chris. He'd met and married a woman who seemed a perfect match.

A month later, Chris wrote to me from his new home in Hattiesburg, Mississippi, where he and his wife were living while he finished his PhD. "It's dull as dirt but we can live a lot easier and with our own sunny little cottage, which, incidentally, is how I will metaphorically describe married life at this juncture," he wrote.

"Our own sunny little cottage." That's how I'd wanted to feel in my marriage, and now that I was out of it, how I longed to feel at home. A sunny little cottage is small and self-contained. Intimate, warm. It's real in its humility, not the seat of endless striving, not a showplace mansion with silver you polish for others and more rooms than you could possibly clean. A sunny little cottage provides a solid setting for a life that's luxurious not in objects but in time. Its windows are flung open to the spring breeze, but the roof is tight. It's also a cheery, safe place from which to go forth. Chris's notion of a sunny little cottage settled into me as a vision of how I wanted to feel in my own space, wherever it wound up being.

While the need to create a home alone can feel sad and exhausting, it's also a chance to take charge of your physical surroundings, to use your space to better reflect and support yourself. "We often lose ourselves in our relationships. The process of creating our nests again can bring us back to ourselves, our values—our dreams, our journey—where we're going and who we want to be," said Karen Lehrman Bloch, author of *The Inspired Home: Interiors of Deep Beauty*. "How you create your individual nest can help you figure out who you are again and who you want to pair with again. It's an opportunity to create something that will touch you and help you get back to yourself."

For some, making a home their own after divorce can be a transformative act. For others, divorce facilitates a beneficial relocation. Even an unwanted move can become a chance to re-create a life in the neighborhood, city, or region of your dreams. Some of us find that divorce allows for a desired relocation together, even as we're creating our new homes, apart.

MAKING YOUR SPACE YOUR OWN

Home is a place of security within an insecure world.

—Kimberly Dovey, Australian architectural critic and professor

People stay put in their marital homes, postdivorce, for various reasons—economics, schools, a general feeling of overwhelm that makes the idea of moving seem impossible. As Clare Cooper Marcus notes in her touching meditation on place, *House as a Mirror of Self*, home is "a place of self-expression, a vessel of memories, a refuge from the outside world, a cocoon where we can feel nurtured and let down our guard."

After divorce, your house can feel like a cocoon that's been knocked from the branch and left cracked open on the sidewalk. But reweaving the silk shell around you can be surprisingly empowering. Jodi Topitz, an interior stylist who launched a divorce décor company, We2Me, after going through her own divorce, sees a home makeover as an action item on the road toward recuperation. Topitz has a two-minute video on her website about getting "your mojo back through color and design" that makes you want to jettison your worldly possessions just to go on an uplifting shopping spree. In one scene, she tells a client, "You need to divorce the coffee table! We need to celebrate with a new piece of furniture that celebrates who you are and fits in your new space."

Topitz encourages people to purge objects holding the past, and buy new ones that make them feel energized and joyful. "I call it a 'space lift.' People just think function, not the emotional baggage of their furniture," she said. You might keep your old coffee table because it's convenient, but forget you bought the table on your honeymoon to Thailand. Emotionally, that memory occupies your living room, dragging you down.

My divorce coach, Amy, stayed put in her house to provide stability for her children. She'd long dreamed of living on the beach in Cape Cod, but for the time being, she needed to feel better about her house in suburban New Jersey. She had to disassociate her house from the memories of her marriage, and the negativity of the divorce. She did "a little voodoo" in some rooms, lighting incense and sweeping about with a broom to shift the energy.

Amy didn't have the funds for a total "space lift" so she decided to create a "sanctuary" instead—one room that felt absolutely safe, a retreat that made her feel nurtured. She advises clients to do the same. "When life feels really rough and unsettled and you're doubting the future, when everywhere you go reminds you of the life you were living, find a space in your home and make it as pleasing as possible," she said.

She also sprung for fresh flowers for her kitchen every week, as she'd done while married, and posted affirmations around her rooms. For Amy, feeling safe and content in her house was part of feeling more "whole" as a person. "If you take care of your outer shell in a way that supports your inner needs, one can feed into another. To me, it's making a connection between feeling at home in your space and at home inside yourself."

Some say that the physical-aesthetic combo of redecorating helped them move forward emotionally. My mother repainted after my stepfather left, wielding the brush and roller herself. "I'd start out angry, painting the kitchen; I always hated that green. But then I'd get so into the painting that I wasn't feeling angry anymore. I just wanted to see the new color of the room," she said. "Painting is self-motivating. It's soothing and liberating. I was doing something productive. It really made me feel good."

Some people feel totally comfortable in their home, with or without their spouse. The technology activist and father of one in Washington, DC, Alex, said his 1909 brick row house stood as a stronghold of stability in the midst of whirling emotions after his wife left. He felt viscerally connected to the house itself.

He also gained comfort from the fact that he was rarely alone in it. When I visited him, on a balmy mid-Atlantic summer weekend, he had houseguests arriving that afternoon, as he often did. "My house has always been kind of a way station. There are always people stopping by. I relied on that to make it feel like my own space. This is DC; people come through. There's literally a calendar where friends and coworkers can block out days."

Alex said he couldn't imagine feeling ill at ease at home, as I did. "Your home should be your sanctuary, your place of rest and relaxation. If instead it's creating angst or stress, it's clearly the wrong place for you. Being honest with yourself and changing the circumstance is crucially important, especially given how much stress is in the rest of our lives."

• • •

If you have to move, the process can feel tremendously liberating—or deeply unnerving—or both. Moving out is a physical manifestation of the fact that you're moving on. Moving to a new home is commonly cited among the top life stressors, up there with, say, divorce. *Moving while divorcing* should be like a double negative, the stressors canceling each other out, resulting in one laugh-riot rollicking good time. Unfortunately, it doesn't always feel that way.

For some, moving out allows them to finally settle in, because it's their first chance in a long time, if ever, to assert their personal style.

"My number one thing was hanging all sorts of art, which I wasn't allowed to do in the old house because I have way more stuff than my ex, and she didn't want me to dominate the place," said Mandrake about the house he bought to facilitate his divorce. "Now I have tons of stuff up—paintings by my grandmother, old art we had around as a kid, framed posters from France because I'm in love with France."

In his postdivorce home, pictures climb the staircase and cluster in the living room, cookbooks crowd into a tall case in the kitchen. The walls are painted peach and rose. His house doesn't look like a bachelor pad. It looks like a cottage your grandmother might have lived in for sixty years. He loves it. "It's great. It's my place. It's my stuff. I put it there because I wanted it there. Boom. Done."

For others, moving out creates a new sense of security. Just as you might arrive at divorce pre-lonely, you could be packing up your belongings after months or years of feeling uncomfortable or unsafe in your marital abode. "Once I left and was alone even for a minute, I felt better," said the chef I spoke to who had moved with her daughter into her parents' home after divorce.

The young Evangelical Christian from Georgia, Morgan, said she felt immediately better in her new place, without her husband. "I thought it would feel terrifying or lonely to be without him, but I just feel safe, safer than in the marriage. He'd wake up with nightmares and be hitting things in the air. He'd never get help for it. It made me scared."

Morgan addressed two divorce-related worries—loneliness and economic insecurity—by seeking an apartment with roommates through her church classified ads. Living with two other young women created an instant social life. "It's like being back in college, but better. We've had roomie movie nights, watching stupid movies, like *High School Musical*, and drinking wine. We've made cookies, done yoga. We hang out. The situation is so much better than where I was before, I'm just in love."

The hardworking mother, Jennifer, who doubted her own intuition after divorce, also said she'd felt uncomfortable in her marital bed. "I'd been living in limbo. I couldn't sleep with him, physically or sexually." Many nights, she'd get up and go sleep in another room. The house itself symbolized some of the problems in the marriage. They owned a glass-walled showplace with a spectacular view, but it was too big and too expensive. It required too much renovation and upkeep. "It was my husband's dream house. I knew it was too much for us, but I went along, I acquiesced," she said.

They had to sell the house in divorce and move into smaller places, a step many find themselves forced to take. While it may sound like a blow to the ego, or an identity assault, the actual lived experience of downsizing can be quite liberating. You're released from the weight of unnecessary rooms to sweep, plants to water, a lawn to mow. You're also cut free from the effort to uphold the image of the Ideal Couple that a big house can seem to proclaim.

Interior stylist Jodi Topitz told me about her own surprisingly uplifting divorce-induced downsizing. She'd sold her large house of twenty years and moved into a tiny rental. She painted the walls of her two-room apartment a deep teal—dark colors make small spaces look larger—and chose one big piece of furniture as a focal point in each room to avoid the "dollhouse effect" of small items in a small space. "My divorce took three years, but it only took me three weeks to make the space feel like a home. I was like, 'Oh my gosh, I never thought I'd wake up in this tiny, two-room apartment and feel safe.' I'd look around at the painted walls and feel safe. I could close my eyes, and feel good."

In fact, most of us could be happy with a lot less than we maintain. But we need to give ourselves permission to spend the time and money to make our space our own. When creating your postdivorce home, chose items, colors, and even a new place based on what speaks to you, rather than on the latest trend. Here are three steps to take:

Creating a Nest of Your Own

Do it fast: Topitz advises clients to set up their new place quickly, ideally in a few weeks. Or at least establish order in the most important rooms. "You have to live in the now. You can't say, 'I'm not going to paint the walls because I'm only living here for two years.' You want to take hold of something concrete, and working on something tangible nourishes you in this transition."

Unpacking and repainting quickly helps re-instill a sense of security and stability for yourself—and for your children, whose routines and even school may have changed due to divorce. You can help a child feel rooted in a new place by letting her choose furniture, paint colors, and drapes for her own bedroom, and giving her responsibility for keeping it clean.

"Setting up the kitchen was important; that's when I feel in my groove, when the kitchen is workable," said Jennifer, of her smaller, post-separation abode. "Now I can make a big weekend breakfast, make the kids their school lunches instead of buying them. As soon as I could establish rituals around food, it felt better for everybody."

Bring in nature: Even if you live in a city, you can open your windows, buy houseplants, and get a dog—or find someone else's to walk—three things that can boost your spirit, said Linda Nebbe, author of *Nature as a Guide*. Tending to a small garden also can help make your house feel like a haven; caring for living things, even leafy green ones, is self-nurturing.

Author Karen Lehrman Bloch stressed the importance of letting in light and spaciousness. "The more you can bring in the grandeur and awesomeness that characterizes nature, the more soulful and inspirational your home will feel," she said. Adding textural details in the décor also can mimic nature in a positive way: think rough tree bark, smooth stones, soft ferns, splashing water. In a home, this might mean a nubby rug, a plush blanket, ceramic planters both rough and glazed, perhaps a little plug-in fountain.

Connect with the home outside your house: Feeling connected to the world outside your front door can help you feel secure at home. Merely getting to know the mail carrier or clerk at your favorite store can increase your sense of being rooted in a place. Better yet? Join a community garden or a gym, volunteer at the library or food bank, or serve as a crossing guard at your child's school.

MOVING AWAY TO MOVE ON

At some point during my second single summer, when I was in Santa Monica for an artist's residency, I had an epiphany about my inability to find a new apartment in New York, or accept the home I had. I hadn't become indecisive to the point of paralysis; I simply didn't *want* any of the choices on offer. My discomfort wasn't about the house, but the *region*. I didn't want to live in the New York area. I wanted to live in California. I had longed to move out West for years. We'd argued about this desire of mine throughout our marriage. My husband couldn't fathom why anyone would move across the country, uproot, give up years of social capital.

People tend to be skeptical about the "geographic solution" as a cure to personal unhappiness, insisting we bring our problems with us. I'm a huge proponent of the geographic solution. To paraphrase what a literary agent told her marriage counselor when discussing divorce, "I know a new relationship will have problems, too. I can handle problems. I just don't want *these* problems. Bring on the new problems."

That summer in Santa Monica, I'd sit straddle-legged on the beach and dig my fingers into the sand like Scarlett O'Hara in *Gone with the Wind*. "As God is my witness, I will never be stuck in a snowstorm on Forty-Second Street, unable to hail a cab, again!"

I had to return, of course. I was divorcing a man from New York, and we had a child. I would not move away from our son, nor sue for the right to take him with me. We'd made a commitment to cooperate, and I would not be the one to break that pact. I read a ream of studies about one parent seeking the legal right to relocate after divorce. The impact on children was inconclusive because many factors contribute to a parent's desire to move. One of the adults, however, was generally unhappy either way the judge ruled. "You made your bed, you lie in it," I said to myself, often.

Divorce releases us from the friction of an incompatible marriage, but if we have children together, our lives remain entwined. This is one reason I was working so hard to have a cooperative relationship with my son's father, but it also meant I wasn't free to do whatever I wanted, wherever I wanted to be. "Think of it as the 'divorce tax,'" said a lawyer I went on a date with that summer in California. "It's the tax you pay to not have to be in that marriage." I found this idea helpful, and added it to my internal refrain. "You made your bed, you lie in it," I'd say to my-self. And, "It's the divorce tax."

I relished that summer in a way that's hard to do if you don't have a ticking clock counting down the hours before your return flight. I also sent photos to my ex of our son glowing with joy while hiking in the red rock canyons. I e-mailed videos of him running freely at the water's edge. The pomegranate-hued, late-afternoon sun, diffused by ocean spray, made every picture look like a Glamour Shots makeover of an ideal summer afternoon.

I was still campaigning, I realized later. I'd given up on moving, and yet . . . I knew that my husband was growing exasperated with New York City himself. It was too loud, too dirty, too expensive, too lacking in open space. He wanted a more outdoorsy life, more time to kick a ball with our son, an environment not quite so work-focused all the time. I was still arguing for life out West, though in a more upbeat, visual way.

A couple of weeks into our trip, I called my ex with an update. I was sitting outdoors on a white couch at a beach center, gazing at the ocean, listening to the call of seagulls on their perpetual quest for french fries dropped by beachgoers.

"How's the boy?" he asked.

"He loves it. It's pretty unbelievably great here," I said.

"It looks like it," he said. "So. I've been looking at schools in Santa Monica."

"What?" *Really?!*

"It just looks great."

"Would you actually consider moving here?"

"I might consider it," my future ex said. Unbelievably. "I might."

. . .

Divorce can be the shift that facilitates a hugely beneficial move—across town, across the state, even across the country. Our surroundings affect us, emotionally and practically. Where we live influences our values. It exposes us to new ideas and new kinds of people, creates work opportunities—or the lack thereof.

Even a micro-move can profoundly upgrade your daily life. Moving from one part of town to another can mean better schools, safer streets, a quieter apartment. Moving into the city from the 'burbs can yield easier access to stores and entertainment, classes, clients, dates. Leaving the city might mean exchanging a cramped apartment for a house with a yard. Carlin Flora, the author of *Friendfluence*, told me about a man she'd interviewed who felt lonely in midtown Manhattan, but found a community at the Starbucks after moving to the less touristy, nearby borough of Queens. One 2015 study examining the draw of high-rent neighborhoods showed that quality of life can vary as much *within* a metro area as it does between two completely different cities.

After selling her house high on a hill, Jennifer rented a modest bungalow on a flat street, a half block from commerce. Suddenly, her children could walk to stores and friends' houses, bike to school rather than take a bus. "That kind of thing really matters to kids. The location has been a godsend. Before, the kids were kind of stranded," she said.

The new house is also much closer to her office, a fact that enabled her to buy a puppy for her children. "I can let the dog out during my lunch hour. The dog has been terrific. There was a heaviness that we all were laboring under. The dog has brought so much light."

A micro-move also might mean relocating to a more fitting landscape. In a recent series of three studies, researchers showed that introverts prefer wooded, enclosed areas, while extroverts gravitate toward open spaces and plateaus. In marriage, this kind of subtle difference can lead to one partner feeling existentially uncomfortable. In divorce, he might move to a nearby area that better suits his personality.

Elizabeth, the young fashion buyer in Texas, stayed in town with her mom after her parents divorced. Her father, Mark, moved twenty minutes away. In that part of Texas, twenty minutes can mean the difference between a small town and deep country. For Mark, it meant finally getting back to his roots. He moved to a ranch house in the deep country, overlooking one hundred head of cattle. "I grew up on the farm. I worked on the farm. We had cows. We had horses. We baled hay," he said. "I'm very much a country boy."

Some people find that nothing short of a total location overhaul will do to break the grip of marriage, or its ending. A mother of two grown children from suburban Illinois said her marriage ended after her husband's series of increasingly public affairs. She felt compelled to leave their hometown to escape the stares and comments of mutual friends. A sixty-something woman from New Jersey said that she wanted a whole new life, postdivorce. For her, too, that meant starting over across the country, revamping her friends, lifestyle, and career.

For my mother, relocation wound up being the act that finally let her recover. While my mother was still in the throes of dealing with her divorce, one of my cousins landed a job in Austin, Texas. My cousin's parents—my mom's younger sister Judie and her husband—decided to move to Austin, too. My sister already lived there with her two kids. They all urged my mother to join them.

I'd grown up in a family that had lost track of its roots during its migration from eastern Europe to Ohio, then got caught in a cyclone of States-based dispersion—moving ever farther from Cleveland for college, for work, for love. Now my family was pulling back together in Texas, like metal filings to a magnet.

Alone, my mother had no one's needs to consider but her own. As much as she'd enjoyed repainting her kitchen in Florida, her sense of loss had resettled once the paint dried. The tree her husband had planted in the front yard was still there. Every day, she'd look out the window and see it. The crown molding they'd hammered up together circumscribed her every move.

She bought a new limestone ranch north of Austin, a four-bedroom far too large for one old lady and a dog. But it felt special, which mattered to her, striking out on her own after her long marriage. And it was hers, alone. "There are no ghosts in Austin," she said. "The closets are mine. There were never his clothes in them. He never used that shower. I think as long as I'd stayed in the house in Florida, the hurt would still be there. Now it's gone. The divorce is just a part of life, an event that happened, but there's not the pain associated with it. I was not expecting it would free me in the way it did."

My mom's voice was hoarse as she was telling me this, partly because of Austin's infamous "cedar fever," but also from emotion. When a home is what keeps you stuck, no amount of paint or purging unbinds you. Leaving it behind can be the ultimate liberation.

RELOCATING TOGETHER, APART

I wanted a massive relocation, too. While some people worry about a divorce contagion, I'd caught relocation contagion. There was my mother, flying free in her airy new house thirteen hundred miles away from her marital albatross. My cousin and his wife and kids were nearby in their new place, my aunt and uncle in theirs. Even my ex-boyfriend Giles, with whom I'd moved to New York from Houston years ago, was relocating to Oregon while I sat around, waiting to hear if my ex would ever leave. I felt petulant, like a toddler denied a cookie. Everyone else got to move but me!

My ex had mentioned looking up schools in California, then gone back to business as usual, focusing on his work and social life. I returned from my summer in Santa Monica and felt like my life was in limbo while I waited for him to decide. If he weren't willing to relocate, I needed to get back to the New York City apartment search. I was leaving our marital house in Hoboken by the end of the year, either way. That much I'd decided.

He needed time to think, he said. Another few weeks passed. I didn't like that my ex had so much say over my life. My desire to find a new home was on hold, subject to his whim.

Working with my divorce coach, I came up with a plan to give me more agency. I proposed to my ex that we have three conversations about moving, one every week, on Sunday, after our son went to sleep. I'd present why I thought we should leave the New York area. He could explain why he thought we should stay. Then, in the fourth conversation, we'd make a decision. I was moving *somewhere* by January. He agreed to this plan.

I started a list on my computer: "Reasons to Leave." Before each conversation, I reviewed it. I felt good about this strategy. Whatever we decided, at least we were actively moving toward something. I would not be sticking around in our too-big house forever, unable to settle or to leave. I was totally obsessed with this, putting each new thought on my list. But I resisted the urge to call him up and pick a fight.

I added research to my notes. Some scholars argue that places have distinct personalities. In one study, researchers mapped attributes of personality onto U.S. regions. The Northeast, they concluded, is "temperamental and uninhibited," a personality characterized by, among other things, residents who score low on agreeableness. Or, in my experience, people who lean on their horns in traffic, and make ordering a bagel at a deli counter feel like a high-stakes competition. Just as the personal style of our friends can inspire us or drag us down, so can the personality of our region. The Pacific Coast? "Relaxed and creative," according to these researchers. That was where I wanted to be.

In November, I joined my mother's side of my family in Austin for Thanksgiving. My dad came, too, now a regular member of our family holiday tradition.

My future ex called while I was there. "I have some news," he said.

"Okay," I said, taking a breath. I braced for the punch. *He's decided to move in with his girlfriend? He wants to change the terms of our financial agreement?*

"Are you there?"

"Yes," I said. "You thought, 'If she's not talking nonstop, she's not there'?"

He laughed. "Yes. I'm ready to move to Santa Monica."

"Really?"

I went outside and sat down on the ground, holding the phone. I leaned against one of the limestone pillars supporting my mom's new wooden pergola. *He would move to Santa Monica?* My desire to move had been a source of ongoing friction. *After all those years of fighting, we get divorced, and he finally agrees to accommodate me?*

The next weekend, back in Hoboken, we sat together on our same old beige couch, under our same front window. I was holding a notebook, ready to delve into logistics. "Don't you want to know why I decided I could go?" he asked.

Sort of. I was so far along in my mind that I'd skipped the "why" and gone straight to the "how." How do you move across the country with your ex? One moving van or two? Would we drive our cars or ship them? Would he turn it into a romantic cross-country road trip with his girlfriend? Would she move, too?

"You and I have a child together," he said. "Our lives are entwined. We are interdependent. When you're interdependent, you have a moral obligation to consider the other person's happiness. You cannot move to L.A. without dramatically impacting me. I cannot insist on staying here without dramatically impacting you. You are unhappy here. I have a moral obligation to compromise."

I stared at him. Who was this man with this ramrod moral center? I mean, that's part of what attracted me to him, but I'd crashed up against that rigidity so often when we were married. Now that same brick-wall solidity was protecting me like the third little pig—no amount of huffing and puffing could blow this good divorce down.

My ex said he'd taken to thinking while hiking. He came up with the premise of necessary compromise, then started asking himself what might be in it for him. When he considered his own preferences, he found many benefits to L.A. In addition to the great weather and cheaper rent, a geographic shift might shake up his identity in a good way, facilitating his desire to leave his career in public policy and launch an Internet business.

This mental flexibility astounded me, this ability to steer his thoughts toward ways that a difficult compromise might benefit him.

It was a version of my divorce coach's notion that we should reframe negative-feeling challenges in terms of how they might serve us. Seeing this from my ex made me vow to be more flexible toward his needs, too.

I've since met other former couples with kids who relocated together after divorce. A newspaper reporter with a son in middle school agreed to move from California to the East Coast because his ex-wife had more work opportunities there. When she landed a good job in DC, he found a stable position in the city, too, For him, this was a career transition that opened a range of future opportunities. A media mogul in Chicago landed a great job launching a television network's new channel on the West Coast; her ex eventually found work there, and followed her out.

Still, I couldn't believe this was happening to me. At the end of December, I was on the airplane to L.A. I looked out the window, then covered my face with my hands, like you do when you're embarrassed by your sudden riches, a surprise party thrown just for you. *Did I deserve to live where I liked?* When you're in an unhappy marriage, that state of discomfort feels like your lot. You become inured to living with less than you desire. It can take a while to accept that your life can more closely resemble your dreams—and that you have a role in that transformation.

• • •

Making a big move is difficult, it turns out, even if you win the jackpot of relocation, as I felt I had. In L.A., I still couldn't settle on an apartment. We found one for my ex right away, near the school we'd chosen, but not for me. What was my problem? Was it psychological? Architectural? Was it still too hard to identify my preferences, after years of trying to adjust to his? We wound up living together, all three of us, while I looked.

Meanwhile, I looked for supplies I'd need. Shopping for housewares alone can be overwhelming. At one point, I found myself reduced to a mass of indecision, laced with longing, topped with regret while shopping in Home Depot. The scale of it. The choices. My dog, with me for moral support, flopped down on the concrete floor in the middle of aisle twenty-one. I sank down next to him, staring up at aisle upon aisle of pipe fittings and shower doors. Home Depot alone! The years of my marriage stared back at me under the glare of the fluorescent lights: the shelves we'd bought together for our first apartment in the city, the vetting of vanities and countertops for the house we'd built in the country, mirrors for our town house in Hoboken.

This is it, I realized. *Me, myself, and my dog*. My son, too, but no adult partner creating a home life with me.

Our son started school. My ex continued working on his new business venture. Two months of camping out together in a one-bedroom was plenty of time to remember why, exactly, we'd decided to part. The forced togetherness probably also helped ease us into the relocation. We'd just left behind everyone we knew; it was nice, in a way, to bump into a familiar face in the hallway.

One morning in February, my temporarily cohabitating separated little family tumbled outside into the brilliant sunshine. "I miss our house in Hoboken," my son said, standing in the velvety grass.

"You do?" I asked, surprised. "What do you miss?"

"The house," he said.

The *house*? "I miss the house, too," I said, realizing that I did. Not those specific walls or that fireplace, but the home life I'd created inside. I *did* have a home culture. I could see it, now that we weren't in it, and so could our son. We had rituals that made our house feel like a sunny little cottage, even if I hadn't noticed it at the time.

In my house, the coffee starts brewing at seven thirty. I open the curtains to let in the light. In our real lives, not this interstitial period of moving and piling in together, most of the action is in the kitchen and our bedrooms. My son's room has pictures from *Richard Scarry's Busy, Busy World* on the wall. He has books in bookcases, trucks under the bed, shirts folded on shelves. My home has a kitchen with baking sheets and cookie cutters in every seasonal shape, a big wooden table for dining and art projects, champagne glasses for a dozen guests. My home life is largely about making my son feel safe and loved. The effort of doing it for him—and welcoming in others—helps make it a home for me. Feeling at home, I finally realized, was not about being married or being divorced. It was about setting up a place in which I could care for others and for myself.

For the first few months in California, I'd go down to the park overlooking the Pacific Ocean at the end of our main street, and grab onto the grass, still afraid it would slip away. I thought of that line from the movie *Willy Wonka & the Chocolate Factory*. Willy Wonka says to Charlie, "Don't forget what happened to the man who suddenly got everything he always wanted."

Charlie asks, "What happened?"

"He lived happily ever after."

CHAPTER ELEVEN

Am I Free Tonight? Let Me Check with My Husband

Dating While Divorced, or Even Just Separated

✵

While some people are eager to find a new partner imme-diately, others need a buffer period between divorce and dating. Some people have to update their dating skills and attitude. When we do enter into a serious new relation-ship, having been married before can help us get it right this time.

Pick yourself up. Dust yourself off. Start all over again.

—"Pick Yourself Up," written by Jerome Kern
and Dorothy Fields for the movie *Swing Time*,
starring Frank Sinatra and Ginger Rogers

was waiting for a flight at the Cincinnati airport with my son, who had apparently eaten a crate of gummy bears when I wasn't looking. He was running down the moving sidewalk in the wrong direction, smacking business travelers in the knees. I was trying to stop him, while also corralling a wobbly carry-on and a plastic fire truck the size of a schnauzer I'd been cajoled into buying. I needed some assistance.

I spotted a handsome businessman holding an iPad, his fingers free of any telltale rings; it's amazing how divorce has improved my long-range vision, at least for small gold details. "Hey," I said to the handsome man, "would you mind keeping an eye on my fire truck while I run after my son?" I flashed what I hoped was still an enticing smile, like I had the last time I was single, back when I was thirty-three and fit, and didn't have these laugh lines around my mouth that I don't find funny at all.

He looked up with a kind and understanding nod. I ran-walked to the moving sidewalk, calling after my son, "Stop running! Stop running!"

We returned ten minutes later. "Would you like to see a picture of my daughter?" the business traveler asked, addressing my son, who responded by making the sound of a fire alarm and slamming his truck into a bank of seats.

I looked at the photo of the cute little girl. Her handsome father had been divorced for six years, it turned out. He'd spent a quarter million dollars on the divorce because his wife, who'd started the proceedings by having an affair, decided she deserved more than they originally agreed upon and dragged out the proceedings.

I felt sorry for him, having had that kind of divorce. Then I felt sorry for me, as he told me that he was engaged again. He gave me an apologetic look, as if he knew that with this commitment, he'd drained the pool of eligible men my age.

Another one down.

I'd expected to be thrilled by dating. I'd enjoyed it so much in the past. I somehow assumed men would fall from trees as I strolled by and land at my feet, clutching flowers and fruit they'd grabbed on their way down. The last time I was single, everyone else had been single, too. I had a social job. I met men at press events, on subways, in airplanes.

I was still meeting men on airplanes—or in airports—but it felt different somehow. They were engaged. Or too young. Or too old. They were too few and far between. I was also less confident about my allure—whether due to age, divorce, or scarcity of good offers, I couldn't tell. Plus, I had loved someone enough to marry him. In contrast, spending evenings with strangers who aroused the most moderate of emotions felt like a waste of time. It was often awkward and uncomfortable.

"Dating is uncomfortable at any age," insisted Nita Tucker, author of *How Not to Stay Single* and *How Not to Screw It Up*. "I say to people, 'Look, when I think of *comfortable*, I think of sitting at home in a robe with no waistband, watching TV and eating. That's comfortable. Everything else in life is uncomfortable. If we have to wait for things to be comfortable for you, it's never going to happen.'"

Dating also can be a great way to meet new people, learn about new places, and see yourself positively in someone else's eyes. Some of us, though, aren't quite ready for it, not in this interregnum, recuperative state. For others, dating successfully requires updating their approach, cultivating a new openness. Whether we fall in love quickly or go out with everyone in our zip code, exercising discretion about sharing the details can help us protect our relationship with our ex, and with a new partner. For all of us, having been through marriage can help us get it right next time.

THE BENEFITS OF A BUFFER PERIOD

Many people—okay, I'm talking about me—leave a marriage without any real desire to *date*. We want a new, serious partner. *Now.* Or nothing.

I'm not saying I didn't go out. I joined OkCupid. I made out with a good friend's brother, only to realize I liked her better. I went out with two different singer-songwriters, each of whom composed a song ostensibly for me. Flattering, but the relationships still fell flat. I met a slender, dark-eyed, thirty-year-old divorced salesman from Long Island who planned to join a Buddhist monastery for life—or at least as long as his passion for celibate poverty lasted. He postponed his ordination to spend the summer considering the opposite of chastity with me.

I even dated a smart, fifty-something attorney who shared my religion and love of the arts, enjoyed good restaurants, had no financial worries, and wasn't happy unless I had the best seat in the house at the theater. Great person. I *wanted* to want to spend my life with him.

But then I didn't fall in love and didn't fall in love, and the repeated disappointment of dating made me feel discouraged. Also, as much as I desired a new partner in theory, I was still preoccupied with pulling myself out of my marriage. I would show up, but I wasn't fully available. The men I was sort of listening to or halfheartedly considering would invariably get angry. I decided I needed a break.

Many divorcées I spoke to said they, too, needed a "buffer period" between marriage and dating, or marriage and the next true love. Some of us remain attached to a former spouse, even if he's found someone new. We've been devoted to caring for this person for so long; letting go of that role, *internally*, takes time. Others want to prove to themselves that they can succeed alone.

For some, the mere thought of giddy romance is nauseating. As biological anthropologist and legendary love researcher Helen Fisher put it, "Romantic love is a need. It's a drive. It's a craving. It's an urge." After years in an unfulfilling marriage, the idea of getting into another relationship can sound like signing up for a calorie-restricted diet designed to induce hunger at all times.

Mick, an executive search consultant in Kansas City, told me he couldn't stomach the thought of dating for the first eighteen months after his separation. "I had a bit of an 'arrangement' that helped on the physical side, but no committed relationship. I didn't want to date just to date. I got involved with someone I used to work with because I knew she was going to be moving. I was comfortable with no commitment."

A woman whose passionless marriage ended after years of no intimacy also said she wanted sex, not romantic involvement. "That first summer, I had a million and a half flings. It was great. This one guy was like, 'You give me two dates and I'll show you we have more in common than sex.' I didn't want more than sex. I was having a great time."

Others, though, find that "sex" and "casual" no longer go together, if they ever did. For me, sleeping with someone new felt wrong, as if I were cheating not only on my husband—who, meanwhile, had his own relationship—but also on my son; how could I be intimate with a man who wasn't his dad?

Chloe in New York said something similar. "As much as he'd betrayed me by sleeping with someone else, it felt like a betrayal to sleep with someone who wasn't him."

Or, as the divorced protagonist of Richard Ford's novel *The Sportswriter* said, "You should never think that leaving a marriage sets you loose for cheery womanizing and some exotic life you'd never quite grasped before. Far from true. No one can do that for long."

Experts and many successfully remarried people I talked to extolled the benefits of taking a break after divorce. Others warned about the pain of going through another big breakup, postdivorce. "You think the divorce was so rough that nothing could be difficult like that again," one man told me. "I was totally unprepared for how disorienting and upsetting it was to break up with someone I hadn't even been married to."

Of course, half the divorcées I met plunged into a new romance within months of leaving the old one. If you fall madly in love with the perfect person right after your spouse moves out, I envy you and wish you luck. But . . . if you don't, if you choose or default to a buffer period, there are plenty of benefits.

The Good News about Feeling Exhausted, Emotionally Drained, and Like You'll Never Want Another Partner Again

A buffer period gives you time to examine your habits and history: Taking time allows you to reflect upon your romantic past. "I really needed to look at myself and what family stuff got me into the marriage," said the art advisor who'd gone to Mexico after her divorce, Katie. "My therapist had this theory that whatever your issues are, you either pick it, project it, or provoke it; you'll re-create the same problems unless you get clear about your own MO. Before you look at it, it's easy for the toxic things to feel nurturing and the nurturing things to feel toxic. I think without that break, I couldn't be in a healthy relationship now."

A buffer period lets you resolve divorce dilemmas: Letting your divorce settle into a comfortable state can help your next relationship succeed. Continued fighting with a former spouse destroys new relationships, said clinical psychologist Barry McCarthy. "So much of the energy is going toward the anger and frustration with the first spouse." Ideally, your new relationship exists in its own clear, open space—not as a foil for ongoing fights with your former spouse.

A buffer period allows negativity to lift: Early on, I met a recently divorced twenty-something with a two-year-old son. Her husband had cheated on her during the pregnancy. She said she couldn't figure out when to tell a new man she already had a child.

"Tell him right away," I said. "Date guys with kids."

"Any guy who's divorced with a two-year-old is an asshole," she said. Matter-of-fact. No questions asked. Her husband's cheating ruled out all men with children, as far as she was concerned.

Many of us leave marriages with a sack of heavy negativity on our backs; a buffer period lets us work through it, rather than lug it along on every date. Residual negativity can warp our view and compromise our judgment. "I used to just look at all the positives, and probably ignored potential problems. Now, I've been through so much, I'm always looking for how it could go wrong," said the stay-at-home mother of one in California, Lauren. "I look for any negatives, and don't really believe the positives."

This sonar for a potential partner's flaws can easily torpedo a new relationship. "In successful relationships, people have the ability to suspend negative judgment about the other person," said Lucy Brown, a neuroscientist at Albert Einstein College of Medicine in New York. Brown works with Helen Fisher conducting brain research on people in romantic partnerships. In one study, they looked at the brain activity of people in the early stages of romantic love, and then reconnected with them five years later. About half were still together. The researchers went back and reviewed the earlier brain scans; the still-happy couples had shown low activity in the region associated with negative social judgment. "To our amazement, it wasn't the activation in any brain area but the decrease in activity in others, such as this one that has to do with social judgment, the ventral medial prefrontal cortex," said Brown.

A surly demeanor also can make us somewhat unpleasant to be around. Lessening negativity might yield more dates, said the University of Arizona's Chris Segrin. "Happiness attracts others, it's contagious. If you can get happier, you make yourself more attractive."

Actually, you *can* attract people at any stage of emotional recuperation, I discovered. Plenty of men, for example, are happy to cheer you up if you're feeling lonely, sad, or incomplete. "Missing the intimacy of marriage? I can help you out with that, little lady." But a more optimistic outlook might make you happier about the type of people who come your way.

• • •

The risk of a buffer period? You forget that you chose it, and start to feel like no one is choosing you. Or you get so comfortable not making the effort to go out that you give up on love altogether. "People tell me they don't want to compromise, that they have very high standards. You should have high standards. And yet I see people compromising all the time in that they're being alone when they don't want to be. That's a compromise," said Tucker.

Setting a time limit on a buffer period can prevent it from becoming a way of life. Commit in advance to joining an activity group or dating site when your buffer period ends. Ending a buffer period can be its own awkward transition, but you may enjoy dating far more for having taken the break.

AN ENDLESS OPPORTUNITY FOR CASUAL . . . FUN?

Some people can't wait to get out there. Dating can be liberating, affirming, a positive part of moving on. After divorce, we have more to bring to a relationship than before. Most of us have worked not only on marriage, but also on ourselves. We've developed new skills and insights. We know how to create a home with another person. I was aware that raising a little boy made me more caring toward fully grown men.

My sister loved dating as a divorced mother in her mid-forties. She had a successful practice as a chiropractor, a beautiful house, two children, enough money of her own to do what she pleased. She also had more confidence and felt more attractive than in her twenties or thirties. She'd taken up tango as a postdivorce diversion, an expressive physical activity that led to a new, slinkier wardrobe and a sense of herself as a fit, embodied being.

She insisted there were *more* men to date as a mother of a certain age. "The dating pool dramatically expanded because I wasn't looking for a man to have kids with. I was free to explore options that weren't appropriate when I had that classic agenda—someone who wants to get married and have a house and family, a financial equal or provider. It's a freedom when you don't have an agenda."

Her sense of expanded options may also have to do with the fact that middle-aged women, it turns out, have been eroticized in the media.

Many younger men seem to see "scoring" an older chick as a coup. I was surprised by the number of twenty- and thirty-somethings who wrote to me online, or approached in person. I heard similar tales from other single women in their forties. What do I think of a retrograde societal shift that has managed to objectify accomplished, mature professionals? I think: any offensive trend that makes a forty-five-year-old woman feel sexy has my support.

My mom described dating after her first divorce, in her early thirties, as a whirlwind of excitement. She'd married at nineteen and had never been single as an adult. Post-marriage, her childbearing desires sated, she found stepping out in the swinging '70s to be one big carousel of arousing non-commitment.

Then again, for every person I met who loved dating, I talked to two or three others who hated it. "Talk to a woman in Cincinnati, she'll say, 'Cincinnati is the worst city to date in.' Talk to a woman in New York, she'll say, 'New York is the worst place to date,'" said Evan Marc Katz, a dating coach who bills himself as a "personal trainer for love." Katz thinks the real problem is time. It takes a while to meet someone you could love.

Dating can be hard at any stage, but dating after divorce adds some curveballs. Society may have changed in the time between your wedding and your divorce. Your ideas about relationships have probably shifted. Old inhibitions, such as fear of pregnancy, or wanting to remain celibate until marriage, may no longer apply. Sex when you're older can be less physically fraught yet more emotionally intense—and you don't know how you'll feel until you try.

Also, as with making new friends, your skills could be rusty. It's basically impossible to remain fluent in dating when married; there's no real way to practice. Even if you spent the waning years of marriage shamelessly flirting with coworkers, you didn't have to figure out how to act on those overtures, and you had a built-in excuse for turning down unwanted advances.

"The biggest complaint I hear from divorced people is that they don't know how to date. But no one knows how to date," insisted Tucker.

And so, in an attempt to help all of us to enjoy going out with the opposite sex, here is a brief primer on dating postdivorce:

The Happy Dater

Keep it light: People often claim they met their perfect match *only after* they stopped looking. But the truth is probably something different: "not looking" translated into bringing an open mind and a relaxed attitude to what they saw.

This is exactly the opposite of what I was doing. I was eyeing every date as a potential husband, then feeling flattened by my lack of desire to rush out and look at wedding rings. "That is not what dating is," insisted Tucker. "Dating is light. It's an entrée to others, an activity, an engagement. It's not a goal. You go on a date to have a date. If you're a woman, it's important to go out with men, to feel like a woman. You don't get that from your friends."

Dating is probably how you'll find your next serious mate, admitted Tucker, but at the moment, you need to be *in the moment*; take a mindful approach to sipping cappuccino with some dude from eHarmony.

Two different divorced men told me they'd reached a similar conclusion. Successful dating—having a good time and eventually connecting with someone—only happened after they let go of the seriousness of marriage and the gravity of its ending. "You've got to be open about it, playful about it," said the divorced restaurateur from New Jersey, Vince. "That's how it was when we were kids. Now we're adults and parents, but we're not in that family life anymore. We've got to start how we started before."

Get yourself out there: Every dating expert I spoke to said a version of the same thing: whether they call it a "numbers game" or "getting a good flow of people going," they agree that successful dating usually requires meeting a lot of people.

You can generate a stream of potentials by subscribing to a few dating sites. Or get yourself out, in person. At first, Airplane Lisa found dating incredibly unpleasant. Fix-ups failed. Married men hit on her.

At one point, her mother created a Match.com profile for her, and spammed her with details of eligible men. The pressure to find someone made her feel worse.

Lisa decided to stop looking, and get more involved in her community. She became the treasurer of her condo association, and she volunteered on service projects, such as cleaning up the park along the town's riverfront. She also focused on work, eventually saving enough to buy a beachfront condo on the Jersey Shore for weekends.

In 2012, Hurricane Sandy wiped out the electrical, cable, and sewer systems in her complex. She threw herself into the task of rebuilding. Working alongside her was another condo owner, a divorced, independent business owner about her age. His take-charge attitude impressed her. "We became friends. We had a common interest, trying to get the electricity back. We got along really well."

When it came to turning the friendship into a romance, she had to take the initiative. "I said to him one day, 'I really like you. If you ever want to hang out sometime, even if it's romantically, like to go to the movies, call me. If you don't, I won't be offended. I would understand.'"

He called a few days later to ask her out, and they've been together ever since. "He said if I hadn't asked, it never would have happened," said Lisa. "He's really strong in his career, but not a good communicator in relationships."

Lisa's story points to another truth about dating: everyone will say you absolutely *must* do some one particular thing, and avoid at all costs something else. "Never ask a guy out!" for example. Or, "You'll only find love when you're not looking." But only you know the details of your situation, and of the people you meet. "I took a gamble. I figured if it doesn't work out, it will be uncomfortable, but I'll get over it. Luckily, it worked out," said Lisa.

The dentistry professional in New York who'd flipped a coin when dividing his assets upon divorce, Adam, said he made a list of eight women he'd met over the years and liked. "As you go through life, you have chemistry with certain people, but you don't pursue it because you're married." Divorced, he decided to pursue it. He started at the top of his list and went out with the first four women. Then he went out with the third woman again. Eighteen months later, they decided to marry.

Through Facebook, Katie, the art advisor, reconnected with a man she'd known as a child—who wound up becoming her second husband. "We'd actually dated when we were eight and nine in summer camp. We have all these friends in common, all these weird things in common."

I was excited by Katie's story, and Adam's. I loved the idea of a new love hiding in an old relationship, the notion that the right person was there all along. We just needed to improve our ability to see.

Forget what you DON'T want: Sometimes we're so focused on *not* repeating past mistakes that we overvalue their apparent opposites, choosing someone who makes us just as unhappy, but in a new way. Or, more likely, the relationship grinds along with basically the same problems dressed in different clothing. We often misdiagnose the source of the problems in the immediate aftermath of a breakup. Our last partner was broke, so this one better have money. But the real snag was selfishness, which Mr. Moneybags also displays.

Or your ex-wife was beautiful but crazy, so you move in with the first sane, homely woman you meet. Then realize, two years later, that both women love conflict and live from crisis to crisis. Or, you think, *I loved my wife more than she loved me. I'll only date people I feel tepid about. That will make me happy.*

I've come to think of overcorrection as the "I need a Norwegian!" syndrome. The Norwegian aviation entrepreneur I spoke to, Roald, careened from one extreme to another *twice* before finding a great partner. "My first wife tended to influence people by manipulation. That contributed to the second person I chose, someone very direct. But she had a combative-type personality that was over-the-top."

After ending his second unsuccessful marriage, Roald decided he needed a Norwegian, like himself. Having the same cultural background would guarantee compatibility, he thought. He dived into a relationship with the first seemingly suitable Norwegian woman he met. Once again, not the right match. "Sometimes you're like a pinball machine. You bounce from one to another until you land somewhere in the middle."

I need a Norwegian!

After being single for a few years, and settling into a new level of comfort with that state, Roald met a woman at his tennis club, about his age, not Norwegian. He found her attractive and genuinely interesting on her own, not in comparison to someone else. Today, they have a great relationship. "I like the way we are together. I think we bring out good things in each other. We have a good mix of respect and love and attraction. And a good balance. Also, I was ready. She was ready, too."

Forget what you DO want: We've all heard that we should write a list of the ten things we want. Tucker thinks that's a terrible idea because it shuts down exploration. "You want to be at the R&D stage—research and development. You don't know what you want. What you want now is very different from what you wanted before. You like different things. You're in a different stage in life. This is about personal discovery."

Tucker advises her clients to be open even in the area of attraction, insisting that 90 percent of the happily married couples she's met or heard about in her workshops were not attracted to each other at first sight. Her rule: give it three dates. Don't rule *out* a guy just because he's distractingly dashing, but give yourself a chance to rule *in* someone with more subtle appeal. "So many people in divorce say, 'Well, we grew apart.' Well, allow yourself to grow. Discover who you are. Have an open mind."

The Puerto Rican hairdresser who'd impressed me by not suing her ex for child support when he lost his job eventually fell hard for a man who was not her usual type. A friend of her cousin's, he'd been around at a few social events over the years, but she hadn't considered him romantically. "My type was more fit, more ethnic looking, shorter. He's Spanish, but he looks white, and he was more on the chunkier side and he's really tall."

After accepting an invitation to see a morning movie with him, she realized her type had changed. "He was different. I liked it. More mature, into work, more family-oriented. He asked about my girls right away. That attracted him to me, and then I just grew to love him."

KEEP YOUR EX OUT OF IT

Sometime after my husband moved out, I was standing in a clothing store while the rain poured down outside, spellbound by Rupert Holmes's "Escape" on the sound system:

> *If you like piña coladas, and getting caught in the rain*
> *If you're not into yoga, if you have half a brain.*

I listened in a misty-eyed fit of romantic longing. A woman in a dead-end relationship writes a personal ad; her forlorn partner answers it. They'd chosen correctly the first time, after all! They'd merely lost sight of their love.

Maybe we, too, could rediscover our common ground and try again! I could stop all this unsatisfying dating!

Then reality reasserted itself. We were not living in a narrative pop ditty from the 1970s. Our relationship hadn't flattened due to familiarity and the passage of time. If I'd come across my ex's personal ad—or today, his online profile—it would have sent me into a tailspin of depression. There he'd be, his chiseled jaw and big brown eyes, a clever description of his athleticism and concern for social justice. I'd be reminded, once again, why I'd wanted him. And then, how unhappy we were while wed. I might obsessively scroll through photos of women on the site and imagine which ones he'd contacted, sinking into a funk.

We agreed early on not to use the same dating sites. We made a pact not to discuss new relationships or sex. We structured our child-care evenings to prevent us from walking in on the other with a date. Neither of us is the jealous type, but we didn't want unnecessary provocation. And as I saw first-hand, watching your former spouse with someone else can make you miserable—even if you're delighted to be free. It doesn't mean you want him back. It means he was yours for many years, and you haven't found another and you don't want what you've lost shoved in your face.

It may be tempting to talk about your new love with your old—to prove how desirable you are to others or to inform her that none of those flaws she cited exist, according to the last five women you dated, several of whom are still calling and texting, trying to get you back. You may feel the urge to lament your latest dating snafus with someone who knows you well, or joke about them.

In most cases, you're better off calling someone else. It can take time for possessiveness to fade, even for healthy attachment to lessen. Hearing about your new love life can make your ex feel betrayed, even if no cheating occurred. For some, jealousy after divorce is a form of grief, sadness over the marriage ending. We may feel incomplete on our own, still "part" of the former "whole."

Being newly single is a labile state, dynamic, liable to change. Discretion protects those we care about from our explorations and experiments, our failed attempts, our wild, passionate, unbridled nights (that I have to believe will happen again).

Collaborative counselor Forrest Mosten said the involvement of new romantic partners can implode mediation sessions, dragging out a divorce. He advises clients to sign a dating-following-separation agreement to clarify their intentions. Such an agreement might stipulate that you'll refrain from talking about dating or new relationships with each other and won't pry for information. It could state that you're each free to date and have sex with others, no further permission slip needed. As painful as it might sound to hash out a dating-following-separation agreement, not doing so might hurt worse. If you have kids, establishing dating guidelines protects the two of you, and them.

Mosten suggested not bringing your new gal-pal to family events the other parent will attend, nor having her sleep over while your kids are home—at least for the first few months or even year after separation. Let time pass. Then, he advised, limit sleepovers to a committed partner, and inform your ex when you're serious enough about someone to include her at home.

Child psychiatrist Mark Banschick agreed. "There needs to be a very clear hiatus for the kids so they can come to terms with the divorce before having to come to terms with someone new. Then, when the new person comes on board, it's not so much a replacement as an addition they can feel good about because Mommy's happy."

Todd, the father in Michigan who'd written a divorce elevator speech with his wife, said he felt optimistic about how his children would adjust to a new partner. Neither he nor his wife had a new serious romance for the first two years after separation. Then he reconnected with a woman he'd dated for about a month in tenth grade. Long before introducing her to the kids, he talked to them about the possibility. "We were out to dinner at Buffalo Wild Wings, just laughing, joking around. It was after my son's football game. I said, 'How would you guys feel if Mommy or Daddy got a boyfriend or girlfriend?' My daughter said, 'We don't want you to be lonely for the rest of your life. We just want you guys to be happy.' She didn't even hesitate for a second about it. My son agreed."

I do think we can go overboard with concern about our children meeting anyone new. A thoughtful, considerate father of three told me he'd remarried too quickly and not very happily, in part because he worried about exposing his kids to a possible revolving door of girlfriends. Lauren, the mother of one in California, finally fell for a guy she met online. She didn't introduce him to her young son, but she talked about him so often that the little boy became fixated on wanting to know why they couldn't meet. Her attempt to keep her dating and home life separate wound up heightening the importance of this new man in her son's estimation, giving him the sense that something secret, possibly wrong, was occurring. A casual, friendly interaction would have been less fraught.

Our son's life always involved other adults. While married, we often had friends stay for the weekend. Single, I still had friends come for dinner and stay over in the guest room or on the couch when visiting. Introducing our son to someone I might like—as a friend, in a casual way—felt more natural and less disruptive than erecting barriers to keep them apart. Others with similarly social lives said the same thing.

A casual interaction is different, however, than encouraging a child to form an attachment to a person you may dump the next year, or trying out partners by inviting them to move into your bedroom.

If your ex finds someone new before you do, you may need an emotional "contract" or dating-following-separation agreement with *yourself*. This agreement might include an internal commitment not to compare your romantic lives, not to dwell on what he might be doing, and to follow Principle No. 6: Resist the urge to compare.

The mother of three in rural Colorado, Hollie, struck me as a great example of someone with a healthy ability to remain self-referential. She focused on her own life—her college courses and her children—rather than comparing her situation to her ex's. She said women in online chat groups often complained when their former spouses moved on. "Everyone says, 'I'm a single mom and he's dating and it's not fair.' I feel like I'm not actually jealous of that life. It's not the life I want. I like being with my kids. I like studying. I don't feel I have a lot to contribute to anyone outside of the kids right now anyway. Maybe in four years, I'll be ready to date."

Some people feel no jealousy when their former spouse finds someone new. Katie was so unperturbed by the idea of her ex dating that she helped him create his online profile, selecting photos and writing copy. "I told him, 'Oh, you can't use that photo; your forehead is all shiny. And you can't say "psyched" and expect to meet quality women.' We'd ended up being much more like brother and sister, since we never had a very passionate sexual relationship. I think if we had, helping him date would have been impossible."

GETTING IT RIGHT THE NEXT TIME

Being divorced may make us better partners the second time around. Despite statistics showing a higher rate of divorce in second marriages, those who succeed bring time-tested knowledge from the first.

McCarthy said people in successful second marriages value them more. "They know they've beaten the odds and take pride in that."

Katz said the divorced women he coaches are quicker to compromise than the never-marrieds. This can be true of divorced men, too. "I'm more flexible in terms of trying to make something work, maybe more mature," said Roald. "You're so grateful that you found someone you get along with. You make more of an effort to make it work."

Age and experience give Roald confidence in his current relationship. "We're both over fifty now. If you meet someone in your twenties, what's the guarantee you'll evolve in the same way as your partner? If you meet at our age, you're less likely to change. You pretty much know what you're going to get."

Still, if you fall in love again at forty, fifty, or sixty, it's easy to look back at your life and lament not having met the right person sooner, perhaps the first time around. "To me that's kind of missing the point," said Roald. "You are the person you are now. The experiences you've had made you that person."

Airplane Lisa also insisted that she's grateful to have met her new partner now, rather than in their youth. "He says he was really arrogant and pushy and selfish. I needed to get more confident myself. It wasn't until I was probably thirty-five that I was confident. Once you establish yourself, you can start to appreciate people for their friendship more. We're both comfortable with ourselves, where we are in life."

Being more comfortable might translate into having more mental bandwidth for your partner's needs, a second major predictor of relationship success, according to neuroscientist Lucy Brown. "People in successful relationships have the ability to put the other person first. We incorporate the other person into our sense of self more than we think we do," she said, pointing to fMRI scans of the happily paired. Those in strong partnerships have decreased brain activity in the regions associated with focus on one's own body. Researchers see this as a kind of brain map of other-centeredness. "As we begin to take this person on, your sense of self becomes partly the other person, this other person's life."

We can work on putting the other first, as well as on other relationships skills such as flexibility, gratitude, consideration, and
decreasing our own negative judgment. After divorce, we bring life
experience, new understanding, and perhaps an increased sense of
urgency to this task.

· · ·

On my third Memorial Day as a single woman, now in California, I drove
with my son to South Pasadena for a playdate with Ruth, a happily married mother of two and a friend of a friend from New York. We were at
the playground, all three of our children up in a tree. "So wait, are you
dating?" she asked.

"Yes. Yes, I am," I said, as if saying it would make it true. "I mean,
you know, I certainly *can*. It's appropriate."

"Who do I know?" she said, looking up at the tree. "I can't believe
you are still single. You are a lottery ticket waiting to be cashed."

A lottery ticket waiting to be cashed! That's the kind of statement an
enamored suitor might let slip, one reason it's worth going out on dates.
I wanted to feel that way about myself, and to believe that the right guy
would come along and feel that lucky to have me.

Later, back home, I wrote her words on an index card and taped
it to my wall. "You are a lottery ticket waiting to be cashed." I'd taken
down that other phrase my friend Abby had uttered: "Your task is to
learn to be alone, temporarily." I'd stopped needing that sticky note
months ago. I was fine being alone.

Still, I would have preferred not to be. I wanted a partner, someone
on my team, a man I'd be excited to come home to at the end of the day,
to go out with at night. I was ready for my buffer period to end.

I looked forward to the day when I'd see the lottery ticket quote as
a useless scribble from a distant epoch, an unnecessary reminder. I'd
peel it off the wall, and toss it away.

CHAPTER TWELVE

Happily Ever After Divorce

The Evolving Post-Marriage Relationship

✦

While we expect marriage to change with time, we often assume divorce freezes a relationship. But divorce evolves, too, sometimes for the better. Increased longevity means more years for many to reconsider and repair.

> For a while we pondered whether to take a vacation or get
> a divorce. We decided that a trip to Bermuda is over in two
> weeks, but a divorce is something you always have.
>
> —American filmmaker Woody Allen

When my future ex told his parents why we were separating, he put it like this: "On a scale of emotional intimacy that runs from one to ten, Wendy is a nine and I'm a four." During our marriage, I grew increasingly angry about this discrepancy between us, and even, perhaps, the values it represented. I worried that our ongoing incompatibilities were squelching my spirit, making me more rigid and less optimistic, more tired, less fun.

Once he moved out, I stopped feeling angry or hurt by his cool emotional style. I no longer worried about its effect on me. As the months passed, my long-standing frustrations faded nearly to the point of nonexistence. Conflicts would recur in little flashes—we were the same people as before and our incompatibilities were real—but we ran up against them infrequently, and they had less impact on my daily life.

Instead, I found myself appreciating him in a new way. He'd occasionally take out my trash or move my car on street-cleaning days to prevent me from getting a parking ticket. He'd done these things in the past, but when we were married, I was often too frustrated by what felt like his lack of emotional presence to value his physical efforts. Now, I was thrilled with the help. *Whose ex-husband takes out the trash?!* I felt his concern about me in a way I couldn't before.

Divorce revealed a new truth about my once-spouse: I'd married the ideal ex-husband.

In marriage, the very singularity of our one and only spouse puts a lot of pressure on that person to be just right. Some people feel as if their spouse is *part* of them. As Cathy said of Heathcliff in *Wuthering*

Heights, "He's more myself than I am. . . . If all else perished, and he remained, I should still continue to be." If all else perished, and my husband remained, and he still refused to put a napkin on his lap, I'd rise from the grave and nag him about it. But my ex-husband forgets his napkin? So he gets a little spaghetti sauce on his khakis? So what? It's no reflection on me. Plus, I'm not doing his laundry.

Of course, I was working hard to create a nice relationship with him, and not only for the sake of our son. I didn't want to lose the twelve years we'd shared, to obliterate my memories under the boot blacking of anger, or the effacing wash of inattention. I was acutely aware of having lost years of my life after breaking up with Giles, my first real boyfriend, an artist I'd loved and lived with for nearly six years. When we split, we divided our friends and our stuff, and went our separate ways. We put our past behind us. But *I* was part of that past, and along with him went his half of my memories.

After my husband and I separated, I looked over photos of trips we'd taken in our breezy thirties. I spoke to our son about our years in the countryside. I wanted to imprint my past, to "take a picture with my brain," as our son used to say when he couldn't recall an event from his toddlerhood. "Uh-oh! My brain forgot to take a picture of that!" he'd say, smacking his forehead like a cartoon character. "Silly brain!" I didn't want to have silly brain about my dozen years with my ex. My life felt too important. My years were dwindling; I needed them all.

Not every separated spouse is going through old photo albums; it may be more common to want to kick them to the curb, jettison any reminders of the marriage. This might feel right in the immediate term. But our emotions and our relationships are elastic, capable of expanding, harboring the will to change.

I reconnected with my ex-boyfriend shortly before my husband moved out. He'd married and was living as a stay-at-home dad in Brooklyn. We talked about our lives back in Houston in our twenties, our move together to New York, the industrial loft we'd sublet in Chinatown. As we reminisced, the years we'd shared came back into focus for me. Reconnecting helped me remember who I'd been.

I saw something similar in my mother's reconnection with my dad. He'd known her in high school. He remembered her parents and her childhood home. He could joke about her days as a "Heights Mocky," a Great Lakes version of a Valley Girl, apparently, an old high school argot that recalled an entire world invisible to others yet salient to them.

Many people find that with time, even a turbulent divorce improves. Sometimes a former spouse finds himself able to express appreciation or remorse years later, paying off a long-overdue verbal debt and creating a more trusting, open interaction. Other times adult children forge reconnection—between former spouses, among step-relations, and even between themselves and a parent distanced by divorce. While some people carry anger to the end, many others find new opportunities to reconcile in their old age.

NEVER TOO LATE TO SAY THANK YOU

Back when we first started telling people about our separation, I was throwing plastic fruit to my son at the cacophonous Children's Museum of Manhattan alongside a happily married friend who'd had a brief, early marriage followed by a rapid divorce. "How's it going?" she asked.

"Good. It's good. We're getting along a lot better now that we're not living together."

"Well, you're in the honeymoon stage of divorce," she said, brushing aside my reality with a matter-of-fact certainty. "It will get worse."

How do people develop this flair for forecasting the negative? Is there an after-school course in bursting other people's bubbles?

Many people assume that hate is the opposite of love. Discord, they therefore presume, must be the flip side of marriage. But *indifference* is love's true counterpart. Our feelings aren't wired to an on/off switch, though it may look like that, at times. "I think it's a faulty understanding of how our emotions and our relationships work," said a thoughtful sixty-something pro baseball player turned real estate magnate. Ten years after separation, he remained close to his wife. Some friends insisted his lack of rancor meant he hadn't moved on emotionally. "I think that's a very narrow view of family. As if family is somehow limited to this one arrangement," he said.

While some once-weds transition smoothly into friendship or benign disinterest, others improve a bad divorce, sometimes merely by retooling how they speak. "I've seen entire cases change because one person looked at the other and said, 'Thank you for being such a good provider all these years,'" said Colorado-based lawyer and mediator Beth Henson. "Or a woman felt undervalued in marriage, and the man says, 'I just want to say what a great job you've done with our children.' It's amazing to see. Never underestimate the power of a sincere 'please' or 'thank you.'"

Or an apology, even years after the split. "The thing that really changed everything for me was when, a couple of years ago, we were having a long conversation, and he apologized of his own accord for the things that he really did owe me an apology for," said Catherine, the mother of one who'd moved from Canada to upstate New York to marry a close friend who then left her shortly after their daughter was born. "When someone hurts you really badly, it's hard to trust them again fully. It was only when he really apologized that everything was okay."

I was amazed to see the "power of one" in one of the worst divorces I'd witnessed up close. A successful film director in Los Angeles told terrible stories about his ex-wife. She'd taken him to court repeatedly, filing frivolous motions involving their children. She was erratic, crazy, scheming. The notion of a good divorce? He'd scoffed. "Cute idea. Limited application."

I saw him a year and a half later. He'd had an epiphany while out of town, he said, partly due to a perspective-altering conversation with another divorced man. *He was committed to this woman for life because they shared the children he loved.* He returned home, called his ex-wife, and thanked her for their children. He told her he'd be there for her forever and upped his child and spousal support. These actions completely flipped a brutal, ugly, ongoing fight. She remained emotionally unstable, he said, but by taking a supportive stance, he was able to minimize flare-ups and manage the interaction.

Some of their old tenderness returned. "She gave me a back rub," he told me in a dazed sort of way. I was shocked. She'd seemed like a moviemaker's villain. But even in a horrible divorce, we may have far more power to influence the relationship than we realize.

Or, as German writer and statesman Johann Wolfgang von Goethe said, "If we take man as he is, we make him worse. But if we take man as he should be, we make him capable of becoming what he can be."

Sometimes a divorce improves because a former spouse changes. Loss can dramatically shift a person's thinking and behavior. In a marriage, people don't improve through criticism, it turns out, at least not in my experience. But the loss inherent in a marriage's end can crack open a carapace hardened over the years, leave space for a new, better being to emerge. Also, your ex still has your complaints in her head. She may now address them on her own. It's important to be open to the real evolution of your former spouse, to keep updating your view. She may become someone you get along with far better.

Other times, a former spouse remains the same, but *we* change. We grow happier, busier, clearer about our priorities and duties. We may not like this person any more than we did when divorcing, but we like *ourselves* better, and that confidence generates a more magnanimous spirit.

The fact that relationships evolve has a risky corollary—even a good divorce can go bad. I've seen old resentments rise up and sabotage a decent divorce years later, or new actions incite unprecedented fights.

The possibility of deterioration exists within all our connections. A favorite nephew could grow into an obnoxious young man. A best friend could become jealous or judgmental. People will warn you that new partners will sour a decent divorce. While that can happen, former couples can mess up a good un-marriage themselves. Just as you can't stick to a weight-lifting routine for three months and expect to be buff for life, you can't create a good settlement agreement and assume your effort is over.

If your parting grows tense with the years, you can stop, reassess, and recommit to re-improvement. New conflicts may even require a return to a therapist, another heart-to-heart with your ex, or the seeking-out of other help.

Some divorce reformers advocate access to mediation services and parenting education years after divorce, a desire that reflects an important fact: while divorce is time-limited, relationships are forever—especially if you have children together. As University of Arizona's Chris Segrin put it, "Co-parenting is a relationship for life that has to be managed almost like a dating relationship has to be managed."

Some people brainstorm—together or individually—about potential new conflicts, and plan how to minimize or avoid them. The technology activist in Washington, DC, Alex, signed a contract with his wife stipulating that neither would take the other to court about child-rearing issues postdivorce. They wanted to protect themselves from the vicissitudes of the future and their own potential reactions. Even if you don't write a contract, recognizing that you may need to attend to your divorce down the line can prepare you to take a thoughtful, active role, should new conflict arise. A good relationship with an ex requires paying attention and making adjustments as circumstances change.

Perhaps more common than some new acrimony surfacing years after divorce is a slow drifting apart, the closeness peeling off in layers as it becomes superfluous. Chloe in New York said that she and her ex-husband talked every week in the beginning, working together to create a calm, stable environment for their daughter. Now that their routine is established and they have more confidence in each other as co-parents, they don't need to stay as connected. For Chloe, the positive adjustment is bittersweet; she misses the interactions with her once-husband. "I can call him up, but there's no urgent reason. Our daughter's fine. We're all fine."

WHEN CHILDREN TAKE THE LEAD

Grown children can catalyze reconnection between former spouses, among step-relations, and even between themselves and a parent—

sometimes after years of hostility. "Kids need both their parents and they will find a way to get them together. Now that my daughter is grown and has kids of her own, it's fun to have holidays with my ex and things are very mellow," said Erica Jong, author of *Fear of Flying*, the smart, racy 1973 bestselling novel about, among other things, a second marriage. "Most of the good divorces I know are bad divorces that mellowed over time."

Michael, a retired dean of a chiropractic college living in Palm Springs, California, divorced in 1979, when his sons were two and four. The divorce was civil, but not amicable. "Then, when the kids were almost done with high school, everything changed dramatically. They wanted us to do everything together. They needed both parents," he said.

All four of them began spending holidays together. As time went on, he and his ex-wife reverted to their original roles, just without the romance. "It took years and years for that to happen. We never discussed whatever resentments we had between us. I think we just matured."

In 2012, his ex-wife was diagnosed with pancreatic cancer, a notably virulent form. They began spending more time together, even taking a trip to Europe for three weeks with another couple. "We ended this trip in Rome. It was like a movie. We knew this was the end," Michael said. "We acknowledged it. We spoke about it. I had no feelings like, 'I wish I had said this,' or, 'I wish this had happened.' We were like old parents, saying, 'Life's good. It sucks that you don't get to stay and enjoy it.' There was no angst between us."

She lived to see their oldest son wed, then died two months later. Michael said he felt grateful not only to have grown closer to his ex-wife, but also to have been there at the end. "What transpired from that is a bond I have with the kids; I was there with them through this. We went through this as a family. Now, with her gone, we still have that. I think that makes us a lot stronger as a unit."

The L.A.-based performance artist, Dan, said he began to finally connect with his father in adulthood. Born and raised in China, his father hadn't grown up in a close family. Had he remained married to Dan's mom, perhaps he would have become more of an involved, ball-throwing, "American-style" dad. As it was, the divorce drove an ever deeper wedge between father and son. "I have this one very vivid memory of a junior high school father-and-son night," said Dan. "Looking at other boys with their dads, I thought, 'What is a father supposed to feel like?' I didn't feel anything. It was this upsetting realization that here was this man I called my dad, but it had no feeling attached to it."

I was at Dan's large live-work studio while he told me this story. We were sitting in his small kitchen, drinking tea at a vintage metal table. His father, tall, slightly stooped, his black hair just thinning, shuffled into the room, smiled vaguely, then shuffled back out. Now in his early eighties, his father had begun showing signs of dementia—some memory loss and confusion. Dan had reached out to him, asking him to come stay for a while.

Fifty years after his parents' divorce, Dan was the one leading the relationship, and finally feeling the closeness he'd missed. "I've been trying to be supportive of him, and we've had some of the most real conversations we've ever had. We've had some talks where I've been like, 'Oh my God, I feel like I'm with my dad. I'm with my dad.' That is really profound. Somehow that chasm got crossed. It's just something you feel."

Relationships with step-parents can grow closer over time, too. Sara, my friend whose beachfront wedding prompted my divorce discussion, was in her twenties when she finally began to develop a relationship with her stepmother. Her father had left her mother for this woman. Her mother had often made bitter, sarcastic comments about the "other woman."

Then Sara saw her stepmother for the first time in a decade at a family funeral. "She seemed much more human," Sara said. Her stepmother began reaching out, arranging dinners, passing down furniture and books. Sara began to question the roles each adult had played in the divorce. "Over time I realized that she didn't cause the breakup of my parents' marriage. Only the people in the marriage are responsible for that relationship. I also saw that my parents were better off apart."

Her mother's vilification of her stepmother, while understandable at first, had become its own reality, not only reflecting the past but also determining the future. "I finally sat her down and told her that her behavior was interfering with my relationship with my dad, and that wasn't fair. To her great credit, she totally heard me and stopped."

Sara and her brother began spending time with her stepmother, and telling each woman about the other. Still, by the time Sara's wedding approached, the two older women still hadn't spoken. Sara's mother, Jonesie, worried that tension would spoil the event. "I had heard things from the kids, that she wasn't that bad," Jonesie said. "I decided, in the interest of not making it difficult for Sara, I'm going to say something. So at the rehearsal at the beach, I thanked them for coming. That was it. Nothing big."

At the cocktail party later that night, Formerly Evil Stepmother approached Jonesie. "She said to me, 'You did a great job raising your children.' That really did break the ice. I said to her, 'Well, in hindsight, I need to thank you for doing me the biggest favor of my life.' I didn't elaborate. I think she knew what I meant."

I saw all three of them together more than a year later, at Sara's baby shower. It was held in a charming, incredibly loud bistro in the East Village. Sara's mother and stepmother sat next to each other on a banquette in the corner, chatting. They looked as pleased as any two expectant grandmothers could be.

"You know what it is? We're both kind of older," said Jonesie. "You realize that you're not going to live for as many years as you already have, and that there are issues you need to put in the right place. We realized that it would be better if we could have a joint relationship with the kids. This ignoring each other needed to end."

THE RISK OF NOT RECONCILING

In her moving, popular memoir *The Top Five Regrets of the Dying: A Life Transformed by the Dearly Departing*, former hospice worker/singer-songwriter Bronnie Ware writes about the laments people express at the end of their lives. Common among them: the wish to have had more courage to express their feelings, and the desire to have stayed in touch with friends.

Both of these regrets plagued a soft-spoken southerner in her late sixties, whom I met while visiting Nubanusit Neighborhood & Farm in New Hampshire. It was the second spring of my separation, back when I still struggled with loneliness. I'd begun fantasizing about living in an "intentional community" such as Nubanusit, a cohousing utopia where everyone agrees on the architectural style and plantings, dines together in a large hall, and collaborates on rules that may sound inane to others but unify the residents in the joint project of collaborative living.

It was spring on the East Coast, and therefore raining. I hurried across the thick lawn in the downpour toward the dining hall, where I met with Marlene and a few other divorcées. Marlene was one of a handful of people who'd moved to the community after divorce.

She said she'd always considered her husband her best friend. Every day, during their long marriage, they'd talked after work, for hours. This sounded like the kind of relationship I'd always wanted, one reflecting Charles Dickens's notion that "a good marriage is a long conversation that always seems too short."

Then, her husband had an affair. Marlene had no interest in ending the marriage. She didn't believe the girlfriend was significant. "I don't even know how he had time to talk to her, given how much we talked," she said. Her husband seemed unable to choose between the two. She finally chose for him. "I could have gotten over *having shared* him with another woman in the past, but I didn't want to keep sharing. The whole thing blew up in about ten days, and then I kicked him out."

Marlene decided to move from the mid-Atlantic region, where they were, up to New Hampshire. Still, their relationship felt too permanent, too much a part of her to really end. They had a warm, loving conversation the day she moved. He promised to visit. He sounded ambivalent about his choice. "I got my hopes up again," she said. They had plenty of time, she figured. They were still young. Or young-ish. He'd had a battle with a non-aggressive form of skin cancer, but he was cured. She thought.

A few months went by with no word from her ex. No call. No visit. Marlene waited. She sank into a depression, and eventually sought psychological help. She forced herself to *get over* her long marriage, to put it behind her. But she didn't forgive her husband. She just sealed up her past and shoved it away.

He finally wrote to her, three years after the split. He was nearby and wanted to meet for lunch. "I was totally torn up again, getting this e-mail out of the blue," she said. After working so hard to get over her hurt, she couldn't bear a visit. She refused to see him.

Marlene stopped talking. She looked at me, and then at the other women in the room. She was sitting on a low, squashy gray couch, resting her forearms on her knees, hunched forward. Rain drummed on the roof.

The skin cancer had metastasized, it turned out. Perhaps he'd called to tell her. Two years later, he was dead. She'd never spoken to him again. She had a full life when we met, friends to dine with or catch a movie in town. But she'd never reconciled with the man she'd loved and considered her best friend. Twelve years later, when I met her, she still didn't know what to do about this fact.

"I regretted all that time, and still do, that we never really talked about it," she said. "We never were able to get out of the throes of the upset to talk about what had happened."

I walked out of there feeling mowed down by her sadness, like the spongy, waterlogged lawn. I thought of the line from the novel-turned-movie *Life of Pi*, "I suppose in the end the whole of life becomes an act of letting go. But what always hurts the most is not taking a moment to say goodbye."

Many people *do* have the time to reconnect before it's too late. Our increased longevity gives us more opportunity than ever to revisit and revise. The life expectancy for a person born around 1900 in the United States was just under fifty. For someone born in 2012, that number has inched up to nearly seventy-nine. Even people my parents' age are out-living their own parents, and we all know of octogenarians who still play tennis or travel or work.

Illness itself can motivate reconnection. Sometimes a former part-ner will return to help out, showing up for better and for worse. A for-mer theater director in Texas, Jacques, was the primary parent for his son, after divorce. He'd realized he was gay around the time of the di-vorce, and eventually formed a close partnership with another man when his son was finishing high school. Years later, his partner got cancer. His ex-wife, single at the time, came to town to help. She was there for Jacques in his partner's last days.

She also was ill, battling hepatitis C, contracted years earlier from a blood transfusion during childbirth. They decided she should move in, set herself up in a wing of Jacques's now too-large house. "She is the mother of my child and I feel it's important for her to have the best ex-perience possible while I'm here," said Jacques. "That's my value sys-tem, and hers as well. I know in my heart, if the situation was reversed, she'd do the same for me."

Psycho-oncologists talk about seeing ex-spouses show up to help out when someone faces cancer. "It isn't every day, but it is every month," said Matthew Loscalzo of City of Hope Cancer Center in Duarte, Cal-ifornia. "It's a very common experience. The first spouse comes back and supports the patient, along with their current spouse. Once you have loved someone, there is something deep in the human spirit that transcends pettiness or anger from the past. You see the goodness of people, the resilience and strength."

• • •

We're not all going to have some beautiful, residential reconciliation with our once-loved, of course. Sometimes an ex refuses to melt. Other times family members cling to and reinforce old hostilities. A new spouse may foment conflict. But we can work on improving our own role in that relationship.

I don't think there is one clear *truth*, one final answer about what the @#$%&! really happened here. Closure in divorce isn't one definite ending. It's more like a DVD with alternative director's cuts. We cycle through them, stopping on one or the other depending on our mood or circumstances. But we need to discard those cuts that trap us in a limiting, defeating story. Keep only the versions that leave us feeling whole. If we're still struggling and angry, we can listen closely for hints of apology, look for signs of change, and keep trying out new narratives that make better sense. We can work on improving our own role in the story.

My parents, it turned out, were not going to have the fairy-tale remarriage I'd envisioned for them. But they had something else. A few years after our first all-family reunion, I took my son to visit my mother. On our second day there, she wrenched her back while dragging a forty-pound patio tile to the front curb. She was in enough pain that she agreed to see a chiropractor and spend the day lying on the couch in her bathrobe—two concessions to overexertion that I'd never seen from my strong, resilient mother.

My dad also was showing his age. A week earlier, he'd had his heart "shocked"—received an electrical treatment meant to correct arterial defibrillation, or irregular heartbeat. My mom and my dad began e-mailing about their health concerns.

I saw one of these exchanges. "I've had a summer of grandchildren and could use some adult company," my mom wrote, encouraging him to get his heart back in working order so he could visit.

My dad responded: "My heart works. It just has developed its own personality disorders. This is true of the rest of the body as well. I have a crick in my neck, a pain in my back, an itch in my scalp. I get up to pee three or four times a night and doubt if I am in good enough shape to walk a mile. All we need is a bench somewhere on a sidewalk and we can be the cartoons we laughed at. At least, I can fulfill my part."

My mom wrote, "I think if you and I sat on that bench 'somewhere on a sidewalk' we would still be glamorous. Let me know what the doctor says tomorrow."

And this exchange between my long-divorced aging parents made me cry. These are the years when you want a dedicated ally on your side, someone to witness the absurdity of life hurtling ever forward, to laugh at the troubles with you, to buffer the lows. You want someone to share the highs, too, and bounce them higher, help secure your grip on some zip line of joy riding above the realities. Pain lessens with laughter and companionship, but happiness also increases.

As my family continued to knit itself back together, I realized that *romance* wasn't the point. My parents *had* reconnected. They cared about each other. They were back on the same team. I believed if my mom and dad sat on that bench together, her back pain would fade as if by some supercharged cocktail, the magical elixir of companionship. Perhaps his heart wouldn't regulate itself, but he might be able to ride over the glitches more easily.

Of course what I really want—as most of us do—is an active, on-duty love of my life to sit on that bench with me. But short of that, I'm glad my mom and dad have each other once again. They're kind to each other, and indulgent of each other's foibles. When we're all together, I find myself hoping my next marriage will resemble my parents' first, all these years after it ended.

But if it doesn't, that's okay. The grand reunification of my family makes me hopeful about my future with my former husband. What I'm seeing is that divorce isn't any more rigid an institution than marriage.

•   •   •

At our new apartment in California, my son and I started a container garden along the balustrade of our balcony. "The basil's not doing too good but the lavender and mint are stribing," my son said to me one day, watering can in hand.

Stribing? "I think you mean *thriving*," I said.

"Right," he said. "The lavender and mint are *striving*."

I looked at my little boy, just learning subtleties of meaning, and thought, *I don't want to confuse striving with thriving in my own life anymore*. In my postdivorce fairy-tale ending, I am never again obsessed with a relationship that feels like a problem needing to be solved. I see myself having come through the tunnel of divorce, earning a living doing work I enjoy, unfettered by financial worries. My first spouse is happy, too, fulfilled. He's in my life, but the intensity of that marriage, that divorce, has faded. It's in the background, the well-worn brocade on a chair I've had for years, not a present-tense preoccupation.

My son is thriving, becoming whoever he is going to be. I'll also have found someone else to love. To paraphrase the Talmudic scholar Hillel, sometimes you have to leave a bad marriage to get into a good one. I do want the next great relationship, the truly fulfilling marriage.

For me, the fairy-tale ending also looks like holding on to the lift of being released from a bad marriage, maintaining that sense of an always-open ending. It's creating a life that is calm and rooted, yet still glimmering with unimagined possibility. Yes, we have a great deal of control over our futures, but I don't want to have to create every good thing that comes my way. For me, the ideal divorce looks like regaining my autonomy but not losing the dream—or the reality—of enchanting events unfolding that I could not have anticipated or created on my own.

Acknowledgments

I am grateful for my parents, who have continued to be my support well past childhood. I am astoundingly lucky in this, as are all of us who can rely on our parents into adulthood, particularly during divorce. My father offered support, opinions, enthusiasm, and his commitment to maintaining good relationships with those he married. My mother talked divorce with me on a weekly basis and was willing to share her difficulties in print. She also allowed herself to be influenced. Over the months and years of reading drafts of chapters, she began to take solace in the stories of others. We all want our work to matter. Seeing someone directly influenced in real time was a huge shot of encouragement for me.

It takes a village to write a book. I had tremendous help throughout the process. In the beginning, George Prochnik sat on a rocky outcropping in Central Park and encouraged me to pursue my interest in working on a book about divorce. "You can do this," he insisted. "It *is* responsible." One of the most fluid, sensitive writers and humans I know, he talked through ideas with me, helped pinpoint themes, scanned drafts of chapters, made time for phone calls during moments of editorial crisis, and believed in the importance of what I was doing. His support was instrumental to this book.

Susan Cain and Ken Cain, both brilliant writers and human beings, were incredibly helpful at the book-proposal stage and during my shaky first single summer. Kimberly Witherspoon at InkWell offered valuable guidance in shaping the proposal and fast sales acumen. Thanks to Dominick Anfuso, former editor in chief of Free Press at Simon & Schuster, for his enthusiasm for the project. Thanks to my editor at Atria, Leslie Meredith, for her incisive, clear-eyed editorial suggestions.

Abby Ellin! Read my proposal. Suggested funnier subheads. Read my manuscript. Edited. Put me up on her couch. Shared her endless well of skepticism, and equally vast pool of warmth, humor, energy, friendship, and *belief.*

I am grateful to a group of talented, generous writers and friends in New York City. My friend Sheri Fink, a brilliant writer, wrote letters of recommendation, supported my inclusion in our author group, and stood as a role model of a woman doing work she believed in. Gretchen Rubin provided inspiration, structural and organizational guidance, endless ideas, and good humor—in person and in print. Randi Epstein read the manuscript and offered wise editorial input and encouragement. Ben Dattner pointed out places where my intentions were vague. He created a rubric for encapsulating the book's message. To paraphrase the acknowledgments of the thriller novelist Harlan Coben, any areas of weak direction are *his.*

Anne Kornhauser was there throughout as a friend and wise counsel. She stepped in at the end to help format the endnotes—perhaps the most onerous task in the life of a writer. Kaja Perina shared invaluable suggestions for top experts in a variety of areas, wrote letters of recommendation, and was a cheerleader for this project. I'm so grateful to Annie Murphy Paul for the creation and dedication of the Invisibles; the group has been a tremendous resource and support to me, and a kind of New York City intellectual home.

The hilarious writer Sharon Krum shared her office space with me in New York, sent related articles, and offered endless encouragement and insight. Kate Foster-Anderson read the manuscript and offered her experience and input. Daphne Anshel talked psychology, children, and my own divorce. I am very grateful for her friendship and insights. Courtney Lancaster Pouzieux kept me company, helped organize my bibliography, tried to help me move to Brooklyn, and then did help me move to California.

In Los Angeles, Hope Edelman welcomed me into her writers' group; thank you, Hope, and much thanks to everyone else in the group. Cindy Chupack offered guidance on plotting. Sandra Barron listened to me talk about my process, helped with research and social media, and celebrated the accomplishment of mini goals. Michelle Fiordaliso helped me set goals and meet deadlines, offered support, and cooked dinner to give me more time to write. Paul Karon listened to me go on and on, and offered stress-relieving back rubs and cookies. Thea Klapwald and Mario Muller lent me their laser printer. David Mamet talked shop, self-belief, and editorial process. Peter Landesman talked divorce, writing, and romance, and encouraged me to ask for what I needed. Rabbi Mordecai Finley provided weekly lessons in how to be a decent person in relationship to others, and to myself. I am indebted to Rabbi Finley for many ideas in here.

Huge thanks and many future lunches to Meagan Mason, who brought much-needed last-minute editing and fact-checking help, offering incredibly thoughtful, detailed suggestions and solid opinions, based on her personal real-time experience.

Law professor and author Naomi Cahn was an incredible resource throughout the nearly three years it took to write this book, despite her own busy schedule and very important work. She offered keen editorial suggestions on the manuscript, forwarded related articles, and repeatedly stepped in to help clarify my understanding of family law in relation to divorce. Thank you, Naomi, for all your help. Thanks also to Rebecca Kourlis, Melinda Taylor, Beth Henson, and everyone at the Institute for the Advancement of the American Legal System for legal guidance and an example of how to concretely improve divorce and unmarried co-parenting.

Sociologist and author Christine Carter provided insight on raising happy children in divorce, read for accuracy, and brought her own keen interest in the role of positive psychology during this life phase. Many other experts read for accuracy, more than I can name here, and I am grateful to them all.

New America Foundation provided essential financial and intellectual support during my 2014 fellowship year. Many thanks to Anne-Marie Slaughter and Andrés Martinez for welcoming me into New America, supporting my project, and exposing me to new ideas. The chance to interact with so many innovators, writers, and leaders was one of the highlights of my career. Becky Schafer and Kirsten Berg at New America did fabulous, painstaking research and fact-checking. Thank you so much for your work. Interns David Allen and Jacob Glenn added strong research and good analysis. Fuzz Hogan slashed unnecessary verbiage. Thanks also to my wonderful colleagues at New America for their intellectual camaraderie, especially Kathryn Bowers, Hao Wu, and Perry Bacon.

Thanks to the MacDowell Colony for time to work on the book, and the 18th Street Arts Center for the time, space, and endless light.

Dan Jones at *The New York Times* published an essay of mine on divorce that helped in the shaping of the book. Lauren Brown at QZ.com published many pieces while I was writing that also let me sharpen my thinking and test ideas. Thanks as well to *The Jewish Week*, *The Weekly Wonk*, and *Zócalo Public Square*. I had great help from Jayme Johnson at Worthy Marketing Group with my blog design and vision.

Many thanks to my once-husband, David Callahan, who chugged along in his own life while I wrote a version of a "tell-all" that told about him. He didn't interfere. He supported me in my effort, watched our son full-time during periods of Total Writing Lockdown, concocted business plans for his version of my potential future, and edited fellowship proposals. He embodied in many ways what has taken me hundreds of pages to say. While I'll always be a little sorry that I wasn't able to love this man well in the context of marriage, I am consistently grateful for his ability to be loving toward me, unwed.

I'd also like to thank his parents, my in-laws, Daniel and Sidney Callahan, for their continued love and support. Sidney, a beautiful, sensitive, cross-disciplinary thinker and writer, shared key studies on marriage and family, and offered encouragement and advice about writing, pacing, research—and parenting.

Dan Callahan, a rigorous thinker and prolific writer, showed me his outlines, talked about his own writing process, gave his opinion about the best way to include the other side (up front!), and railed at me to fess up that I was "writing this book to defend your family's way of life!" At the time, I disagreed with this assessment. Over the years, I've come to concur. I am writing this book to defend my family's way of life, Dan. And also yours. The Callahans have an unflagging commitment to rationality, clear and *charitable* thinking, temperance, hard work, the taking in of others, and the harnessing of their talents in the service of a better society. These family values I also defend, and hope to promote.

Alexander Paris-Callahan drew supportive pictures to tape to my wall, and offered opinions about how to start chapters, as well as title suggestions and creative embellishments such as including poems and maybe pictures! My deadlines at times absorbed my attention. I want to thank him for his mature forbearance, intelligence, presence, and love.

Writing a book, like getting divorced, can be lonely. I wrote much of the first half at Anthony David's in Hoboken. Thanks to the owners for accommodating me. I wrote the second half at R+D Kitchen on Montana Avenue in Santa Monica, spending six mornings a week for the past year and a half shuttling between booth and bar. Thanks to the management, staff, and community of fellow coffee drinkers for cheering me on every morning as the marine layer slowly burned off in the ascending sun. Hanna Brewer in particular brought water, asked about my progress, and discussed relationships with me. My morning routine created a sense of community and "mattering." As one regular said, "We don't call it R+D for 'Research and Development.' We call it 'Rich and Divorced.'" I called it "the office."

I'm grateful—and frankly, astounded—that my MacBook Air held up without crashing.

Finally, I owe a tremendous debt of gratitude to everyone who talked to me about divorce, particularly those willing to have their experiences shared here, whether under their own name or a pseudonym. The divorced people profiled here are amazing—amazingly resilient and creative and optimistic and strong. But they're also regular folks who've found good ways to step outside of bad marriages and keep all parties whole. It's a real service to share your struggles and accomplishments; I believe your stories will aid others. An endless well of thanks from me, and please acknowledge to yourselves the valuable contribution you have made.

Resources for Readers

For updates, interviews, self-assessments, and inspiring stories, check out my site, WendyParis.com; sign up for my newsletter; or e-mail me at wendy@wendy paris.com.

To join the *Splitopia* conversation . . .

Twitter: @WendyParis1 [https://twitter.com/wendyparis1]
LinkedIn: Wendy Paris [https://www.linkedin.com/in/wendyparis]
Facebook: Wendy Paris [https://www.facebook.com/wendyeparis]
Pinterest: Wendy Paris [https://www.pinterest.com/wendyparis/]

GENERAL DIVORCE INFORMATION AND MONEY MATTERS

WEBSITES

CollaborativePractice.com
Use the member directory to find a collaborative lawyer, mental health professional, or financial advisor who is a member of the International Academy of Collaborative Professionals, the leading organization for collaborative lawyers and others focused on holistic, healthy divorce.

Family.FindLaw.com
Click on "Divorce" and find information about topics such as state laws, processes, and property division.

FindLegalHelp.org
Click on your state and "Lawyer Referral" to locate your local chapter of the American Bar Association and affiliated lawyers.

InstituteDFA.com
Find a certified divorce financial analyst.

LSC.gov
Legal Services Corporation provides free or low-cost legal aid for low-income Americans. Select your state and county under "Find Legal Aid."

MakingDivorceWork.com

Click on "Really Useful Free Stuff" to access a form to guide your Divorce Mission Statement and worksheets.

Mediate.com

Enter your city for a list of local mediators.

MyMoney.gov

The U.S. Department of Treasury's website offers information and tools for making good financial choices during and after divorce. Click on "Life Events," then "Life Partners."

UpToParents.org

This free website offers pre-mediation guidance for parents caring for their children in the midst of divorce.

Wevorce.com

Find local attorneys and mediators, articles on divorce, and advice.

BOOKS

Emery, Robert. *Renegotiating Family Relationships: Divorce, Child Custody, and Mediation.* Guilford Press, 1994.

Gold, Louis. *The Healthy Divorce: Keys to Ending Your Marriage While Preserving Your Emotional Well-Being.* Sphinx Publishing, 2009.

Margulies, Sam. *Getting Divorced Without Ruining Your Life: A Reasoned, Practical Guide to the Legal, Emotional, and Financial Ins and Outs of Negotiating a Divorce Settlement.* Touchstone; rev. upd. edition, 2001.

Tesler, Pauline, and Peggy Thompson. *Collaborative Divorce: The Revolutionary New Way to Restructure Your Family, Resolve Legal Issues, and Move On with Your Life.* HarperCollins, 2006.

PARENTING AND CO-PARENTING

WEBSITES AND APPS

EmeryOnDivorce.com

Great site for parents, by Robert E. Emery, PhD.

KidsHealth.org/teen/your_mind/Parents/divorce.html

For teens whose parents are divorcing, part of the pediatrician-led Nemours Foundation's Center for Children's Health Media.

MGaryNeuman.com/consultation/the-sandcastles-program

Information on the Sandcastles program, an excellent, inspiring half-day workshop for kids, created by Gary Neuman. You can also order books and workbooks.

OurFamilyWizard.com

A subscription-based online calendar, court-mandated in some states, which helps divorced parents manage and organize their children's schedules in a neutral zone.

SesameStreet.org/parents/topicsandactivities/toolkits/divorce

SesameStreet.org's tool kit for helping young children face and understand their parents' divorce.

TheIntelligentDivorce.com

The website of Mark Banschick, author of The Intelligent Divorce: Taking Care of Your Children, offers an online Family Stabilization Course.

TwoHappyHomes.com

Online parenting dashboard for sharing schedules, photos, phone numbers, and more with a co-parent. Also offers tools, expert tips, and a support forum.

Family organizing apps

For smartphones, check out: 2Houses.com, Cofamilies.com, Coparently.com, and Kidganizer.com.

BOOKS

Ahrons, Constance. *The Good Divorce: Keeping Your Family Together When Your Marriage Comes Apart*. HarperCollins, 1994.

Banschick, Mark. *The Intelligent Divorce: Taking Care of Your Children*. Intelligent Book Press, 2010.

Emery, Robert, E. *The Truth about Children and Divorce: Dealing with the Emotions So You and Your Children Can Thrive*. Plume, 2006.

Neuman, M. Gary. *Helping Your Kids Cope with Divorce the Sandcastles Way*. Random House, 1999.

Pedro-Carroll, JoAnne. *Putting Children First: Proven Parenting Strategies for Helping Children Thrive through Divorce*. Avery, 2010.

BOOKS FOR KIDS

DiCamillo, Kate. *Flora & Ulysses: The Illuminated Adventures*. Candlewick, 2013.

Honig-Briggs, Rebecca. *Two-Hug Day*. Sesame Street, 2012. Downloadable at *SesameStreet.org/parents/topicsandactivities/toolkits/divorce*.

RESOURCES FOR THRIVING . . . OR SURVIVING

WEBSITES

CompassionPower.com

Find a wealth of resources, workshops, and ideas for dealing with anger, developing compassion, parenting, and more.

ContemplativeMind.org/practices/tree/loving-kindness

Learn the basics of the "gateway practice" of loving-kindness meditation.

EvWorthington-Forgiveness.com

Psychology professor Everett Worthington details his R.E.A.C.H. approach to forgiveness, and lists links to other helpful organizations.

GreaterGood.Berkeley.edu

Read a trove of information and the latest research on gratitude, altruism, compassion, empathy, forgiveness, happiness, and mindfulness.

Happier.com

Legendary positive psychologist Martin Seligman offers his latest thinking about happiness on this beautiful, upbeat site, as well as exercises to raise yours (requires a small subscription fee).

HighConflictInstitute.com/individuals

Find help with and information about those who seem determined to escalate strife. Lawyer/social worker Bill Eddy founded this institute, based on his experience with what he calls "high-conflict" personalities.

Locator.APA.org

Type your zip code into the American Psychological Association Practice Organization's search engine to find a psychologist in your area.

PsychologyToday.com

Psychology Today *magazine's website lets you connect with local social workers, certified counselors, psychologists, and other professionals. Click on "Find a Therapist."*

SelfCompassion.org

Learn about self-compassion on psychologist Kristin Neff's site, and try exercises to build yours.

CoachFederation.org

Type your city into the member directory of the International Coach Federation site to find a life coach in your area. Or search for "divorce coach" online to pull up an ever-growing list of results, as more people are turning to this field. Since coaching requires a great deal of marketing, you can learn a lot about a coach from his or her site. Many also offer a free trial session.

BOOKS

Burns, David D. *The Feeling Good Handbook*. Plume, 1999.

Cohen, Gabriel. *Storms Can't Hurt the Sky: A Buddhist Path through Divorce*. Da Capo Press, 2008.

Fredrickson, Barbara L. *Love 2.0: Finding Happiness and Health in Moments of Connection*. Hudson Street Press, 2013.

Joseph, Stephen. *What Doesn't Kill Us: The New Psychology of Posttraumatic Growth*. Basic Books, 2011.

Langer, Ellen J. *Mindfulness*. Da Capo Lifelong Books, 2014.

Lopez, Shane J. *Making Hope Happen: Create the Future You Want for Yourself and Others*. Atria Books, 2014.

Neff, Kristin. *Self-Compassion: The Proven Power of Being Kind to Yourself.* William Morrow, 2011.

Orlick, Terry. *Embracing Your Potential*. Human Kinetics, 1998.

Rubin, Gretchen. *Better Than Before: Mastering the Habits of Our Everyday Lives*. Crown, 2015.

Salzberg, Sharon. *Real Happiness: The Power of Meditation; A 28-Day Program*. Workman Publishing, 2011.

Seligman, Martin E. P. *Authentic Happiness: Using the New Positive Psychology to Realize Your Potential for Lasting Fulfillment*. Atria Books, 2013.

Trafford, Abigail. *Crazy Time: Surviving Divorce and Building a New Life*. William Morrow Paperbacks, 2014.

SELF-ASSESSMENTS

AuthenticHappiness.SAS.UPenn.edu/testcenter

This site links to a variety of useful research-based assessments. Identify your signature strengths (and then use them to rebuild a more resonant life). Rate your happiness, depression, positive and negative affect, and more.

**Fetzer.org/sites/default/files/images/stories/pdf/selfmeasures/Self_
    Measures_for_Loneliness_and_Interpersonal_Problems_UCLA_
    LONELINESS.pdf**

Rate your loneliness.

PositivityRatio.com/single.php

Rate your positivity-to-negativity ratio.

Resources for Professionals

Whether you're a lawyer, a mental health professional, a financial advisor, a student, a communicator, or anyone else looking for a way to help families facing divorce, the need is great and the opportunities plenty for getting educated about alternative dispute resolution, supporting organizations making a difference, spreading the word about best practices, and advocating for policy changes to protect families.

Here are a few places to look for more information:

ACADEMY OF PROFESSIONAL FAMILY MEDIATORS

A professional organization offering divorce mediation training, an annual conference, and topic-specific workshops for lawyers, mediators, social workers, and others. (APFMnet.org)

ASSOCIATION FOR CONFLICT RESOLUTION

A professional organization for mediators, arbitrators, educators, and others who work in conflict resolution offering live and online training and an "advanced practitioner" certification. (ACRnet.org)

ASSOCIATION OF FAMILY AND CONCILIATION COURTS

The leading interdisciplinary, international association of lawyers, researchers, teachers, and policymakers in the family court area. Members have been involved with reform and development of a variety of dispute resolution processes such as child custody mediation, parenting coordination, and divorce education. The AFCC also works on improving family law training, and puts out the quarterly *Family Court Review*, the leading interdisciplinary family law journal. (AFCCnet.org)

CENTER FOR OUT-OF-COURT DIVORCE

This national umbrella organization is based on the Resource Center for Separating and Divorcing Families (covered in chapter eight), a three-year pilot program started by the Institute for the Advancement of the American Legal system.

The COCD directly helps families with all aspects of the divorce and separation process, and keeps the entire effort out of the court system. The COCD is in the process of helping start and support non court-based family service centers in other cities around the nation. (CenterForOutOfCourtDivorce.org)

HIGH CONFLICT INSTITUTE

Cofounded by lawyer/licensed clinical social worker Bill Eddy, creator of the high-conflict-personality theory, HCI offers resources and training for lawyers, mediators, and mental health professionals. The institute also provides speakers and organizational consulting. (HighConflictInstitute.com)

INSTITUTE FOR DIVORCE FINANCIAL ANALYSTS

This national organization offers education and certification for financial professionals interested in working with divorcing clients, and promotes the use of financial professionals in divorce. (InstituteDFA.com)

INSTITUTE FOR THE ADVANCEMENT OF THE
AMERICAN LEGAL SYSTEM

This think tank on the campus of the University of Denver, started by former Colorado justice Rebecca Kourlis, created the prototype for the Center for Out-of-Court Divorce. IAALS is supporting the creation of a national nonprofit, the Center for Out-of-Court Divorce, National, which will work with partners around the country to start more centers. (IAALS.DU.edu)

Read a white paper about IAALS's mission in *Family Court Review* 51, no. 3 (2013): 345–49/doi: 10.1111/fcre.12031.

INTEGRATIVE LAW INSTITUTE AT COMMONWEAL

Founded by collaborative law pioneer Pauline Tesler, the institute offers workshops and retreats for lawyers seeking to integrate neuroscience, positive psychology, and body/mind awareness in their practice. It also certifies integrative lawyers. (IntegrativeLawInstitute.org)

INTERNATIONAL ACADEMY OF COLLABORATIVE PROFESSIONALS

The leading international community of legal, mental health, and financial professionals focused on holistic, "client-centered" conflict resolution and the establishment of unified standards of practice for collaborative law. Offers information, training, and an annual networking and education forum. (Collaborative Practice.com)

PROGRAMS FOR BECOMING A DIVORCE COACH

Certified divorce coaching is a growing specialization of life coaching. Many life coaching programs are online, and are approved by the International Coach Federation, a nonprofit founded in 1995 that has helped professionalize life coaching by establishing core competencies, a code of ethics, curriculum standards, and a certification program. Today, coaching programs around the country follow ICF guidelines. (CoachFederation.org)

A few divorce-coach-training options: CertifiedDivorceCoach.com, CoachTrainingAlliance.com, and DivorceCoachTrainingProgram.com.

BOOKS

Margulies, Sam. *Working with Divorcing Spouses: How to Help Clients Navigate the Emotional and Legal Minefield.* Guilford Press, 2007.

Mosten, Forrest S. *Collaborative Divorce Handbook: Helping Families without Going to Court.* Jossey-Bass, 2009.

Schepard, Andrew. *Children, Courts, and Custody: Interdisciplinary Models for Divorcing Families.* Cambridge University Press, 2004.

Tesler, Pauline. *Collaborative Divorce: The Revolutionary New Way to Restructure Your Family, Resolve Legal Issues, and Move On with Your Life.* HarperCollins, 2006.

Webb, Stuart. *The Collaborative Way to Divorce: The Revolutionary Method That Results in Less Stress, Lower Costs, and Happier Kids—Without Going to Court.* Plume, 2007.

PAPERS

To read about the recent history of divorce mediation and standards established:

"Model Standards of Practice for Family and Divorce Mediation," developed by the Symposium on Standards of Practice. Approved by the ABA House of Delegates, February 2001.

(http://www.americanbar.org/content/dam/aba/migrated/family /reports/mediation.authcheckdam.pdf)

Policy Suggestions & Reforms

Today's good divorce is a direct result of flexible, supportive laws and policies that reflect a public health approach to divorce and co-parenting. But even as families benefit from these new laws, some states are making it harder to part in peace. Arkansas, for example, now has an eighteen-month waiting period between separation and divorce for a no-fault divorce. The only other option for divorce in that state is to prove fault—to show that your spouse has committed a felony or adultery, for example, or is incurably insane. The eighteen-month waiting period for a no-fault divorce is a paternalistic, potentially damaging requirement that restarts anytime a couple makes a repair effort through cohabitation—or, say, if one parent moves in briefly to help during a hurricane, as mine did before we'd legally split.

The waiting period between separation and divorce or filing and divorce varies state by state. Opinions differ on the ideal length, but the eighteen-month period and the default "reset button" impede an individual's ability to move on and remarry, squelch attempts to reconcile, and can easily drive a wedge between co-parents. It also doesn't protect marriage: Arkansas has one of the highest divorce rates in the nation.

We don't want laws that increase conflict and harm children under the guise of supporting marriage, let alone that lessen the possibility of recommitment. We need policies that avoid polarized position-staking and support today's real families, as they are being lived.

Some issues for action include:

PROMOTE FAMILY POLICIES FOR TODAY'S FAMILIES

Experts from all political sides agree that family policies should support children. However, policies and programs aimed at promoting

283

marriage alone, rather than bolstering *family stability* more broadly, are becoming decreasingly useful as fewer people marry, more live together outside of marriage, and more unmarried couples and singles have children.

As Johns Hopkins scholar Andrew Cherlin notes, a family policy exclusively promoting and supporting marriage does not serve the needs of many children. "American policymakers eager to promote marriage are unlikely to be able to raise U.S. family stability to levels typical of other developed countries."

As we've all read, the United States lags behind other industrialized nations in policies that support two-income families, such as paid day care and family leave. As we find better ways to address the needs of today's working families, we want to ensure that children of divorce are included.

CREATE INCENTIVES TO REDUCE FIGHTING IN COURT

Divorce reformers are working on *institutional incentives* to reduce fighting between divorcing spouses. These are important both to protect children and to reduce the load on the courts caused by frivolous divorce filings. Two proven solutions that could be more widely available are parent education and early intervention of spiraling conflict through mediation and/or counseling.

Many courts now have some version of mandatory parent education classes for divorcing couples and/or a parenting-plan facilitator. Some have begun instituting practices that can help parents learn to behave more like business partners in the job of raising their children. Maryland, for example, has a family division that, in some jurisdictions, provides court-based mediators to help spouses reach an agreement themselves, rather than asking a judge to decide. Channeling these services more widely toward couples early in the divorce process, as well as increasing mental health resources and financial education, could help more couples make decent decisions, protect their kids, and avoid an escalatory, adversarial court spectacle. Families need information, education, and assistance to create viable, positive parenting plans and separation agreements. Resources for divorcing parents, such as parent education classes, also should be expanded to never-married parents.

We also need more systematic evaluation of the programs that currently exist, and better dissemination of the findings. As a 2013 study in *Family Court Review* showed, despite the popularity of parent education courses for separating and divorcing families, there's no rigorous evaluation of them, nor are they consistent across the states. The quality of information you receive is completely dependent on where you happen to live at the time of your divorce. (Here's one such review and resulting recommendation: NCBI.NLM.NIH.gov/pmc/articles/PMC3638966/.)

Additionally, access to legal aid needs to be improved. In low-income areas such as the Bronx, about 70 percent of divorcing couples don't get any legal help, says Hofstra University law professor Andrew Schepard, due to not being able to afford it and to mistrusting lawyers. As budgets are being cut, court-based resources are shrinking and access to mediators is being reduced. This at a time when reformers stress the need for the court process to be simplified to enable the large number of people without a lawyer to more easily navigate it on their own.

MOVE MORE NON-ADVERSARIAL DIVORCES AND RESOURCES OUT OF COURT

Most uncontested divorces today do not need to be processed through the general court system. At the Resource Center for Separating and Divorcing Families in Denver that I visited, for example, after a couple worked with a mediator and other professionals at the center to draft their separation agreement and parenting plan, a judge came to the center to grant the final divorce decree there. Housing divorce in court is a remnant of the pre-no-fault days, when divorce was a "remedy" granted by a judge to a grievously wronged spouse.

Moving non-adversarial divorce into a community center frees up the court to handle high-conflict cases and intervene more quickly when someone really needs protection. It also puts divorce more squarely in line with the other emotional, physical, and financial issues that we never step inside a courthouse to address. We visit a psychiatrist or child psychologist in her hushed private office. We work with the physical therapist at a medical center. We go to H&R Block or Charles Schwab to handle taxes and investments. We do have to get our marriage certificate at the court, but we're free to conduct every other detail of our wedding at the church or local Marriott.

Having to stand in line at a metal detector in a sterile or frightening courthouse every time you need information is enough reason for many to skip it. Moving important family services out of court means many more people might actually use them.

In their new book, *Divorced from Reality: Rethinking Family Dispute Resolution*, law professors Jana Singer and Jane Murphy recommend pilot programs offering inexpensive, divorce-related services in a non-court setting, such as the Resource Center, to familiarize Americans with the concept. The Center for Out-of-Court Divorce in Denver (an outgrowth of the Resource Center for Separating and Divorcing Families) is a good example of this. Another great model—with an extensive website and long track record—is the Australian Family Relationship Centres. (FamilyRelationships.gov.au)

ADOPT A LIFE-SPAN APPROACH TO DIVORCE SUPPORT

The Family Relationship Centre idea reinforces an important truth: divorce is not a onetime event primarily of legal import. Particularly when there are children involved, it's a continuing aspect of family life. Services such as mediation, financial counseling, and parenting education should be available to parents until their children reach maturity, not only until their divorce papers are signed.

Ironically, more couples return to court postdivorce today than in the "bad divorce" era of the past: shared custody means parents now must agree on the nitty-gritty details of their children's lives. Having a life-span orientation toward co-parenting, and easy access to regular services, would help parents guide their children without constant fights. It would also better serve children, and prevent families from returning to court every time a change or challenge arises.

INCREASE COMMUNICATION OF BEST PRACTICES

When I started this book, I assumed there was a lack of good ideas for divorcing families. What I've found instead are amazingly creative, innovative, proven strategies—and abysmal communication of them between disciplines and among states. We need far better communication of best practices.

A national best-practices database could aid policymakers seeking better options in their states, as well as lawyers, mental health practitioners, parents, and other divorcing couples. Additionally, while couples can find online legal forms, go to a court-based self-help center, or call a telephone hotline in some states, all of these resources should be expanded, made more widely known, and better evaluated.

DECRIMINALIZE NONPAYMENT OF
CHILD SUPPORT BY THE POOR

While divorce has improved for most, it has gotten arguably worse for the very poor because of old, punitive "bastardy" laws and newer, overly aggressive child-support enforcement policies. States impute income to the unemployed and charge child support against these fictitious earnings. They levy fines for noncompliance. Some states even terminate parental rights and throw a parent in jail or prison for failure to pay—even if nonpayment is due to unemployment.

Seventy percent of unpaid child support debt is owed by parents with no or low reported earnings, according to the Office of Child Support Enforcement. If a state collects the back child support, it often goes back to the state for supporting the brood, *not to the mother and children*. This is the opposite end of the spectrum from today's good divorce, and a set of issues needing dramatic and immediate remedy.

In Texas, a parent can be incarcerated even *after* he's paid back his child support debt. Texas is infamous for overcrowded courts, too. In one court in Harris County, Texas, a court master decided five hundred paternity and child support cases in one day.

While a parent is in jail or prison, child support arrears are allowed to mount in many states, some of which consider incarceration "voluntary impoverishment." Studies from a few states show that on average, a parent with a child support case enters jail or prison about ten thousand dollars behind and leaves owing more like thirty thousand. This debt is unlikely ever to be paid, as data show. It also creates huge obstacles for a parent trying to land a new job, secure housing, get a credit card, and even pay his current child support once released.

Part of the problem is that child support tables are based on the assumption that the noncustodial parent has a reliable income, and that this adequately covers a family's needs. These tables don't work for the very poor, who are nonetheless subject to them. "Most policy is driven by discussion about cases where both parents are working, middle-class families on up. Most people don't talk about the low-income side," says University of Maryland law professor Daniel Hatcher. "You plug in both parents' income, and then transfer money to the custodial parent."

If a custodial parent—usually the mother—applies to Temporary Assistance to Needy Families (TANF, the program that replaced welfare) or seeks food stamps, she's required to name the father, establish paternity, and sue him in court for support, even if they have an in-kind arrangement that's working or if she's safer and more stable by keeping a violent or addicted parent out of the family's daily life.

Solutions exist, but they are far from widespread. As reformers note, child support should be assessed based on the reality of a person's resources, not a mythological number a parent "could" be earning. Some states have experimented with the practice of assessing child support only if a noncustodial parent has a minimum reserve of income. States including California and Ohio have passed statutes requiring the exercise of discretion rather than automatic referral of child welfare cases to enforcement. The exercise of discretion by judges and other officials should be required nationwide, as should the practice of considering every family's *actual set of circumstances*, rather than shoving everyone into an auto-pursuit, family-grinder.

In Virginia, some child support enforcement workers have begun reaching out to employers to find work for non-compliers, rather than jail time. The state also has retooled its child support guidelines and begun launching programs aimed at helping poor fathers improve job-hunting and parenting skills.

In Maryland, Hatcher has worked on legislation to allow the state to automatically disable child support arrears during incarceration, rather than having child support debt add up while a parent is behind bars and clearly unable to work. This reform passed but is not widely enforced. "The child support agency has not sufficiently used the statutory authority," says Hatcher, who notes that one stumbling block to reform is poor communication between child support enforcement and the criminal justice system.

Other possible reform efforts include:

- Challenging the legality of many current practices, such as enforcing child support enforcement plans that conflict with federally required reunification services and case plans.
- Challenging the constitutionality of terminating a parent's rights based on back child support.
- Encouraging and assisting parents to create their own child support and visitation schedules.
- Consider and credit in-kind assistance a parent provides.
- End the practice of routing child support payments to the government, rather than to the children.

CREATE NEW MODELS FOR FAMILY LAWYERS

Many lawyers today seek training in alternative dispute resolution on their own, a positive trend for families—and for lawyers. Some lawyers also offer "unbundled services"—à la carte help for clients. Bar associations are endorsing both of these trends, but more could be done within the legal community to encourage family lawyers to expand their problem-solving skills, stop taking a default adversarial approach in divorce, and offer more unbundled, affordable legal aid.

Other good ideas are circulating for remodeling the practice of family law. Singer and Murphy recommend that bar associations consider the "urgent care center" approach to legal services—setting up drop-in law shops where families could pay for one-off consultation on discrete issues. This idea models the urgent care medical centers that have sprung up around the nation to relieve some of the load on emergency rooms, and could be beneficial to those facing divorce and needing answers to specific questions.

Some reformers push for more freedom for lawyers to represent both parties in an uncontested divorce, to serve as "counsel for the divorce," as opposed to counsel for one. This could greatly help couples who are working together on their divorce. Many of us cooperatively uncoupling spouses would like one lawyer to help figure out a good plan, and are completely uninterested in paying for two to fight between themselves. It's not a conflict of interest for a lawyer to represent the *divorcing couple* in a no-fault, amicable un-marrying.

UPDATE LAW SCHOOL CURRICULUM TO TRAIN
FAMILY LAWYERS FOR TODAY'S DIVORCE

Law schools should train lawyers to guide families toward the appropriate dispute-resolution model, and to consider a family's overall interests, not merely one client's *legal interests*. The curriculum is changing in this way in many law schools around the country, but legal scholars say it still lags behind the need.

Law students should develop an expanded skill set for their future as family lawyers, one that includes mediation, conflict management, and the ability to work with other professionals, such as social workers and financial advisors. They also should learn about the psychology of conflict and crisis.

As Singer and Murphy write, the current curriculum sends "the misleading message that most legal disputes are resolved by judges and that a lawyer's core function is to win in court, regardless of the financial and emotional costs and with little attention to a client's underlying interests."

As an avalanche of research shows, this old-school approach to divorce can cause harm, and at a time in people's lives when thoughtful, measured help is sorely needed.

Notes

My thinking in this book is influenced by the work of Martin Seligman, the father of positive psychology and author of the seminal work *Authentic Happiness: Using the New Positive Psychology to Realize Your Potential for Lasting Fulfillment*. Many writers and thinkers have contributed to this line of inquiry before and since, but Dr. Seligman activated the mission of elevating the study of happiness within mainstream American psychology.

The ideas of courage and hope researcher Shane Lopez also run throughout this work. While writing this book and "rewriting" my life, I found myself hauling out two key ideas I'd gleaned from him over the years, from various conversations: (1) sometimes we need to create a meaningful plan B, and (2) courage does not mean lack of fear. It means feeling the fear and acting anyway.

NOTE TO READER: WHAT WE TALK ABOUT WHEN WE TALK ABOUT DIVORCE

Unwed mothers are among the poorest: For a great overview of how family is changing, see Andrew J. Cherlin, "American Marriage in the Early Twenty-First Century," *The Future of Children* 15, no. 2 (Fall 2005): 33–55, http://www.princeton.edu/futureofchildren/publications/docs/15_02_03.pdf.

Then there's the early study: Judith S. Wallerstein and Sandra Blakeslee, *Second Chances: Men, Women, and Children a Decade after Divorce* (New York: Ticknor & Fields, 1989). Also Wallerstein and Joan B. Kelly, *Surviving the Breakup: How Children and Parents Cope with Divorce* (New York: Basic Books, 1980); Wallerstein, Julia M. Lewis, and Sandra Blakeslee, *The Unexpected Legacy of Divorce: The 25 Year Landmark Study* (New York: Hachette Books, 2001).

But family scholars criticize: Paul R. Amato, "Reconciling Divergent Perspectives: Judith S. Wallerstein, Quantitative Family Research, and Children of Divorce," *Family Relations* 52, no. 4 (October 2003): 332–39, doi: 10

.1111/j.1741-3729.2003.00332.x. Also, Joan B. Kelly and Robert E. Emery, "Children's Adjustment Following Divorce: Risk and Resilience Perspectives," *Family Relations* 52, no. 4 (October 2003): 352–62, doi: 10.1111 /j.1741-3729.2003.00352.x. Also, University of Cambridge's Michael E. Lamb, telephone interview with author, July 4, 2014. "The majority of the researchers either pay little attention to Wallerstein or point to the fundamental problems and move on. But if you look at the popular literature or work by the people with axes to grind, they give it more attention."

Four decades of research show that 75 to 80 percent of kids: Lamb, "Mothers, Fathers, Families, and Circumstances: Factors Affecting Children's Adjustment," *Applied Developmental Science* 16, no. 2 (2012): 98–111, doi: 10.1080/10888691.2012.667344.

Most people get through divorce fine: George A. Bonanno, Maren Westphal, and Anthony D. Mancinci, "Resilience to Loss and Potential Trauma," *Annual Review of Clinical Psychology* 7 (April 2011): 511–35, doi: 10.1146/ annurev-clinpsy-032210-104526.

In New York, for example, a couple might collude: Ilyon Woo, *The Great Divorce: A Nineteenth-Century Mother's Extraordinary Fight against Her Husband, the Shakers, and Her Times* (New York: Atlantic Monthly Press, 2010). Also, Ilyon Woo, "Breaking Up Is Hard to Do," *Wall Street Journal*, August 13, 2010, wsj.com/articles/SB1000142405274870490110457542334 1295531582.

In California, where cruelty: In re the Marriage of Norma and Paul Attley McKim. Norma McKim v. Paul Attley McKim 6 Cal. 3rd 673 (1972). For more on Mosk and Hollywood's history of divorces, see Jacqueline R. Braitman and Gerald F. Uelmen, *Justice Stanley Mosk: A Life at the Center of California Politics and Justice* (Jefferson, NC: McFarland, 2012).

Economists Betsey Stevenson and Justin Wolfers: "Bargaining in the Shadow of the Law: Divorce Laws and Family Distress," *Quarterly Journal of Economics* 121, no. 1 (2006): 267–88, doi: 10.1093/qje/121.1.267.

Suicide rates among women: Ibid.

The negative impact of living in a bad marriage: Psychologist Lawrence Birnbach, telephone interview with author, May 25, 2012.

One of the great advances in psychology: This is a basic tenet of cognitive behavioral therapy. For more information: Rational emotive behavior therapy, created by psychologist Albert Ellis, http://www.rebtnetwork.org/ and http://albertellis.org/; cognitive therapy, developed by Aaron Beck, http://www.beckinstitute.org/.

About 20 percent of American adults: "Any Mental Illness (AMI) among Adults," National Institute of Mental Health, National Institutes of Health, accessed July 7, 2015, http://www.nimh.nih.gov/health/statistics /prevalence/any-mental-illness-ami-among-adults.shtml. "The Numbers Count: Mental Disorders in America," National Institute of Mental Health, National Institutes of Health, cached October 1, 2013, http:// www.lb7.uscourts.gov/documents/12-cv-1072url2.pdf.

About two million people divorce: "National Marriage and Divorce Rate Trends," Centers for Disease Control and Prevention, http://www.cdc.gov/nchs /nvss/marriage_divorce_tables.htm. Also, Cherlin, "Goode's *World Revolution and Family Patterns*: A Reconsideration at Fifty Years," *Population and Development Review* 38, no. 4 (December 2012): 577–607, doi: 10.1111/j.1728-4457.2012.00528.x.

CHAPTER ONE: THE JOY OF EX

But then it was summer: Sara LeTrent, "In January, 'Ex' Marks the Spot," CNN, January 17, 2014, http://www.cnn.com/2014/01/17/living/january-divorce -month-matrimony/.

She gave us a statistic that sounded hopeful: Robert Schoen and Nicola Standish, "The Retrenchment of Marriage: Results from Marital Status Life Tables for the United States," *Population and Development Review* 27, no. 3 (2001): 553–63. Also, Susan L. Brown and I-Fen Lin, "Age Variation in the Remarriage Rate, 1990–2011," National Center for Marriage and Family Research, https://www.bgsu.edu/content/dam/BGSU/college-of -arts-and-sciences/NCFMR/documents/FP/FP-13-17.pdf. Also, Esther Lamidi, "Single, Cohabiting, and Married Households, 1995–2012," National Center for Marriage and Family Research, https://www.bgsu.edu /content/dam/BGSU/college-of-arts-and-sciences/NCFMR/documents /FP/FP-14-01.pdf.

In 1985, Harvard sociologist Lenore Weitzman published: Lenore J. Weitzman, *The Divorce Revolution: The Unexpected Social and Economic Consequences for Women and Children in America* (New York: Free Press, 1987).

As Arizona State University professor emeritus: Sanford L. Braver and Diane O'Connell, *Divorced Dads: Shattering the Myths* (New York: Penguin, 1998).

Finally, in 1996, Weitzman allowed: Richard R. Peterson, "A Re-evaluation of the Economic Consequences of Divorce," *American Sociological Review*

61, no. 3 (1996): 528–36, http://www.jstor.org/stable/2096363. Weitzman's response: Weitzman, "The Economic Consequences of Divorce
Are Still Unequal: Comment on Peterson," *American Sociological Review* 61, no. 3 (1996): 537–38, http://www.jstor.org/stable/2096364?
seq=1#page_scan_tab_contents. Also see, Felicia R. Lee, "Influential
Study on Divorce's Impact Is Said to Be Flawed," *New York Times,* May 9,
1996, http://www.nytimes.com/1996/05/09/garden/influential-study-
on-divorce-s-impact-is-said-to-be-flawed.html.

Even the amended results: Braver and O'Connell, *Divorced Dads.*

The outlook is also better for women: George Washington University law professor Naomi Cahn, author with June Carbone of *Marriage Markets: How
Inequality is Remaking the American Family* (New York: Oxford University Press, 2014). Naomi Cahn, telephone interview with author, February 11, 2014. Also, Stephen J. Brake, "Equitable Distribution vs. Fixed
Rules: Marital Property Reform and the Uniform Marital Property Act,"
Boston College Law Review 23, no. 3 (1982): 761–88, http://lawdigital
commons.bc.edu/cgi/viewcontent.cgi?article=1706&context=bclr.

In the U.S., divorce rates are highest in the Bible Belt and the West: Cahn and
Carbone, *Red Families v. Blue Families: Legal Polarization and the Creation of Culture* (New York: Oxford University Press, 2011). Also, Cahn
interview: "People with higher incomes and higher education tend to
marry later, and later marriage makes them less likely to get divorced."

As of 2010, the states with the highest divorce rates: Cahn and Carbone, *Red
Families v. Blue Families.*

What a violent and cruel thing: John Milton, "The Doctrine and Discipline of
Divorce," in *The Works of John Milton, Historical, Political, and Miscella-
neous,* vol. 1 (London: A. Millar, 1753), 184. For a good overview of English marriage law in the seventeenth century and Milton's objection,
see the *Norton Anthology of English Literature*'s explanation: http://www
.wwnorton.com/college/english/nael/17century/topic_1/divorce.htm.

In 1643, a judge granted her: "First Divorce in the Colonies," History.com
(A+ENetworks, 2010), http://www.history.com/this-day-in-history/first
-divorce-in-the-colonies.

This hostility toward divorce makes sense: The idea that our needs and desires
for marriage are influenced by shifts in culture, health, and technology
is described by many people. For this section, I referred primarily to
these works:

- Cherlin, "Goode's *World Revolution and Family Patterns.*"

- Cherlin, "American Marriage in the Early Twenty-First Century."
- Cherlin, "The Deinstitutionalization of American Marriage," *Journal of Marriage and Family* 66, no. 4 (November 2004): 848–61, doi: 10.1111/j .0022-2445.2004.00058.x.
- Stephanie Coontz, *Marriage, A History: How Love Conquered Marriage* (New York: Penguin Books, 2006).
- Ron Lesthaeghe, "The Unfolding Story of the Second Demographic Transition," *Population and Development Review* 36, no. 2 (June 2010): 211–51, doi: 10.1111/j.1728-4457.2010.00328.x.
- Paul R. Amato et al., *Alone Together: How Marriage Is Changing* (Cambridge, MA: Harvard University Press, 2009).
- Betty Friedan, *The Feminine Mystique* (New York: W. W. Norton, 2001).
- Elizabeth Gilbert, *Committed: A Love Story* (New York: Riverhead Books, 2011).

There began to be an "emphasis on emotional satisfaction": Cherlin, "The Deinstitutionalization of American Marriage."

One way to think about: Abraham Maslow's original hierarchy of needs had five stages. In the 1970s, he added three more: cognitive, aesthetic, and "transcendence"—helping others achieve self-actualization.

During the past twenty years, the divorce rate: Susan L. Brown and I-Fen Lin, "The Gray Divorce Revolution: Rising Divorce Among Middle-Aged and Older Adults, 1990–2010," National Center for Family & Marriage Research Working Paper Series (March 2013), https://www.bgsu.edu /content/dam/BGSU/college-of-arts-and-sciences/NCFMR/documents/Lin/The-Gray-Divorce.pdf.

CHAPTER TWO: PRINCIPLES OF PARTING

Some of us are seized by loss aversion: Loss aversion explains what University of Chicago behavioral scientist and economist Richard Thaler calls "the endowment effect," our habit of investing *our* relationships and objects with special meaning. One classic study involved college students' unwillingness to part with mugs given to them. See Daniel Kahneman, Jack Knetsch, and Richard Thaler, "Experimental Tests of the Endowment Effect and the Coase Theorem," *Journal of Political Economy* 98, no. 6 (December 1990): 1325–48, http://www.jstor.org/stable/2937761. Also, Kahneman's *Thinking, Fast and Slow* (New York: Farrar, Straus and Giroux, 2013).

Some people get a surge of energy: Gallup senior scientist and psychologist
Shane Lopez, telephone interview with author, May 24, 2012.

. . . *as the Census Bureau reports:* In 2010, blended or stepfamilies became the
most common form of family in America. U.S. Census Bureau.

"A lot of times I ask people": Social worker MJ Murray Vachon, telephone interview with author, June 24, 2013.

David Sbarra at the University of Arizona: David A. Sbarra, Hillary L. Smith,
and Matthias R. Mehl, "When Leaving Your Ex, Love Yourself: Obser-
vational Ratings of Self-Compassion Predict the Course of Emotional
Recovery Following Marital Separation," *Psychological Science* 23, no.
3 (2012): 261–69, doi: 10.1177/0956797611429466. Also, Sbarra, telephone interviews with author, May 30, 2013, and June 26, 2014. See his
great TEDxTucson talk "Surviving Divorce": https://www.youtube.com
/watch?v=vg92QEL4w4I&feature=youtube.

Self-compassion is a composite idea: Sbarra et al., "When Leaving Your Ex."

"The research shows that self-compassionate people": Psychologist Kristin D.
Neff, telephone interview with author, August 19, 2013.

Self-compassionate people also have better romances: Neff and S. Natasha Be-
retvas, "The Role of Self-compassion in Romantic Relationships," *Self
and Identity* 12, no. 1 (2012): 78–98, doi: 10.1080/15298868.2011.639548.

Research links mindfulness with a slew: Erika N. Carlson, "Overcoming the
Barriers to Self-Knowledge: Mindfulness as a Path to Seeing Yourself
as You Really Are," *Perspectives on Psychological Sciences* 8, no. 2 (March
2013): 173–86, doi: 10.1177/1745691612462584. J. David Creswell et al.,
"Mindfulness-Based Stress Reduction Training Reduces Loneliness and
Pro-Inflammatory Gene Expression in Older Adults: A Small Randomized Controlled Trial," *Brain, Behavior, and Immunity* 26, no. 7 (October
2012): 1095–1101, doi: 10.1016/j.bbi.2012.07.006. Kirk Warren Brown
and Richard M. Ryan, "The Benefits of Being Present: Mindfulness and
Its Role in Psychological Well-Being," *Journal of Personality and Social
Psychology* 84, no. 4 (April 2003): 822–48, doi: 10.1037/0022-3514.84.4
.822. Gaëlle Desbordes et al., "Effects of Mindful Attention and Compassion Mediation Training on Amygdala Response to Emotional Stimuli in
an Ordinary, Non-meditative State," *Frontiers in Human Neuroscience* 6
(November 1, 2012), doi: 10.3389/fnhum.2012.00292.

Meditation can deactivate the brain's "default mode": Neff interview.

Ellen Langer, a psychologist at Harvard: For her research into mindfulness, see
http://www.ellenlanger.com/ and http://langermindfulnessinstitute

.com/ellen-langer/. Also, her book *Mindfulness, 25th Anniversary Edition* (Boston: Da Capo Lifelong Books, 2014).

One way to bolster self-forgiveness: Leah B. Shapira and Myriam Mongrain, "The Benefits of Self-Compassion and Optimism Exercises for Individuals Vulnerable to Depression," *Journal of Positive Psychology* 5, no. 5 (2010): 377–89, doi: 10.1080/17439760.2010.516763.

If you're seeking divine forgiveness: Rabbi Mordecai Finley, interview with author, Los Angeles, July 24, 2013.

"It is a way of seeing yourself": Nita Tucker, *How Not to Screw It Up: 10 Steps to an Extraordinary Relationship* (New York: Three Rivers Press, 1998).

By seeing your contributions: Lisa Capps and George A. Bonanno, "Narrating Bereavement: Thematic and Grammatical Predictors of Adjustment to Loss," *Discourse Processes* 30, no. 1 (2000): 1–25, doi: 10.1207/S15326950dp3001_01. Jack Bauer and Bonanno, "I Can, I Do, I Am: The Narrative Differentiation of Self-Efficacy and Other Self-Evaluations while Adapting to Bereavement," *Journal of Research in Personality* 35 (2001): 424–48, doi: 10.1006/jrpe.2001.2323.

William Glasser, a psychiatrist who pioneered: Glasser's *Reality Therapy: A New Approach to Psychiatry* (New York: Harper Perennial, 1975) was the first in a series teaching that accepting responsibility is a key to happiness. Quote from Elaine Woo, "Obituaries: Dr. William Glasser, 1925–2013, 'Reality Therapy' Psychiatrist," *Los Angeles Times*, August 28, 2013, http://articles.latimes.com/2013/aug/28/local/la-me-william-glasser-20130828.

"There are five levels of separation": Attorney Forrest Mosten, interview with author, Los Angeles, July 8, 2014.

"The more you can befriend": Attorney Regina DeMeo, telephone interview with author, March 19, 2014.

Some find help from cognitive-behavioral therapy: See the National Alliance on Mental Illness, http://www.nami.org/Learn-More/Treatment/Psychotherapy.

I could finally avoid using the "four horsemen": John M. Gottman and Nan Silver, *The Seven Principles for Making Marriage Work* (New York: Three Rivers Press, 1999). Gottman is known for being able to predict if a couple will divorce, based on their use of the "four horsemen" in conversation.

"That's the real purpose of anger": Steven Stosny, therapist, author, and founder of Compassion Power, telephone interview with author, October 30, 2013. See also Steven Stosny, *Living & Loving after Betrayal: How to Heal from*

Emotional Abuse, Infidelity, Deceit, and Chronic Resentment (Oakland: New Harbinger Publications, 2013). Also Cecilia Capuzzi Simon, "The Lion Tamer," *Psychology Today*, July 1, 2005, https://www.psychology today.com/articles/200506/the-lion-tamer.

We think the origin of empathy: Primatologist and ethologist Frans de Waal, telephone interview with author April 1, 2010. Also see Jennifer L. Goetz, Dacher Keltner, and Emiliana Simon-Thomas, "Compassion: An Evolutionary Analysis and Empirical Review," *Psychological Bulletin* 136, no. 3 (May 2010), 351–74, doi: 10.1037/a0018807.

You may believe you'll feel better if you exact revenge: Psychologist Ben Dattner, telephone interview with author, November 14, 2012. See also Dattner and Darren Dahl, *The Blame Game: How the Hidden Rules of Credit and Blame Determine Our Success or Failure* (New York: Free Press, 2012).

. . . divorced people, when taken as a group: Sbarra interviews.

In general, we maintain a basically stable level of well-being: Bereavement researcher George Bonanno, interview with author, New York City, April 18, 2013.

Researchers are increasingly excited by new modeling methods: Bonanno interview.

They can create an "upward spiral of positivity": Online class with Barbara Fredrickson through MentorCoach.com, September 24–November 19, 2013. Also, Fredrickson, *Love 2.0: Finding Happiness and Health in Moments of Connection* (New York: Hudson Street Press, 2013).

A couple of recent studies: Heather A. Wadlinger and Derek M. Isaacowitz, "Positive Mood Broadens Visual Attention to Positive Stimuli," *Motivation and Emotion* 30 (March 2006), 89–101, doi: 10.1007/s11031-006-9021-1. Alice M. Isen, Andrew S. Rosenzweig, and Mark J. Young, "The Influence of Positive Affect on Clinical Problem Solving," *Medical Decision Making* 11, no. 3 (August 1991): 221–27, doi: 10.1177/0272989X9101100313.

Fredrickson promotes a three-to-one positivity-to-negativity ratio: Fredrickson, "Updated Thinking on Positivity Ratios," *American Psychologist*, July 15, 2013, advance online publication, doi: 10.1037/a0033584.

CHAPTER THREE: THE EXPANDED FAMILY

Sure, research shows that 75 to 80 percent of kids: So many people study childhood adjustment that it can seem as if there are as many opinions about parenting as there are parents. But this statistic is pretty consistent.

Check out:

- E. Mavis Hetherington and John Kelly, *For Better or Worse: Divorce Reconsidered* (New York: W. W. Norton, 2003). Hetherington, a University of Virginia emeritus professor and a preeminent divorce scholar, followed 2,500 kids of divorce for three decades, finding that 75 to 80 percent were "coping reasonably well and functioning in normal range." See also oral history interview by Lloyd Borstelman, December 4, 1992, Society for Research in Child Development.
- Constance Ahrons, *We're Still Family: What Grown Children Have to Say about Their Parents' Divorce* (New York: Harper Perennial, 2005) and *The Good Divorce: Keeping Your Family Together When Your Marriage Comes Apart* (New York: HarperCollins, 1994). Ahrons interviewed 173 grown children of divorce; most adapted well and thought they were better off for the divorce; many thrived.
- Lamb's meta-study on childhood adjustment is quick and enlightening: "Mothers, Fathers, Families, and Circumstances."
- Psychologist Joan B. Kelly, telephone interview with author, October 15, 2013.

Many factors affect a child's well-being: Joan B. Kelly and Emery, "Children's Adjustment Following Divorce."

When kids of divorce falter: Joan B. Kelly, "Children's Adjustment in Conflicted Marriage and Divorce: A Decade Review of Research," *Journal of the American Academy of Child & Adolescent Psychiatry* 39, no. 8 (August 2000): 963–73, doi: 10.1097/00004583-200008000-00007.

"One of the things that happened in the mid-nineties": Joan B. Kelly interview.

"I was giving long lists of places": Lamb, telephone interviews with author, August 26, 2013, and July 3, 2014.

He needed only nine pages: Lamb, "Mothers, Fathers, Families, and Circumstances."

Divorce is a risk factor for sure: Studies showing the resilience of most children in divorce also point to the risks of conflict, instability, economic insecurity, mental illness, etc. Johns Hopkins University public policy professor Andrew Cherlin said: "Most children cope successfully with divorce and live a normal, happy life. But the risk goes up that your kid will have some problems. It's as if there's an illness going around and most children won't get it, but your child is at more risk. So what might you do? Give him medicine. Keep him home." Telephone interview with author,

March 12, 2013. Also, Paul Amato and Jacob Cheadle, "The Long Reach of Divorce: Divorce and Child Well-Being across Three Generations," *Journal of Marriage and Family* 67, no. 1 (February 2005): 191–206, doi: 10.1111/j.0022-2445.2005.00014.x.

"There are many ways to be involved in a child's life": University of Maryland law professor Jana Singer, telephone interview with author, January 29, 2015.

Indiana-based social worker Murray Vachon asks clients: Vachon interviews.

Studies show that a nonresidential parent: Amato, Jennifer B. Kane, and Spencer James, "Reconsidering the 'Good Divorce,'" *Family Relations* 60, no. 5 (December 2011): 511–24, doi: 10.1111/j.1741-3729.2011.00666.x.

For generations, the father's role was as constrained: Lamb, "The Changing Faces of Fatherhood and Father-Child Relationships: From Fatherhood as Status to Father as Dad," in *Handbook of Family Theories: A Content-Based Approach*, ed. Mark A. Fine and Frank D. Fincham (New York: Routledge, 2013), 87–102, doi: 10.4324/9780203075180.ch6. Also, Paul Raeburn, *Do Fathers Matter? What Science Is Telling Us about the Parent We've Overlooked* (New York: Farrar, Straus and Giroux, 2014). Also, Raeburn, interview with author in New York, September 30, 2013. Lamb interviews, August 26, 2013, and July 3, 2014.

In the late 1940s developmental psychologist Pauline Sears: Robert R. Sears, Margaret H. Pintler, and Pauline S. Sears, "The Effect of Father Separation on Preschool Children's Doll Play Aggression," *Child Development* 17 (1946): 219–43. Also, Pauline Sears, "Doll Play Aggression in Normal Young Children: Influence of Sex, Age, Sibling Status, Father's Absence," *Psychological Monographs* 65, no. 6 (1951).

. . . many states have a presumption of joint custody: "A Review of the Year in Family Law, Chart 2: Custody Criteria," *Family Law Quarterly* 46, no. 4 (Winter 2013): 524–27, http://www.americanbar.org/content/dam/aba/publications/family_law_quarterly/vol46/4win13_chart2_custody.authcheckdam.pdf. Also, June Carbone and Naomi Cahn, "The New Math of the Single Mother: Why the Ranks of America's Unmarried Moms Keep Growing," *Politico*, October 13, 2014, politico.com/magazine/story/2014/10/the-new-math-of-the-single-mother-111842.html#ixzz3dIGEo27z.

Divorced mother of two Traci Whitney: Telephone interview with author, May 2, 2013.

Intense, ongoing conflict is a major stressor: Joan B. Kelly interview: "The kind
of conflict that's most highly associated with negative outcomes for kids
is when parents use the kids to express their disputes. They put them in
the middle and say 'You tell that bastard to give me the check.' Or the
dad says, 'So how many guys has your mom had in her bed this week?'
That kind of conflict is really toxic."

"When you put down your child's parent": M. Gary Neuman, author and creator
of the Sandcastles workshop for children of divorce, telephone interview
with author, August 16, 2013.

"But the wild things cried": Maurice Sendak, *Where the Wild Things Are*, 50th
anniversary ed. (New York: HarperCollins, 2012).

"Nobody fights over custody anymore": Mediator and lawyer Sam Margulies,
telephone interview with author, March 27, 2013.

Nearly every state has: Susan L. Pollet and Melissa Lombreglia, "A Nationwide
Survey of Mandatory Parent Education," *Family Court Review* 46, no. 2
(April 2008): 375–94, doi: 10.1111/j.1744-1617.2008.00207.x. Also, Peter
Salem, Irwin Sandler, and Sharlene Wolchik, "Taking Stock of Parent Edu-
cation in the Family Courts: Envisioning a Public Health Approach," *Fam-
ily Court Review* 51, no. 1 (January 2013): 131–48, doi: 10.1111/fcre.12014.

"Children fear that something irreparable": Psychiatrist Mark Banschick, telephone interview with author, May 1, 2013.

Stimulating, demanding activities can moderate: Kathleen B. Rodgers and Hil-
ary A. Rose, "Risk and Resiliency Factors among Adolescents Who Experience Marital Transitions," *Journal of Marriage and Family* 64, no. 4
(February 2002): 1024–37, doi: 10.1111/j.1741-3737.2002.01024.x.

The presence of other stable adults: Rodgers and Rose, "Risk and Resiliency Factors among Adolescents."

This sense of our own utter significance: Lamb, "The Changing Faces of Fatherhood."

"A lot of denominations take youth service trips": Lutheran minister Amy Ziettlow, telephone interview with author, March 12, 2014.

A "parentified child" may grow up to stifle: Banschick interview.

CHAPTER FOUR: THE OPPOSITE OF ENGAGEMENT

"At no other point in my life": Katie Roiphe, *In Praise of Messy Lives* (New York:
Dial Press, 2012).

As Salman Rushdie said: Salman Rushdie, from "One Thousand Days in a Balloon," in *The Rushdie Letters: Freedom to Speak, Freedom to Write*, ed. Steve MacDonogh (Lincoln: University of Nebraska Press, 1993).

We mimic each other's gestures: A huge amount has been written on emotional contagion. When people say, "Smile and the world smiles with you," they could cite plenty of studies to back up this point. Check out "Duchenne smile" on any search engine. Elaine Hatfield, John T. Cacioppo, and R. Rapson, "Primitive Emotional Contagion," in *Review of Personality and Social Psychology*, ed. M. S. Clark (Newbury Park, CA: Sage, 1992), 4: 151–77. Hatfield et al., "New Perspectives on Emotional Contagion: A Review of Classic and Recent Research on Facial Mimicry and Contagion," *Interpersona* 8, no. 2 (2014): 159–79, doi: 10.5964/ijpr.v8i2.162. Also, Marco Iacoboni, *Mirroring People: The Science of Empathy and How We Connect with Others* (New York: Picador, 2008). Also, social psychologist Dana Arakawa, telephone interview with author, May 10, 2013. Dacher Keltner, an evolutionary psychologist at the University of California, Berkeley, and the director of the Greater Good Science Center, made an encouraging observation about emotional contagion: "The findings are that the positive stuff is more contagious than the negative stuff." Telephone interview with author, August 4, 2014.

A guide to elevator speeches: Pepperdine University's Graziadio School of Business and Management online "Career Toolbox," https://bschool.pepper dine.edu/career-services/toolbox/.

New York City therapist Hollis Brown: Telephone interview with author, August 18, 2012.

I think of American author Peter de Vries's quote: Peter de Vries, *The Tunnel of Love* (New York: Penguin, 1982).

Self-affirmation theory proposes: For a good overview of self-affirmation theory, see Lisa Legault, Timour Al-Khindi, and Michael Inzlicht, "Preserving Integrity in the Face of Performance Threat: Self-Affirmation Enhances Neurophysiological Responsiveness to Errors," *Psychological Science* 23, no. 12 (December 2012): 1455–60, doi: 10.1177/0956797612448483. Also, Joshua Correll, Steven J. Spencer, and Mark P. Zanna, "An Affirmed Self and an Open Mind: Self-Affirmation and Sensitivity to Argument Strength," *Journal of Experimental Social Psychology* 40, no. 3 (2004): 350–56, doi:10.1016/j.jesp.2003.07.001.

. . . a recent study in which college students listened: Ibid.

"What school they'll go to": Banschick interview.

"I've always been about 'projective techniques'": Neuman interview.

"I find the quieter I am": Ziettlow interview.

"'Sad' can be distinguished from 'disappointed'": Geraldine V. Oades-Sese, principal investigator and advisor, Sesame Workshop's Childhood Resilience Initiative. Telephone interview with author, July 30, 2013. E-mail exchange, June 18, 2015.

One way to write an inner elevator story: Martin E. P. Seligman, *Learned Optimism: How to Change Your Mind and Your Life* (New York: Alfred A. Knopf, 1991).

Or, as it says in the Proverbs: Proverbs 11:25 (Amplified Bible).

CHAPTER FIVE: FRIENDS . . . AND LACK THEREOF

Chronic loneliness is a risk factor: Louise C. Hawkley et al., "Loneliness Predicts Increased Blood Pressure: Five-Year Cross-Lagged Analyses in Middle-Aged and Older Adults," *Psychology and Aging* 25, no. 1 (March 2010): 132–41, doi: 10.1037/a0017805. Cacioppo, Hawkley, and Gary G. Berntson, "The Anatomy of Loneliness," *Current Directions in Psychological Science* 12, no. 3 (June 2003): 71–74, doi: 10.1111/1467-8721.01232. Christopher Masi et al., "A Meta-Analysis of Interventions to Reduce Loneliness," *Personality and Social Psychology Review* 15, no. 3 (2011): 219–66, doi: 10.1177/1088868310377394. Or check out this article on the latest research on loneliness, published on IGSB.org (January 25, 2011): http://www.igsb.org/news/psychologist-john-cacioppo-explains-why-loneliness-is-bad-for-your-health.

"Marriage fills us in a very big way": Vachon interviews.

"When we depended on friends": Carlin Flora, author of *Friendfluence: The Surprising Ways Friends Make Us Who We Are* (New York: Doubleday, 2013). Telephone interview with author, August 10, 2012.

As University of Arizona behavioral scientist Chris Segrin: Telephone interview with author, May 10, 2013.

A recent meta-analysis by John Cacioppo: Masi et al., "A Meta-Analysis of Interventions to Reduce Loneliness."

There's some evidence of divorce contagion: Rose McDermott, James H. Fowler, and Nicholas A. Christakis, "Breaking Up Is Hard to Do, Unless Everyone Else Is Doing It Too: Social Network Effects on Divorce in a Longitudinal Sample," *Social Forces*, 92, no. 2 (2013): 491–519, doi: 10.2139/ssrn.1490708.

Two married couples might "date": Nora Ephron, *Heartburn* (New York: Vintage, 2011).

"Cities have booming subcultures": Eric Klinenberg, telephone interview with author, August 30, 2012.

There's a classic book on mindfulness meditation: Jon Kabat-Zinn, *Wherever You Go, There You Are: Mindfulness Meditation in Everyday Life* (New York: Hachette Books, 2005).

Michael Cobb, a professor of English at the University of Toronto: From Thomas Rogers, "In Defense of Single People," Salon.com, July 8, 2012.

CHAPTER SIX: HURRICANE

"Almost one hundred percent of my clients": DeMeo interview.

"Most people don't even realize": Banschick interview.

Psychiatrist Elisabeth Kübler-Ross: Elisabeth Kübler-Ross, *On Death and Dying: What the Dying Have to Teach Doctors, Nurses, Clergy and Their Own Families* (New York: Scribner, 2014).

"Many people have been harmed by this idea": Bonanno interview.

Resilience is part of our makeup: Mancini, Bonanno, and Andrew E. Clark, "Stepping off the Hedonic Treadmill: Individual Differences in Response to Major Life Events," *Journal of Individual Differences* 32, no. 3 (2011): 144–52, doi: 10.1027/1614-0001/a000047.

. . . even clinically diagnosable depression: Seligman, *Learned Optimism*, 11.

Our emotions evolved along with us: James J. Gross and Robert W. Levenson, "Emotion Elicitation Using Films," *Cognition and Emotion* 9, no. 1 (1995): 87–108, doi: 10.1080/02699939508408966. Norbert Schwarz, "Warmer and More Social: Recent Developments in Cognitive Social Psychology," *Annual Review of Sociology* 24 (August 1998): 239–64, doi: 10.1146/annurev.soc.24.1.239. Justin Storbeck and Gerald L. Clore, "With Sadness Comes Accuracy; With Happiness, False Memory: Mood and the False Memory Effect," *Psychological Science* 16, no. 10 (2005): 785–89, http://queensaffectiveneuroscience.com/Storbeck_Clore2005.pdf. Nancy Eisenberg et al., "Relation of Sympathy and Distress to Prosocial Behavior: A Multimethod Study," *Journal of Personality and Social Psychology* 57, no. 1 (1989), 55–66. Lihong Wang et al., "Amygdala Activation to Sad Pictures during High-Field (4 Tesla) Functional Magnetic Resonance Imaging," *Emotion* 5, no. 1 (March 2005): 12–22, doi: 10.1037/1528-3542.5.1.12.

As new insights from the field of bereavement studies: Stephen Joseph, *What Doesn't Kill Us: The New Psychology of Posttraumatic Growth* (New York: Basic Books, 2011). Also, Bonanno interview.

Psychologist Mavis Hetherington: Hetherington and Kelly, *For Better or Worse: Divorce Reconsidered.*

"My idea was that any marriage": Gabriel Cohen, interview with author, Hoboken, New Jersey, December 22, 2012.

"What I learned astonished me": Gabriel Cohen, *Storms Can't Hurt the Sky: A Buddhist Path through Divorce* (Boston: Da Capo Press, 2008).

But some kind of philosophical: Joseph, *What Doesn't Kill Us.* Also, Stephen Joseph, telephone interview with author, January 29, 2015.

He has said that the difference: Terry Orlick, *Embracing Your Potential: Steps to Self-discovery, Balance, and Success in Sports, Work, and Life* (Human Kinetics, 1998).

"A principle that was highlighted by Frankl": Wendy Lichtenthal, clinical psychologist at Memorial Sloan Kettering, New York City, telephone interview with author, November 14, 2014.

A suspicion that you're stronger and wiser: Joseph, *What Doesn't Kill Us.*

"Approach-oriented" coping: Joseph, *What Doesn't Kill Us.* Also Gabriele Prati and Luca Pietrantoni, "Optimism, Social Support, and Coping Strategies as Factors Contributing to Posttraumatic Growth: A Meta-Analysis," *Journal of Loss and Trauma: International Perspectives on Stress and Coping* 14, no. 5 (2009): 364–88, doi: 10.1080/15325020902724271.

CHAPTER SEVEN: I LOVE YOU, YOU'RE PERFECT (NOW THAT YOU'RE GONE)

"It takes very special, low-conflict people": Mosten interview.

"Here's a story that drives people nuts": American University professor and clinical psychologist Barry McCarthy, telephone interview with author, May 13, 2013.

"It's hard to get their words out of your head": Amy Minkoff, telephone interview with author, November 6, 2014.

There's a lot of support out there for recommitment: Murray Vachon interview.

William Doherty, author: William J. Doherty, *Take Back Your Marriage: Sticking Together in a World That Pulls Us Apart* (New York: Guilford Press, 2013).

Research on memory shows that we have a "positivity bias": There's a huge amount of scholarship on memory. For a good overview, see Benjamin

Storm and Tara Jobe, "Retrieval-Induced Forgetting Predicts Failure to Recall Negative Autobiographical Memories," *Psychological Science* 23, no. 11 (2012): 1356–63, doi: 10.1177/0956797612443837.

CHAPTER EIGHT: DON'T BUY YOUR LAWYER A COUNTRY HOUSE

I spoke to many people to gain an understanding of family law in relation to divorce, as explained throughout this chapter. Primary sources include:

- Margulies interview. Margulies is one of the country's most experienced mediators and the author of many books, including *Getting Divorced Without Ruining Your Life: A Reasoned, Practical Guide to the Legal, Emotional, and Financial Ins and Outs of Negotiating a Divorce Settlement* (New York: Touchstone, 2001). See sammargulies.com.
- Naomi Cahn, George Washington University law professor. I spoke to Naomi many times over the course of working on this book, and am grateful for her insight and forbearance.
- DeMeo interview.
- Karen Winner, New York–based attorney, telephone interview, May 8, 2014.
- Andrew Schepard, law professor and director of the Center for Children, Families and the Law, Hofstra University, and author of *Children, Courts and Custody: Interdisciplinary Models for Divorcing Families* (New York: Cambridge University Press, 2004). Telephone interview, June 6, 2014.
- Pauline Tesler, author of *Collaborative Divorce: The Revolutionary New Way to Restructure Your Family, Resolve Legal Issues, and Move On with Your Life* (New York: HarperCollins, 2006) and founder of the Integrative Law Institute (integrativelawinstitute.org). Telephone interview, June 6, 2014.
- Melinda Taylor, executive director, Resource Center for Separating and Divorcing Families, University of Denver. Interviews and tour, Denver, October 22–24, 2014.
- Mosten interview and ongoing e-mail correspondence.
- Beth Henson, Colorado attorney/mediator who has been active in Colorado's family law reform effort for two decades. In-person mediation session and interview, October 23–24, 2014, and ongoing e-mail correspondence.
- Singer interview.

In one twelve-year study, couples who took part in mediation: Emery, Sbarra, and Tera Grover, "Divorce Mediation: Research and Reflections," *Family Court Review* 43, no. 1 (January 2005): 22–37, doi: 10.1111/j.1744-1617 .2005.00005.x.

"Everyone is advising you because they love you": Jim Halfens, CEO of Divorce-Hotel, telephone interview with author, March 25, 2015.

Minnesota-based family lawyer Stuart Webb: Gregory R. Solum, "Collaborative Law: Not Just for Family Lawyers," *Bench & Bar of Minnesota* 67, no. 2 (February 2010), http://www2.mnbar.org/benchandbar/2010/feb10 /family.html. Also, Stuart Webb, *The Collaborative Way to Divorce: The Revolutionary Method That Results in Less Stress, Lower Costs, and Happier Kids—Without Going to Court* (New York: Plume, 2007).

"The courtroom makes you want to punch your way out of it": Robert Hyatt, Denver District Court's chief judge 2010–13; district court judge 1987–2010, interview with author, Denver, October 24, 2014.

In many states, the noncustodial parent can be incarcerated: Daniel Hatcher, "Don't Forget Dad: Addressing Women's Poverty by Rethinking Forced and Outdated Child Support Policies," *Journal of Gender, Social Policy & the Law,* 20, no. 4 (2012): 775–96. Available at Social Science Research Network: http://ssrn.com/abstract=2133344. Also, Hatcher, University of Baltimore School of Law, telephone interview with author, January 6, 2015.

Family lawyers increasingly offer guidance on an hourly basis: Luz Herrera, ed., *Reinventing the Practice of Law: Emerging Models to Enhance Affordable Legal Services* (Chicago: American Bar Association, 2014). See especially chaps. 1 and 2. Also, Mosten interview.

All services take place at the center, which, when I visited: Site visit and interviews at the Resource Center for Separating and Divorcing Families, Denver, CO, October 23–24, 2014.

CHAPTER NINE: TRANSFORMATIVE ACTS

When we trade in a loveless life: A riff on the Bhagavad Gita, chapter 2, verse 22. For more on the idea of rebirth, Jivamukti style, see: http://jivamukti yoga.com/teachings/focus-of-the-month/p/renaissance.

To really bring closure: Renne Beck, marriage and family therapist, telephone interview with author, January 16, 2015.

Or, as Carl Jung said: Jung talked about the value of ritual at a seminar in 1939

at the Guild for Pastoral Psychology, London. Read an excerpt at www
.jung.org/readingcorner.html.

After finalizing her divorce: Charlotte Eulette, international director, Celebrant Foundation and Institute, telephone interview with author, May
12, 2012. For more about Eulette's ceremony and others, see Abby Ellin's excellent *New York Times* article, "Untying the Knots, and Bonds,
of Marriage," April 27, 2012, http://www.nytimes.com/2012/04/29
/fashion/weddings/leaving-a-spouse-behind-for-good.html?pagewant-
ed=all&_r=0.

"Officiant" was recently listed: Susan Adams, "5 Second-Act Careers to Sail
through Retirement," *Forbes*, January 7, 2013, http://www.forbes.com
/sites/susanadams/2013/01/07/5-second-act-careers-to-sail-through-
retirement/.

Rhodes, a corporate event planner in Vegas: Bella magazine, January 14, 2014,
http://www.foxnews.com/travel/2014/01/14/extravagant-divorce
-parties/.

Joelle Caputa, author: E-mail interview with author, January 14, 2015.

Steven Rogat, a licensed professional counselor and cofounder: Steven Rogat,
e-mail interview with author, January 6, 2015; telephone interview with
author, January 14, 2015.

"A lot of people are stuck": Karen Schaler, author of *Travel Therapy: Where Do
You Need to Go?* (New York: Seal Press, 2009). Telephone interview with
author, June 15, 2015.

Being with animals and being in nature: Linda Lloyd Nebbe, retired counseling
professor at the University of Northern Iowa, telephone interview with
author, June 17, 2015. Also, Nebbe, *Nature as a Guide: Nature in Counseling, Therapy, and Education* (Spotsylvania, VA: Educational Media Corp,
1991).

"Sometimes in unhealthy relationships, we lose sight of who we are": Barry Shingle, director of guest relations and programming at Rancho la Puerta,
e-mail interview with author, June 17, 2015.

CHAPTER TEN: DOES THIS COUCH
MATCH MY PERSONALITY?

"We often lose ourselves": Karen Lehrman Bloch, author of *The Inspired Home:
Interiors of Deep Beauty* (New York: Harper Design, 2013). Telephone
interview with author, January 1, 2014.

As Clare Cooper Marcus notes: Clare Cooper Marcus, *House as a Mirror of Self: Exploring the Deeper Meaning of Home* (Lake Worth, FL: Nicolas-Hays, 2006), 2.

Jodi Topitz, an interior stylist: Telephone interview with author, June 1, 2015.

Even if you live in a city: Nebbe interview.

I read a ream of studies: Nicola Taylor and Marilyn Freeman, "International Research Evidence on Relocation: Past, Present, and Future," *Family Law Quarterly* 44, no. 3 (2010): 317–39, doi: 10.2307/23034358.

One 2015 study examining the draw of high-rent neighborhoods: David Albouy and Bert Lue, "Driving to Opportunity: Local Rents, Wages, Commuting, and Sub-Metropolitan Quality of Life," *Journal of Urban Economics* (in press, June 2015), doi: 10.1016/j.jue.2015.03.003.

In a recent series of three studies, researchers showed that introverts: Shigehiro Oishi, "Introverts Like Mountains," *Psychological and Personality Science* (forthcoming, 2015).

In one study, researchers mapped attributes of personality: Peter J. Rentfrow et al., "Divided We Stand: Three Psychological Regions of the United States and Their Political, Economic, Social, and Health Correlates," *Journal of Personality and Social Psychology*, 105, no. 6 (2013): 996–1012, doi.org/10.1037/a0034434. Two good books on the role place plays in our lives: Richard Florida, *Who's Your City? How the Creative Economy Is Making Where to Live the Most Important Decision of Your Life* (New York: Basic Books, 2008) and Eric Weiner, *The Geography of Bliss: One Grump's Search for the Happiest Places in the World* (Twelve: 2008).

CHAPTER ELEVEN: AM I FREE TONIGHT? LET ME CHECK WITH MY HUSBAND

"Dating is uncomfortable": Nita Tucker, telephone interview with author, July 9, 2015.

As biological anthropologist: Helen Fisher, "What Is Romantic Love?" The Anatomy of Love, https://theanatomyoflove.com/what-is-love/what-is-love/.

Continued fighting with a former spouse: McCarthy interview.

"In successful relationships, people have the ability to suspend negative judgment": Lucy Brown, telephone interview with author, July 13, 2015. Also, Xiaomeng Xu, Lucy Brown, Arthur Aron, Guikang Cao, Tingyong Feng, Bianca Acevedo, and Xuchu Weng. "Regional brain activity during early-stage intense romantic love predicted relationship outcomes after 40

months: and fMRI assessment," *Neuroscience Letters*, 526, no. 1 (2012): 33-38. doi: 10.1016.

Lessening negativity might yield more dates: Segrin interview.

"Talk to a woman in Cincinnati": Evan Marc Katz, telephone interview with author, May 23, 2013.

He advises clients to sign: Mosten interview.

"There needs to be a very clear hiatus for the kids": Banschick interview.

CHAPTER TWELVE: HAPPILY EVER AFTER DIVORCE

"I've seen entire cases change": Henson interview.

In her moving, popular memoir The Top Five Regrets*:* Bronnie Ware, *The Top Five Regrets of the Dying: A Life Transformed by the Dearly Departing* (Hay House, 2012).

The life expectancy: Life expectancy isn't a perfect science, but check out Laura B. Shrestha, "Life Expectancy in the United States," Congressional Research Service Report for Congress, updated August 16, 2006. Also: Jiaquan Xu et al., "Mortality in the United States, 2012." *NCHS Data Brief* 168 (October 2014), http://www.cdc.gov/nchs/data/databriefs/db168.pdf.

"It isn't every day, but it is every month": Matthew Loscalzo, executive director, Department of Supportive Care Medicine, City of Hope Hospital, Duarte, CA, telephone interview with author, September 18, 2014.

Index

About the Author

Wendy Paris is a journalist and personal essayist whose work has appeared in *The New York Times*, *Psychology Today*, *Quartz* (QZ.com), Salon.com, *The Guardian*, *Travel & Leisure*, Portfolio.com, and *Brides* magazine. She is the coauthor of the perennially popular wedding-planning guide *Words for the Wedding* (Perigee 2011; original edition 2001), and the author of a humorous book of dating advice, *Happily Ever After: The Fairy Tale Formula for Lasting Love* (HarperCollins, 2002). She was a 2013 Encore Fellow, working at an environmental and educational nonprofit in the South Bronx, and a 2014 Fellow with the New American Foundation in Washington, DC. She has a master's degree in nonfiction creative writing from Columbia University. She volunteers as a Mentor Editor with the Op-Ed Project in New York City, and with the Children's Lifesaving Foundation in Venice, California. She lives in Santa Monica, California, with her son, Alexander, a few blocks up the beach from her first husband, with whom she shares a warm co-parenting relationship.